MW01071022

THE WAYS

OF

MENTAL PRAYER

BY

THE RIGHT REV. DOM VITALIS LEHODEY

ABBOT OF BRIQUEBEC, O.C.R.

TRANSLATED FROM THE FRENCH

BY

A MONK OF MOUNT MELLERAY

Martino Fine Books
Eastford, CT
2019

Martino Fine Books
P.O. Box 913,
Eastford, CT 06242 USA

ISBN   978-1-68422-405-0

Copyright 2019
Martino Fine Books

All rights reserved. No new contribution to this publication may
be reproduced, stored in a retrieval system, or transmitted, in any form or
by any means, electronic, mechanical, photocopying, recording, or
otherwise, without the prior permission of the Publisher.

Cover Design Tiziana Matarazzo

Printed in the United States of America On 100% Acid-Free Paper

THE WAYS

OF

MENTAL PRAYER

BY

THE RIGHT REV. DOM VITALIS LEHODEY

ABBOT OF BRIQUEBEC, O.C.R.

TRANSLATED FROM THE FRENCH

BY

A MONK OF MOUNT MELLERAY

DUBLIN

M. H. GILL & SON, Ltd.

50 UPPER O'CONNELL STREET

AND WATERFORD

1912

Nihil obstat :

JOANNES WATERS,
Censor Theol. Deput.

Imprimi potest :

✠ GULIELMUS,
Archiep. Dublinen.
Hiberniæ Primas.

DUBLINII, die 11ᵉ Aprilis, 1912.

TO

THE SERVANT OF GOD

SISTER TERESA OF THE CHILD JESUS

AND OF THE HOLY FACE

"THE LITTLE FLOWER OF JESUS"

WHO DIED IN THE ODOUR OF SANCTITY
AT THE CARMELITE CONVENT OF LISIEUX
SEPTEMBER 30TH, 1897, AGED 24

THIS TRANSLATION

IN THE FIRM HOPE THAT ALL ITS READERS
MAY GET A SHARE OF HER

"SHOWER OF ROSES"

IS DEDICATED

BY

THE TRANSLATOR

DILECTO FILIO VITALI LEHODEY

ABBATI EX ORDINE CISTERCIENSIUM REFORMATORUM

PIUS P. P. X.

Dilecte Fili, salutem et apostolicam benedictionem.

Is tuus liber de *Les Voies de l'oraison mentale*, cujus Nobis dedisti exemplar, quanquam in argumento sacris auctoribus usitato versatur, non tu tamen rem supervacaneam fecisti scribendo ; imo valde utilem, nec solum religiosis hominibus, sed etiam omnibus quicumque perfectionem christianæ vitæ assequi contendunt. Certe de opere isto tale intelligentium est judicium, quibus tua et doctrina et peritia jure probatur. Nos igitur cum gratias tibi agimus, tum gratulamur ; et quos ex labore tuo fructus communis pietatis expectas, ii ut uberes sequantur exoptamus. Divinorum autem munerum auspicem, et benevolentiæ Nostræ testem, tibi, dilecte fili, apostolicam benedictionem peramanter impertimus.

Datum Romæ apud S. Petrum, die XIII Decembris MCMVIII, Pontificatus Nostri anno sexto.

PIUS P. P. X.

(*TRANSLATION*)

BRIEF OF HIS HOLINESS PIUS X.

TO OUR BELOVED SON VITALIS LEHODEY

ABBOT OF THE ORDER OF REFORMED CISTERCIANS

PIUS X. POPE

Beloved Son, health and apostolic benediction.

Your book *On the Ways of Mental Prayer*, of which you have sent us a copy, treats of a subject familar to spiritual writers. Nevertheless, by writing it you have not laboured in vain; on the contrary, you have accomplished a work very useful, not only to religious, but to all who, in any walk of life, are striving after christian perfection. Such, assuredly, is the judgment which all enlightened persons, who do justice to your knowledge and experience, must pass upon this book.

We, therefore, both thank and congratulate you, and it is Our earnest desire that your work may produce abundantly all those fruits you expect from it, for the spiritual advantage of all.

As a pledge of the Divine favour, and in testimony of Our benevolence, We impart to you with all Our heart, dear son, Our apostolic benediction.

Given at Rome, at St. Peter's this 13th day of December, 1908, in the sixth year of Our Pontificate.

PIUS POPE, X

LETTER OF THE MOST REV. AUGUSTINE MARRE
BISHOP OF CONSTANCE
ABBOT GENERAL OF THE REFORMED CISTERCIANS

RIGHT REVEREND FATHER,

We learn with pleasure that your treatise *On the Ways of Mental Prayer* is at length about to be printed.

We have no need to approve this work, which has already received the approbation and the praise of our General Chapter; but we wish once again to congratulate you upon this book inspired by an enlightened zeal, and we fervently pray that it may contribute to revive the spirit of prayer in the souls of its readers.

✠ AUGUSTINE MARRE,
Bishop of Constance, Abbot General.

LETTER OF THE RIGHT REV. JOSEPH GUÉRARD
BISHOP OF COUTANCES AND AVRANCHES

COUTANCES,
27th October, 1907.

RIGHT REVEREND FATHER,

I feel very happy in giving you the approbation which you ask for your work.

The Reverend Father Superior of the Diocesan Seminary whom I commissioned to examine it writes to me:

" This work, the doctrine of which appears to me to

be irreproachable, can be very useful not only to the religious for whom it has been written, but also to priests and to all souls called by God to a life of perfection."

I am glad of this testimony, and I sincerely hope that your work may be appreciated as it deserves, and have a rapid and widespread success.

Receive, Right Reverend Father, the renewed assurance of my most respectful affection, and pray for us.

✠ JOSEPH,
Bishop of Coutances.

LETTER OF THE RIGHT REV. ALEXANDER LE ROY

BISHOP OF ALINDA
SUPERIOR GENERAL OF THE CONGREGATION OF
THE HOLY GHOST

CHEVILLY PAR L'HAY (SEINE),
18th October, 1907.

RIGHT REVEREND AND VERY DEAR FATHER,

. . . . , having read your work myself, and given it to others to read, I am of opinion, along with these competent judges, that it is excellent, and that many religious, many priests, and many of the simple faithful will owe you a great debt of gratitude for having opened to them or made easy for them the *Ways of Mental Prayer*.

You wished to compose a full treatise which might furnish the soul, at every stage of the supernatural life, with a guide and support to enable her to recognise her path, to persevere in it, to look forward and to ascend still higher. You have succeeded.

It is a *hand-book* you say. Yes, it has the characteristics of a hand-book: it is practical, and purposely avoids controverted and purely speculative questions; its mode of exposition is very clear and renders the highest teachings accessible to the humblest readers; finally, its doctrine is perfectly safe, grounded as it always is upon the most competent authorities.

Publish your work, and may God give it his blessing! In this age of hatred, of tyranny over consciences, of sensuality, materialism and folly, it is well to attach ourselves to *Him who is :* for He alone is everlasting. . . .

Receive, Right Reverend and very dear Father, the religious homage of my most affectionate respect.

✠ ALEXANDER LE ROY,
Bishop of Alinda, Sup. Gen. C. S. Sp.

LETTER OF MONSIGNOR LEGOUX
PROTONOTARY APOSTOLIC

PARIS,
1st December, 1907.

RIGHT REVEREND FATHER,

Your deep devotion towards her, whom we shall soon call "The Blessed Mary Magdalen Postel," and your friendship for the humble author of her "Life," induced you to ask a few lines from me upon your work, *The Ways of Mental Prayer.*

Your desire evidently was to obtain for your readers and for yourself a special blessing from that heroic Lover of our Saviour, whose whole life, like that of her Divine Master, was "one perpetual prayer." I congratulate you and thank you in her name: who, indeed, better than she could understand and relish a work so pious and so learned?

How often while her wonderful cause was under examination, how often while writing the "story of her life," have I not regretted that her invincible humility made her observe an absolute silence concerning the special ways by which Our Divine Lord guided her in her interior life! What a powerful charm and what a precious instruction in fact the knowledge of her inward life would have procured us!

Now, whilst reading your work with much pleasure, I seemed to discover on every page the key to the mysteries of the holiness of that life, "unique in its kind": it is thus, said I to myself many a time, that she must have prayed, since it is thus she lived.

Starting from this principle, your book seemed to me a real model, capable by its simplicity, its clearness and its method of serving as a guide, not only to those who are mere beginners in this holy exercise of mental prayer, but also to souls the most experienced in the secrets of the mystical life.

Better still: the multitude of "Manuals" and of "Methods" of mental prayer which have been published up to the present, and with which, through duty or opportunity, I became acquainted, never gave me so clear, so simple an idea of the necessity and the facility of performing this important exercise as does this work, and I am persuaded that it is destined to produce the same impression upon all who shall have the good fortune to read it, to study it and to use it as their ordinary manual. Just as all those, whom " Providence will favour with the grace to read the life of the Venerable Mary Magdalen Postel, will become almost of necessity better and more desirous of advancing in the path of christian and religious perfection," so those who know your book will feel themselves drawn to the love and practice of mental prayer, and of those "sublime virtues of which it is the best school."

May that Venerable Servant of God deign to bless and thank you herself for the good you have done me, and obtain for you the legitimate satisfaction of seeing what you call your "modest work" known and relished by all.

I am, Right Reverend Father, with profound respect and most sincere affection,

Your very humble

A. M. LEGOUX,

Protonotary Apostolic.

LETTER OF THE REV. FATHER AUG. POULAIN, S.J.
AUTHOR OF THE "GRACES OF PRAYER"

PARIS, 1st *October*, 1907.

RIGHT REVEREND FATHER,

The peace of Our Lord be with you.

You are performing a great act of humility when you ask me to place at the head of your book a letter introducing it to the public. A bishop would, in such a case, be qualified to speak; when pronouncing judgment, he might hope for a special assistance of the Holy Ghost. As for me, who am of such small consequence in the Church of Christ, I can hardly reckon upon anything more than my natural lights. I will try, however, to make use of them.

Now, they assure me that your work is an excellent one. Your descriptions of divine graces are exact; it is easily perceived that not only you have consulted books, but that you have also come in contact with favoured souls, which is an indispensable corrective of theoretical knowledge. Your ascetic counsels are very solid. You unceasingly urge your readers to abnegation, to detachment from the creature, to the love of God and to the virtues

xii

which are its consequence. Finally, throughout your work, there reigns a tone of piety which will elicit responsive echoes in every soul.

In spite of the unfavourable conjunctures in which your work is being published, I hope that it will have a wide circulation. When the Church is undergoing such rude assaults, it seems very daring to invite souls to contemplation. But Moses did not consider it useless to remain inactive, with his arms raised, upon the mountain, whilst his people were fighting valiantly upon the plain. And then, there are so many souls that need to be consoled for the afflicting spectacles of the present time! You will behold coming to you those who are sickened by the hatred and injustice of our adversaries, saddened by the effeminacy of certain christians, and by the compromises and apostasy of others. Flying from earthly contentions, they will come to ask of your book to speak to them heavenly words, and to enable them to get a glimpse of the heavenly Jerusalem, the city of peace.

I beg of you, Right Reverend Father, to accept the expression of my profound respect, and to kindly send me your holy blessing.

AUG. POULAIN, S.J.

PREFACE

St. Alphonsus relates [1] that St. Teresa would have wished to ascend to the top of a high mountain, and be able to make her voice heard by the whole world, for the sole purpose of crying out to it: "Pray, pray, pray." She had rightly understood the words Our Lord addresses to each of us: We ought always to pray and not to faint." [2]

In the spiritual life there are two great principles which should never be forgotten: Without grace we can do nothing; [3] with it we can do all things. [4] Sometimes it anticipates our desires; ordinarily, God waits till we ask for it. This is a general law thus expressed by Our Lord: "Ask, and it shall be given to you." [5] Prayer is, therefore, not only a precept, it is a necessity. God places the treasure of His graces at our disposal, and its key is prayer. You desire more faith, more hope, more love; "ask, and it shall be given to you." Your good resolutions remain sterile, resulting always in the same

---

[1] St. Liguori, *True Spouse of Jesus Christ*, xx.
[2] Oportet semper orare et non deficere. Luke, xviii. 1.
[3] Sine me nihil potestis facere. John, xv. 5.
[4] Omnia possum in eo qui me confortat. Philip, iv. 13.
[5] Petite et dabitur vobis. Matthew, vii. 7.

failures: "ask, and it shall be given to you."
Precepts are numerous, virtue painful, temptation
seductive, the enemy ruthless, the will weak: "ask,
and it shall be given to you." Prayer will draw
down into your soul the omnipotence of God, "it
is stronger than all the demons."[1]—But I pray
and I do not obtain.—"It is because you ask
amiss."[2]—I have been asking now for a long
time.—"Ask" again, "seek, knock";[3] reanimate
your desires, importune heaven, make the voice of
your soul loud and shrill as a piercing cry, and,
provided that your prayer possesses the necessary
conditions, "you shall ask whatever you will, and
it shall be done unto you."[4]—The Master of grace,
Truth itself has pledged His word for it, a promise
supremely encouraging, the only reproach He
makes us is that we do not ask enough;[5] a
promise too, which leaves faint-heartedness no
excuse; for we can always pray, and nothing is
easier. The mind remains without light, because
it does not draw nigh to God;[6] the heart is dried up
because the soul has forgotten to eat her bread,[7]
and the will is hard as iron, and resists grace
because we have neglected to heat it in the fire of
prayer. This is the doctrine which St. Augustine
preaches: "The body is nourished by material

---

[1] St. Bernard, *De modo bene viv.* "Oratio dæmoniis omnibus malis prævalet," c. 49.

[2] Jac., iv. 3.   [5] Joan., xvi. 24.
[3] Matth., vi. 7.   [6] Ps., xxxiii. 6, and Jac. i. 5.
[4] Joan., xv. 7.   [7] Ps., ci. 5.

food, and the interior man by prayer."[1] St. Chrysostom declares with not less energy : "As the body cannot live without the soul, so the soul without prayer is dead and fetid."[2] And St. Liguori gives us this memorable admonition : " He who prays shall certainly be saved, he who does not pray shall certainly be damned."[3]

The ordinary Christian must have recourse to prayer, in order to fulfil his duties and to conquer temptation. Much more must a religious give himself to it ; for, in addition to the ordinary precepts, he has to observe his vows and his rules, and has bound himself to tend to perfection, by ever seeking to die to self, and so to advance ever in virtue and in holy love. Such an enterprise, the noblest and most fruitful of all, but also the most elevated above the reach of human weakness, requires a broad and continuous flow of graces, and consequently a superabundance of prayer. Besides, is it not meet and just that a soul consecrated to God should seek the presence and the conversation of her Divine Spouse? This is true for even the active religious Orders; how much more is it so for a contemplative Order like ours, all whose observances are ordained with a view to a life of prayer !

[1] Sicut escis alitur caro, ita orationibus homo interior nutritur St. Aug., *De Sal. doc.*, c. ii. 8.

[2] Sicut corpus sine anima non potest vivere, sic anima sine oratione mortua est et graviter olens. St. Chrys., *De oratione.* D. b. 1st.

[3] St. Liguori. *Great Means of Salvation*, c. 1 at end.

b

None have so many motives and means as we, to make us conceive an affection for prayer, give ourselves to it with love and seek, above all things, union with God. The world, alas! absorbed by its pursuits and its pleasures, hardly ever thinks of God. Martha, overburdened with the pious labours to which she devotes herself all day long in the service of God and of souls, has but little leisure for repose and contemplation. Our vocation is that of Mary, who, keeping at Our Lord's feet, looks upon Him, loves Him, listens to Him and speaks to Him; our function in the house of God is to be attached to the person of Our Divine Master, to have frequent and familiar intercourse with Him, to be united to Him in a life of prayer; we are contemplatives by the peculiar duties of our profession. Can any lot be more sweet or more desirable?

It is true that we are also penitents. But penance and contemplation are, so far as we are concerned, as closely connected as our two eyes or our two hands. We have need of one and we cannot do without the other. They are like the two tables of the law: it is impossible [1] for us to please God without our austerities, and not less impossible to be acceptable to Him without our life of prayer; and, of course, it is not enough to give to God only the half of what we have promised. They are the two wings which can raise us from earth and bear us

[1] For Cistercians, of whom the author is speaking here.—*Trans.*

aloft to God, but only by acting in harmony and lending each other mutual support. Penance, by its fasts, watchings, toils and, above all, by interior mortification, detaches the soul from all things and allows her to raise herself freely towards God by contemplation; the life of prayer, in its turn, inflames us with zeal for penance; and at times, in the hour of dryness and sterility, it may itself be not the least of our sacrifices. These are two sisters who live together in perfect concord, and do not want to be separated. Penance, assuredly, is noble and fruitful; contemplation is incomparably more beautiful, richer and happier; the former tears us painfully away from earth, the latter unites us to God.

Of all the ways which obedience opens up to us to lead us to God, the shortest, the easiest and the most certain is a life of prayer. Our life may be very penitential, at least corporally, and yet not be by any means perfect; but no one can be courageously and perseveringly a man of prayer without becoming a saint. Faith, hope, charity, humility, all the virtues bloom easily in prayer, and are there in turn developed. A single outburst of the heart may even express them all at one time; and it is the best exercise of perfection. And when one's prayer is ended, for prayer is not the only duty even in the life of a monk, we remain enlightened by faith and rich in graces, which enable us to act supernaturally, to suffer with fruit, to correct our faults, to grow in virtue and to do whatever God wills; during our actions we will be in touch with God, because prayer shall have filled our mind and our heart with Him. Thus it was that forty days' conversation with the Lord upon the holy mountain left upon the brow of Moses two rays of light;[1] the presence of God, with which he was filled within, being reflected upon his countenance, and doubtless also in his words and works. Such ought we ourselves to be, angels at prayer and men of God in our conduct. St. Peter of Alcantara strongly reproves those who, " after having experienced the inestimable advantages of prayer, and recognised that the whole conduct of the spiritual life depends upon it, take it into their heads that prayer alone is everything, . . . and give way to relaxation in all their other duties. For all the other virtues act as a support to prayer, and, if this foundation happens to be wanting, the whole edifice must fall. . . . When an instrument is played upon, it is not a single string, but several sounding together, which produces the harmony. . . , A clock stops altogether if a single piece only of the mechanism is out of order."[2] Thus, too, the spiritual life cannot get on if a single wheel be wanting, whether that wheel be prayer or works.

[1] Exodus, xxxiv. 29.
[2] St. Peter of Alcantara, *Prayer and Meditation*, 2nd part, c. v. 7th counsel.

Prayer should, therefore, nourish in us faith, hope and charity, develop the other virtues and effectually tend to make us grow in holiness. This is its end, and by this we can judge whether our prayer is well made, and whether we devote enough time to prayer. Bodily health requires that nutriment, work and rest should bear a due proportion to each other; so too, sanctity demands that the soul be nourished by prayer, should labour at acquiring virtues and should have rest in God, who is found in prayer. We know that the body has all it wants, when it can do its work without difficulty; and the interior man is sufficiently nourished by prayer, when he shows vigour in cultivating virtue, bearing trials and making sacrifices. On the contrary, if he has lost his strength and his energy, it is food that he wants; he requires to pray more or to pray better.

In the beginning of this work on mental prayer, we deemed it well to remind our readers of the necessity of prayer in general, and of the supremely important part it plays in the work of our sanctification. If we wished to describe all the exercises of the contemplative life, it would have been sufficient to annotate the short but solid treatise, which our holy father St. Bernard, or, rather, some other author, has composed on this subject so full of interest for us. "One day, when engaged in manual work, he began to reflect upon the exercises of the spiritual man, and four degrees suddenly

presented themselves to his mind : reading, meditation, the prayer of petition and contemplation.
Here we have the ladder of the dwellers in the
cloister, by means of which they ascend from earth
to heaven.[1] . . . Reading *seeks* the sweetness
of the beatific life, meditation *finds* it, prayer *asks
for* it, contemplation *tastes* it. . . Seek by reading, and you shall find by meditation; knock by
prayer, and the door shall be opened to you by
contemplation." [2] This would certainly be an interesting study, but very long and too complex for
a single treatise. We refer our readers, therefore,
for information concerning our other exercises of
piety to the Directory,[3] which treats sufficiently of
them, and in order not to extend that work already
too long, we thought it better to treat, in this
separate work, of mental prayer and of all the developments so grave a subject implies.

Mental prayer is, in fact, the soul of the contemplative life. It is this exercise, which fertilises,
animates and renders ten times more efficacious
all our other means of attaining to union with God.
Without this, the Divine Office, which occupies so
considerable a portion of our day, and in which the
same expressions so continually recur, would run
some risk of producing a mere system of routine,
distracting thoughts, disgust and weariness; but,
when once the fire of meditation has inflamed the

[1] St. Bernard (?), *Scala Claustralium*, c. i.
[2] *Ibid.*, c. ii.
[3] *Direct. Spirit. des Cist. Réf.* (Trans.).

heart, the holy liturgy is no longer a dead letter, it
speaks to our mind and heart, and everything in us
sings the praises of God.   So, likewise, without the
hunger after God derived from mental prayer,
spiritual reading is frigid and almost unfruitful;
with it, spiritual books move us and shed their light
not merely upon the intellect, but make it penetrate
even to the depths of the heart and of the will.
Nothing is more powerful than the Holy Sacrifice
and the Sacraments; yet even they never produce
so much fruit as when fervent prayer has thrown the
doors of the soul wide open to the effusions of grace.
A life of prayer it is, which raises a religious above
the paltry thoughts of earth and the pitiful cares of
nature; this it is, which establishes us in God, and
makes us live in recollection and watchfulness over
ourselves; this it is, which communicates to us the
supernatural spirit of devotion, thus vivifying our
fasts, our watchings, our manual labours and all
our works; without it, our observances, admirably
conceived though they be, would run the risk of
becoming a body without a soul.

Since, then, mental prayer is so vital an element
in our contemplative life, we ought to esteem it, to
love it, and to apply ourselves to it with a holy
ardour.   But it is a divine art, and by no means
one of the easiest to acquire.   Beginners require to
learn a method of prayer, just as even the most in-
telligent apprentice must be initiated into the secrets
of his trade.   They will find it useful to know the

various processes which may serve as substitutes
for meditation, in order not to remain idle when this
latter fails them. Those who are making progress,
as well as those who are still more advanced in the
ways of prayer, have need to know when they
should pass on to affective prayer or to active contemplation, and how they should conduct themselves therein. Later on, should it please God to
raise souls to the different degrees of mystical contemplation,—and this ought not to be of rare
occurrence amongst religious, especially in a
contemplative Order,—they will need to have a
clear light thrown upon their road and an experienced guide to direct their steps. Otherwise the
soul would be exposed to all kinds of illusions.
This is what makes many promising beginners
stand still upon the road, or keep performing the
goose-step upon the one spot without ever advancing; they have not a sufficient knowledge of this
art of prayer, which should be the groundwork of
their whole life. It would be inexact to say that
the evil arises wholly from ignorance, for the weakness of the will has a great share in it; but ignorance is the primary pest, and, so to speak, a fundamental evil.

It is true that good books treating of mental
prayer abound and are in everybody's hands.
Nevertheless, the greater number of authors hardly
treat of anything but the method of prayer which is
proper to beginners; and it is difficult to find a clear

and precise explanation of the kinds of prayer which, without yet leaving the common ways, are suitable to souls more advanced. Many authors have, as it were wantonly, confused this matter, which is, nevertheless, very simple; they have created a disconcerting confusion by their parallel descriptions of acquired contemplation and infused contemplation. They are a labyrinth, especially when there is a question of passing from the common to the more elevated ways of prayer. The authors have to be patiently studied, collated with and controlled by each other, in order to bring them into harmony, and to discern the truth amidst such various systems. A study so arduous has all that is required to repel even the best constituted minds.

The author of this modest work thinks, therefore, he is rendering a helpful service to his brethren by offering them a clear, simple, and short explanation of all this matter, a little guide in the ways of prayer, a handbook wherein they will find practical counsels for all their needs, according as they advance in the common kinds of prayer, and even, should it so please God, in mystical contemplation; so that they will have always at hand briefly stated, the information they should otherwise have to seek for in twenty different books.

This work is not presented as a scientific treatise, and contains nothing very new, except, perhaps, the order in which the subject is treated. The writer made use of all the treatises on prayer which he was able to procure. Sometimes he quotes them, sometimes he summarises and combines them, and he has said hardly anything of his own, like the bee which goes pilfering from flower to flower, gathering its honey wherever it can find it.

His sole desire is to excite souls to mental prayer, to recall to their mind the beaten tracks, as well as the less explored paths which lead to union with God, to put them in mind of the dispositions which secure success in prayer, of how they should conduct themselves in it, of the fruit they should draw from it, of the necessity of making perfection keep pace with prayer, and thus to give a fresh impulse in our Order to the contemplative life, and, by its means, to those lofty virtues of which mental prayer is the best school; for, it was in meditation that the Psalmist warmed his heart and inflamed his soul with the fire of divine love.

May God deign to bless this modest work and communicate to it the grace to revive in many souls their zeal for mental prayer.

The work is divided into three parts, in which we shall successively study prayer in general, ordinary prayer, and mystical prayer.

CONTENTS

SECOND PART

ON ORDINARY MENTAL PRAYER 83

CONTENTS

FIRST PART

ON PRAYER IN GENERAL

CHAPTER I

OF PRAYER AND ESPECIALLY OF VOCAL PRAYER

§ I.—Notion of Prayer in General.

In its widest sense, "prayer is an elevation of the soul to God." [1] This formula, borrowed from St. John Damascene, has become classical.

The soul, therefore, leaves aside the useless thoughts, the nothings, the frivolities, which too often invade it; it abandons the thoughts which are good at another time, such as all questions of business, of work, of office; it raises itself above the earth and the things of earth; its mind and its affections ascend to heaven; they stop not even at the choirs of Angels and of Saints, unless indeed, our prayer is directly addressed to them; they ascend even to God, they rest in God, *ascensus mentis in Deum*. There, fixed in God, we look affectionately

---

[1] Ascensus mentis in Deum. St. John Dam., *De Fide Orth.*, l. iii. c. 24

at God,[1] we enter into *conversation with God*,[2] and God deigns to listen to us with love, as a father to his children, and to reply to us by granting us interior lights and affections.—Oh, to what a height does prayer raise the soul, and what an honour it is for a being sprung from nothing!

Prayer, in its widest sense, does four things: it adores, asks pardon, gives thanks, and begs for graces.

1°.—It adores. By prayer we kneel before the infinite Majesty and perfections of God, making ourselves quite little, we contemplate, admire, believe, hope, have confidence, love, praise, rejoice in the glory which God finds in Himself and in His creatures, we are afflicted to see Him so little known and so much offended, desire to glorify Him and make Him glorified, and arm ourselves with a holy zeal. Or, considering God as its Creator and its sovereign Master, the devout soul adores Him, and subjects itself humbly to Him, it admires and blesses the ways of Providence, it resolves to obey, and even reaches to the height of abandoning itself with confidence and love into the hands of God.

2°.—It asks pardon. Recalling all its years in the bitterness of a contrite and humbled heart, the soul confesses its faults before God, feels shame and confusion, expresses its repentance, appeals to

[1] Oratio est namque mentis ad Deum affectuosa intentio. St. Aug., *Serm.* ix. n. 3.

[2] Oratio conversatio sermocinatioque cum Deo est. St. Greg. Nyss. *Orat. I. de Orat. Dom.*—Oratio colloqui est cum Deo. St. Chrys., *Hom.* xxx. *in Gen.*

the Divine mercy, takes salutary resolutions, performs penance, and accepts willingly the austerities prescribed by the Rule and the crosses sent by Providence.

3°.—It traces up to God with thanksgiving all the general and particular benefits which it has received from Him. And often while it overflows with sentiments of gratitude, struck by the Divine goodness and infinite charity of which all these benefits are the manifestation, it rises easily from gratitude to love, thus discharging the primary function of prayer.

4°.—Finally, the soul begs new graces, temporal and spiritual, for herself and for all who are dear to her, pleading in turn the cause of God Himself, of His Church, militant or suffering, of her own country, of the clergy and religious, especially of her own Order, of the just and of sinners, &c., &c.

To repeat, prayer is an elevation of the soul to God, to adore Him, to thank Him, to beg pardon and ask for graces.

Schram [1] makes a very just remark which he borrows from Suarez.[2] "Prayer can apply itself to any one of the acts we have just enumerated in preference to any of the others. Nay, more, vocal or mental prayer, however prolonged, may limit itself to a single one of these acts, because there is no obligation nor necessity to join them always together, and also because it may happen that more fruit, more fervour and devotion may be

[1] Schram, Ed. Vivès, 1874. *Theol. Myst.*, t. 1st § xxii. bis.
[2] Suarez, *De Relig.*, l. ii. c. 3.

derived from the continuous dwelling upon a single one than from dwelling upon them all at one time. In such a case we ought to confine ourselves to that one which is more profitable, without trying to go through them all in the one prayer."

It must, however, be noted, that, if we confine ourselves to praising, to thanking God, and expressing our repentance for the past, we have indeed performed excellent acts of virtue, but we have not been praying, in the strictest sense of the word, for the first three functions belong to prayer only when taken in its widest sense. In its strict sense, it consists in petition, and may be then defined with St. John Damascene: "The asking of seemly things from God," [1] that is, things which may glorify God and do good to our soul, and hence which are conformable to the Divine good-pleasure. It is also defined: an act by which the intelligence as interpreter of the will expresses a desire of the soul and strives to induce God to grant it to us.

Prayer, considered as petition, consists entirely in expressing to God some desire in order that He may hear it favourably; a real desire is, therefore, its primary and essential condition; without this, we are merely moving the lips, going through a form of words which is not the expression of our will; and thus our prayer is only an appearance without reality. The means, then, to excite ourselves to pray, to put life and fervour into our prayer, and to make of it a cry which, breaking

[1] Petitio decentium a Deo. *De Fide Orth.*, l. iii. c. 24.

forth from the depths of the soul, penetrates even
to heaven, is to conceive the real desire mentioned
above, to excite it, to cherish it; for the fervour of
our prayer will be in proportion to the strength of
the desire we have to be heard; just as what we
have but little at heart we ask for only in a half-
hearted way, if even we ask it at all; so what we
desire with our whole soul we ask for with words of
fire, and plead for it before God with an eloquence
that is very real.

§ II.—Vocal Prayer and Mental Prayer.

Leaving aside whatever belongs not to our
present subject, we will confine ourselves to saying
that prayer is divided into vocal and mental.

Vocal prayer is that which is made by using
words or signs, or, perhaps, more exactly by
using some approved form of words, which we
read or recite; such as, the divine office, the beads,
the Angelus, grace before and after meals, &c.
Mental prayer is that which is made without employing either words or formulas of any kind.

A large share is given to the former in our daily
exercises. The liturgical prayers are imposed by
the laws of the Church; by our rules also we are
enjoined certain vocal prayers; and others, like the
beads, are in such constant use amongst the faithful
generally, that a good religious would not wish to
omit them. Vocal prayer is not to be despised,
for, if well made, it pays to God the homage of our
body as well as that of our soul. A heart full of

devotion pours itself out quite naturally in words and signs which express externally its interior sentiments; on the other hand, when there is need to excite such sentiments, these pious formulas fix the attention of the mind, and call forth the devotion of the heart. " It is for this reason," says St. Thomas,[1] " we must, in private prayer, make use of these words and signs *as far as they are useful* to arouse the mind interiorly; but if they *should end by distracting it* or causing it any hindrance, we must cease to make use of them, and this is the case especially of those whose mind is sufficiently prepared for devotion without these external expressions."

This last observation of St. Thomas shows to what extent each one ought to devote himself to vocal prayer, outside prayers of obligation or those prescribed by the rules.   According to Schram,[2] for those who are not called to a more elevated prayer, vocal prayer well made may well suffice to enable them to lead a Christian and even a perfect life, especially if they are urged to this by a special movement from God—an impulse which may be recognised by its effects. . . .   Nay more, St. Bonaventure recommends vocal prayers to the more devout, that they may have the good custom of ruminating them when their devotion flags.

St. Teresa knew several who from vocal prayer were raised by God to a very sublime degree of contemplation." " I know," says she, " a person

[1] 2, 2, q. 83, a. 12.
[2] Schram. *Theol. Myst.*, § 36.

who never being able to pray otherwise than vocally, was yet in possession of all the other degrees of prayer. . . . She came to me one day much afflicted at not being able to make mental prayer nor to apply herself to contemplation, finding herself reduced to saying only some vocal prayers. I asked her what they were, and I found that while saying continually the *Pater,* she used to enter into so high a contemplation that it was evident Our Lord raised her even to divine union; and her actions indeed showed it, for she lived a holy life. So I praised Our Lord and envied such a vocal prayer." [1] That does not prevent the saint from strongly urging mental prayer upon her daughters, and even telling them that *they should make every effort* to arrive at mystical contemplation *if it is God's will.*[2] Religious will generally derive more profit from practising mental prayer, all the more because a considerable part of their time is already devoted to the exercise of vocal prayer in common. At all events, it is better to recite fewer vocal prayers, and to say them with recollection and devotion, than to try to get through a great number hastily; neither should we take upon us so many as to end by being disgusted. And "if during vocal prayer," says St. Francis of Sales,[3] "you feel your heart drawn and invited to interior or mental prayer, refuse not to follow this attraction, but allow your thoughts to flow freely in that

---

[1] *Way of Perfection,* xxxi.
[2] *Ibid.,* xviii.
[3] *Devout Life,* 2nd part, c. i. n. 8.

direction, and be not troubled at not having finished the vocal prayers which you had intended to say; for the mental prayer which you will make in their stead will be more agreeable to God and more useful to your soul." Vocal prayers of obligation, however, are always to be said.

§ III.—ATTENTION IN VOCAL PRAYERS.

We must not confine ourselves to reciting the words with our lips; it is necessary that we should raise to God our mind by attention, our heart by devotion, and our will by submission. "If any one," says St. Thomas, "is voluntarily distracted it is a sin, and that hinders the fruit of the prayer."[1] We must herein be all the more watchful over ourselves, because habit easily begets routine. It is not, however, *of obligation,* in fact it is morally impossible, that the attention of the mind be always actual. "It is sufficient," says M. Ribet,[2] "that the will perseveres, and the will to pray is suspended only by a distraction freely consented to."

Nay, more, according to St. Thomas,[3] in order that *vocal* prayer be *meritorious* and obtain its effect, it is not necessary that the attention remains actual to the end; it suffices to have begun with an attention which is not afterwards retracted by any voluntary distraction. But prayer so made does

---

[1] S. Th., 2, 2. q. 83, a. 13, ad 3.

[2] M. Ribet, *Ascét. Chrét.,* c. xxv. 7.

[3] S. Th., 2, 2. q. 83, a. 13.

not nourish the soul with the sap of devotion. Some bring forward as an objection to this the words of St. Gregory [1] : " God listens not to him who while praying listens not to himself." St. Thomas teaches that this holds good only when prayer is begun and continued without attention. According to this consoling doctrine, when we begin well, and afterwards in spite of us our mind wanders, the prayer, which we continue to say with this involuntary distraction, will not be entirely devoid of merit and effect. But then it must be admitted that if the soul could only keep herself more attentive the merit and fruit would be greater.

It is, therefore, of great importance to commence vocal prayer well, and to preserve always an actual attention. For this reason it is well to put oneself at first in the presence of God, in order to withdraw all the powers of the soul from exterior things, to recollect them within oneself, and to fix them upon God. It is also very useful to renew one's attention at certain fixed times. Further on [2] we will point out different ways of recollecting oneself. We might, if we liked, keep our eyes fixed upon the holy tabernacle, or look at a crucifix or some pious picture, represent to ourselves God in Heaven, or Our Lord in the Crib, at Nazareth, during the Passion, upon the cross, &c., and speak to Him *as if we saw Him*.

St. Teresa, [3] treating of *vocal* prayer (or rather of

[1] S. Greg., l. 22, *Moral.*, c. 13.
[2] *Cf.* 2nd part, c. ii. § ii., p. 106.
[3] St. Teresa. *Way,* xxix. and xxx.

vocal prayer meditated), and starting from the principle that God dwells in the just soul as in a magnificent palace and a little paradise, highly praises what she calls the prayer of active recollection.[1] We close our bodily eyes; and the soul, collecting together all her powers, enters into herself with God. She ceases not to look upon Him interiorly while the lips are reciting some pious prayer, and, knowing for certain that He is quite near, and that she has no need to cry out aloud, she speaks to Him lovingly and noiselessly as to her Father, her Brother, her Spouse, her Lord. Since God is ever within us the saint exhorts her daughters not to leave such an august companion alone; she wishes them to look at Him while speaking to Him; it is the means to excite attention, to inflame devotion, and to prepare the soul for a higher kind of prayer. She declares that she herself never knew what it was to pray with satisfaction until the day that God taught her to act in this way. This is a method which depends on our will, and though we had to spend six months or a whole year in acquiring it neither our time nor our trouble would be lost.

St. Ignatius [2] teaches a manner of praying vocally which " consists in saying some prayer very slowly, leaving the space of a full breath

----

[1] See *St. Teresa's Own Words: or Instructions on the Prayer of Recollection*, a short treatise (pp. 39), by the Rt. Rev. James Chadwick, Bishop of Hexham and Newcastle, published by Messrs. Burns & Oates.—*Trans.*

[2] S. Ign., *Spir. Ex.*, 3rd. manner of prayer.

between each word. Let us apply this method as follows to the prayer :—Soul of Christ, sanctify me.

1°. Recollect yourself and ask yourself : What is it I am going to do ?

2°.—Beg the grace to derive much fruit from this exercise.

3°. Commence the prayer : Soul—of Christ—sanctify me. — Body—of Christ—save me.—Blood—of Christ—inebriate me : and so on.

During this time we think on the sense of the word we have just pronounced, or on the dignity of Him to whom we pray, on our own baseness, on our miseries, on our needs.

This method is suitable for every one, for any time in the day, and may be practised during almost every kind of manual work. It is very useful for such as may have contracted a bad habit of reciting their vocal prayers too quickly ; but it is particularly recommended to religious.''

It is easy to understand that this method should contribute much to excite attention and devotion ; it is already as it were a timid attempt at meditation.

CHAPTER II

MENTAL PRAYER—ITS OBJECT

§ I.—Of Mental Prayer in General.

MENTAL prayer in general is an interior and silent prayer, by which the soul raises itself to God without the aid of words or formulas, in order to discharge its duty towards Him and to become better.

There is ordinary mental prayer and mystical mental prayer; in other terms, active prayer and passive prayer.

Prayer, like every other meritorious act, requires God's grace and man's co-operation; but sometimes the soul's effort is more manifest, sometimes the divine action.

In active prayer the soul's effort predominates, God's action is less evident; the supernatural, though very real, remains latent.

In passive prayer God's action is stronger and goes so far as to reduce the soul to a certain passive state, more or less accentuated according to the degree of mystical union; and when this is well marked, the supernatural is plainly perceptible—almost palpable. This passive condition, however, interferes with only certain operations of the mind and of the senses; the soul, under God's action, remains free and capable of meriting even in the state of ecstasy, and it is altogether occupied in contemplating and loving God, sometimes with a marvellous intensity.

Further on, we will speak of these mystical kinds of prayer; for the present, we shall confine ourselves to the ordinary kinds of mental prayer, after having made some general considerations applicable to both.

§ II.—Of Ordinary Mental Prayer.

Active prayer is a kind of mental prayer in which a person raises his mind to God by considerations or by a simple look, and his will by pious affections, petitions, and resolutions.

God gives His interior and hidden grace, and the soul endeavours to turn towards Him. According to the saying of St. Teresa, the soul in this stage is like a gardener, who, with much labour, draws the water up from the depths of the well to water his plants and flowers.

These efforts of the soul consist of two operations; one belongs to the thinking faculty which applies the imagination, the memory, the understanding to consider some truth or mystery, to turn it over and over, to convince itself of it and to penetrate it. This is what is called the consideration or the meditation. Later, it will concentrate the mind's attention upon God without the roundabout ways and turmoil of reasonings, and this will be the simple look of contemplation. The other operation is dependent on the will, and makes us love, desire, ask the good proposed by the mind, and make resolutions to arrive at it ; this is prayer—mental prayer properly so called.

The considerations are not a mere speculative study ; they are not made in order to learn or to know, but to inflame the heart, and set the will in motion. The mind's eye is fixed upon some truth in order to believe it, upon some virtue in order to love and seek it, upon some duty to fulfil it, upon moral evil to detest and fly from it, upon some danger to avoid it. In a word, meditation ought to lead to love and to action.

In the early stages of the spiritual life, considerations occupy a large place, because we have need to strengthen our faith ; later on, in proportion as the practice of mental prayer and of virtue has penetrated the soul with profound convictions, considerations progressively diminish, and end by giving place to a simple thought, to a simple attentive look. On the other hand, affections, at first rare and wordy, go on increasing ; they gain all the ground that considerations lose ; they, too, are after a time simplified, becoming shorter and more numerous, and the soul ends by attaching itself to a few affections only, which suffice for its needs and its attractions.

§ III.—Of the End of Mental Prayer.

All mental prayer, active or passive, whatever be its object, form or method, has for its end *to glorify God,* and in order to this, as we have already seen,[1] it may perform the four functions of

¹ C. i. § 1st, p. 2.

prayer, or some of the four, or only one, according to the attraction or need of the soul. But, in addition to this, and we beg our readers to pay special attention to this remark, it has always for its end *to make us better.*

We make mental prayer in order to be converted from evil to good, from good to better, from better to perfection, as we have promised. This constant and progressive conversion, or this tending to perfection, as it is now called, is the chief point of our rules, the object towards which should tend all our observances. All our spiritual exercises, without exception, are directed to this end, and have no other; but mental prayer, by its very nature and its divers acts, is pre-eminently the source of this transformation.

Those who are as yet only at the beginning of the spiritual life should propose to themselves as the result of their mental prayer, the extirpation of some sin or some defect, above all of their predominant vice; the victory over some temptation, the correction of some bad inclination, the governing of such and such a passion. When one evil is corrected they should turn their prayer against another for as long as may be necessary in order to triumph over it; and thus mental prayer well practised will purify their souls.

Those who are making spiritual progress should, without abandoning altogether this struggle against evil, employ their prayer chiefly in cultivating the virtues, especially the fundamental virtues, or those of which they have most need; above all, the spirit of faith, humility, self-renunciation, obedience, recollection and the life of prayer, in order to arrive at perfect love.

Those who are already united to God in spirit, heart, and will, should employ their prayer in strengthening this union. They should love in order to develop holy charity; their prayer should consist chiefly of love, confidence, conformity, and abandonment to the divine will, particularly amidst the crosses sent by Providence.

It is thus that our prayer will attain its end. Its principal object is not to instruct us, pious reading would suffice for that; it is rather to inflame the heart, that it may discharge better its duty towards God, and especially to conform our will to that of God, so that prayer may detach us from everything else, attach us to Him alone, and so transform our habits and our life.

During prayer, pious considerations replace our human thoughts with thoughts more divine; the entering into ourselves puts before us a mirror in which we contemplate our defects; affections and petitions unite us to God and draw down the grace, which clothes us with strength from on High. We leave off this communing with God in a closer relation with Him. These are already so many fruits ripe and gathered for Heaven. But all this tends further to good resolutions, which as yet are only flowers, and should become fruits.

After prayer has ended, all is not yet done. It is not a drawer, from which we take out during half an hour convictions and affections, and then shut it up for the rest of the day. Lights have been received, to which we should henceforth strive to conform our thoughts and conduct; we retire from prayer with a perfume of devotion which we must not allow to evaporate; we have made good resolutions and asked the help of God's grace to keep them; it now remains to put them in practice. In a word, mental prayer prepares us for action; a life of prayer calls for a life eminent in all virtues. Otherwise, mental prayer has not produced all its fruit; it has brought forth flowers in abundance; let us take care that these flowers, rich in promise, be not burnt up by the icy breath of dissipation, routine, and tepidity.

CHAPTER III

ADVANTAGES AND NECESSITY OF MENTAL PRAYER

As we shall point out later on the happy effects of affective prayer and of contemplation, we shall here more especially keep in view those of meditation.

The tending to perfection, which sums up all our obligations, meets with obstacles in us, both on the part of the understanding and on the part of the will.

§ I.—On the Part of the Understanding.

On the part of the understanding there is 1° ignorance of the supernatural life. The remedy is the word of God which we can find in instructions and in pious reading. To listen attentively to the word of God or to read it carefully is already a beginning of meditation.

There is 2° want of reflection, levity, routine, inadvertence to the truths of faith, that milder form of forgetfulness which makes such havoc even amongst us religious; a baneful pest, which dries up devotion and destroys the energy of the soul, and which St. Benedict exhorts us absolutely to avoid.[1] This is

---

[1] Reg. S. Ben., c. vii., 1st degree of humility.

why the earth is laid desolate, and even, alas! the cloister, the very home of sanctity; because no one thinks sufficiently in his heart.   Hence it comes to pass that even amongst good souls, who live by grace, there are so many weak, so many slumbering.   When we forget God and the things of God, we have still the eye of faith, but it is half closed by spiritual drowsiness.   The end to be aimed at, the rocks to be avoided, the virtues to be practised,— everything is clouded over, nothing distinctly outlined.   While faith sleeps, fear, hope, and love, which should carry us to God, slacken their course, and wander about aimlessly.   Hope is without desire, charity without fervour; the other virtues lose their activity; torpor reigns everywhere; the sleep which deadens faith gains upon our whole supernatural life, and the enemy profits of it to sow cockle in the field of our soul.   We sleep and we dream; and while our eyes are closed towards God, our imagination is taken up with a thousand foolish fancies as in a dream, our memory is filled with a thousand frivolous recollections, our intellect exhausts itself in useless thoughts and in the preoccupations of our work and office.   We have been sleeping long enough and too long; "it is time for us to awake at last," to "open our eyes to the deifying light, to act in a manner which may profit us for eternity," and "by our progress in faith and in a good life, to dilate our hearts and to run in the way of the precepts and counsels."[1]

But what, then, can arouse us from this wretched

[1] Reg. S. Ben., prolog. passim.

sluggishness, if not the practice of mental prayer? Little by little, mental prayer well made will render our faith more lively, will strengthen our convictions, will penetrate us deeply with the things of God, will keep the supernatural always present to our mind. And then there will be no more forgetfulness, no more sleep. It will then be easy for us to live by faith, to fear, to hope, to love and to act as we ought, because the eye of our faith will be always open.

There is 3° ignorance of ourselves. Self-love blinds us; humiliated by our many miseries and discouraged by the difficulty of remedying them, we prefer to shut our eyes. Hence, no longer seeing the faults we have to correct, and the enemies we have to combat, we either cease to fight, or merely beat the air. So also, if we hardly know the virtues we want, the weak points we should strengthen, our spiritual life will drift away aimlessly at the mercy of every passing impulse.

The remedy for this pest is the examination of conscience, especially the self-examination which is made during mental prayer. For, after showing us the ideal we should follow, mental prayer invites us to consider the reforms we have to make. Thus it is the torch which illumines our spiritual work, it is especially the school of humility. He who neglects mental prayer " has no horror of himself, because he feels not his miseries "[1]; on the other hand, mental prayer enables us to put our finger upon the multitude of our faults, defects, and im-

[1] S. Bern., *De Consid.*, l. i. c. 2.

perfections, to see clearly how poor we are in
virtues and merits, what pitiful creatures we are,
when contrasted with the saints who are the glory
of the Church and of the Cistercian Order, and above
all to realise our nothingness and wretchedness
before Him who is greatness and sanctity itself.
Thus mental prayer becomes the grave of pride.

§ II.—ON THE PART OF THE WILL.

1°.—The first obstacle to our progress is to be
found in our affections; it is a certain weariness of
God which makes us cold and languid in His service, while at the same time we are in a fever of
anxiety for all which is not God. Sin has drawn
us aside from our end and turned us towards the
creature. The remedy is mental prayer, which
detaches us from obstacles, and unites us to what
helps us. It detaches us from sin, from perishable
goods, from the world, above all, from ourselves;
and it unites us to the one and only Good.

First, it detaches us from sin. " This it is,"
says Fr. Crasset, " which leads us down in spirit
to hell, to behold our place there; which brings us
to the grave-yard, to behold there our abode; to
heaven, to behold there our throne; to the valley of
Josaphat, there to behold our judge; to Bethlehem,
there to see our Saviour; to Thabor, there to
behold our love; to Calvary, there to contemplate
our model."

It detaches us from perishable goods, such as
riches, honours, bodily comfort, of all which things

it is so easy to make an ill use. It shows us the
vanity of all that cannot satisfy a heart hungering
after God, the inconstancy and frailty of all that
passes away, the anxieties and dangers these false
goods bring with them, and their utter worthless-
ness in comparison with what lasts for ever. And
if it renders these things so contemptible in our
eyes, it detaches us still more from them by teaching us to love God. "How empty appears the
earth to him who contemplates heaven!" How
its joys and honours lose all their charm once the
soul has tasted God!

It detaches us from the world. It teaches us to
make no account of the world's promises or threats,
of its esteem or its contempt; for the world can
neither make us happy nor virtuous; we are no
better because it extols us to the clouds, nor any
worse when it tramples us under foot. We are
worth only just what we are worth in God's eyes.
Mental prayer makes us dread the corruption of the
world, the danger of its praises, the perfidiousness
of its caresses, far more than its impotent fury. It
makes us understand that God alone is to be considered; that no other's anger is to be feared, no
other's esteem to be desired, that there is no other
friendship on which the heart can securely rest.

Above all, it detaches us from ourselves. The
grave of pride, as we have called it, it is also that of
sensuality. "It substitutes the spirit for the flesh,
the soul's delights for bodily pleasures. If there is
any fact evident in the history of Christian and
religious life, it is that the love of mortification

keeps pace in a soul with the love of mental prayer. This exercise also enriches with treasures of patience those who seriously give themselves to it. They bear pains and afflictions, whencesoever they may come, without a murmur, and even with joy." [1]

Finally, mental prayer unites us to God. Detached from all things, the soul is no longer held back by anything; it is so thoroughly emptied that God hastens to fill it with Himself, there to establish His Kingdom. What treasures, what a deliverance, what a happiness a soul enjoys, in proportion as the habit of mental prayer withdraws her from beneath the sway of her passions and subjects her to her good Master, first by fear, afterwards by hope, and lastly by love! A day comes when the heart is taken captive; then it is a mutual friendship, the sweetest intimacy. The soul knows God and His infinite charms, and this view enchants and inflames her; everywhere, in nature and in grace, in Our Lord's life, and in her own, she sees a thousand touching proofs of the mercies and of the love of Him who ravishes her heart. Notwithstanding her nothingness and her faults, she dares to raise towards a God so high and so holy the eyes of her heart and to ask for a return of affection, she loves God and is beloved by Him. God does not disdain to lower Himself even to her, and often she is astonished at the tenderness which her God manifests towards her. Oh, how consoling and strengthening are these precious but all-too-short moments! How superabundantly they compen-

---

[1] Fr. Chaignon, *Méd. rel.*, 1st. vol., p. 10.

sate for all past sufferings, and give courage to face
new trials! Because the soul loves and wishes to
be loved, she cannot endure that anything in her
should offend the most pure eyes of her Well-
Beloved, and so love watches with a jealous eye
over the purity of the heart. What sacrifices
would she not make to preserve or to bring back
the visits of Him who is her all? The more we
love the more we forget ourselves, and the more we
leave ourselves in order to go to God. We seek
God alone, and, therefore, we would think only of
God, speak only of God, live all the day long only
with God, spend ourselves and suffer for Him, and,
after having employed all our energies in serving
Him, still think we had done nothing. Now,
mental prayer is the source whence springs this
holy love: " My heart grew hot within me; and in
my meditation a fire shall flame out." [1]

Louis of Blois thus describes this transformation
of the soul by mental prayer :—" The soul, putting
off everything human, and putting on what is
divine, is, as it were, transformed and changed into
God, as iron placed in the furnace receives the form
of fire and is changed into fire. . . . So the
soul was cold before, but now it has become all inflamed; it was in darkness before, but now it
shines; it was hard before, but now it has become
soft. Its entire being takes on a celestial aspect,
because its essence is all penetrated by the divine
essence." Now that the soul has found God it

[1] Ps. xxxviii., Cor meum concaluit intra me et in meditatione
meâ exardescet ignis.

willingly renounces creatures. She possesses in fact, light, strength, peace, joy, liberty; for in finding God, she has found all good.

2°. The second obstacle which the will offers to our progress regards our resolutions; it is sluggishness, weakness, cowardice, inconstancy. The sole remedy for this evil is God's grace, without which we can do nothing, and with which we can do all things. Now, nowhere is it asked for so well as in mental prayer, when meditation has made us feel the need of it, and the heart is inflamed with holy affections; we have then the eloquence of a poor man who is sensible of his misery, and prayer, as a loud cry, bursts forth from the depths of the soul. Then it is that we gain more strength to do violence to God's mercy, who wants to be implored, who wishes to be constrained, who wills to be overcome by a kind of importunity on our part.[1]

§ III.—WHAT THE SAINTS HAVE THOUGHT OF MENTAL PRAYER.

They have devoted to it long hours day and night, and no argument is equal to that. Many amongst them have praised it very highly in their writings.

St. Bonaventure, quoted or analysed by St. Peter of Alcantara,[2] makes the following poetic eulogy of it:—" If you would suffer with patience the adversities and miseries of this life, be a man of

[1] S. Greg., in Ps. pœnit., 6.
[2] St. Peter of Alc. *Treatise on Prayer*, 1st part, c. i.

prayer. If you would obtain courage and strength to conquer the temptations of the enemy, be a man of prayer. If you would mortify your own will with all its inclinations and appetites, be a man of prayer. If you would know the wiles of Satan and unmask his deceits, be a man of prayer. If you would live in joy and walk pleasantly in the ways of penance, be a man of prayer. If you would banish from your soul the troublesome flies of vain thoughts and cares, be a man of prayer. If you would nourish your soul with the very sap of devotion, and keep it always full of good thoughts and good desires, be a man of prayer. If you would strengthen and keep up your courage in the ways of God, be a man of prayer. In fine, if you would uproot all vices from your soul and plant all virtues in their place, be a man of prayer. It is in prayer that we receive the unction and grace of the Holy Ghost, who teaches all things. I say more : if you would raise yourself to the heights of contemplation and enjoy the sweet embraces of the Spouse, practice mental prayer. It is the way by which the soul is raised to the contemplation and enjoyment of heavenly things."

"In mental prayer," adds St. Peter of Alcantara,[1] the soul is purified from its sins, nourished with charity, confirmed in faith, and strengthened in hope; the mind expands, the affections dilate, the heart is purified, truth becomes evident; temptation is conquered, sadness dispelled; the senses are renovated; the drooping powers revive;

[1] St. Peter of Alc. *Treatise on Prayer*, 1st part. c. i.

tepidity ceases; the rust of vices disappears.   Out of
mental prayer issue forth, like living sparks, those
desires of heaven which the soul conceives when
inflamed with the fire of divine love.   Sublime is
the excellence of mental prayer, great are its
privileges; to mental prayer heaven is opened; to
mental prayer heavenly secrets are manifested and
the ear of God is ever attentive."

St. Teresa, who may be called the doctor of
mental prayer, never ceases to urge her daughters
to practice it and would have wished to lead them
up to its heights.   It is mental prayer that saved
her.   "There, nothing is to be feared, and
everything that can be desired is to be found.   Progress is slow, be it so. . . .   But, at all
events, we learn by degrees to know the road
to heaven. . . .   It is not in vain that we
have chosen God for our friend.   For, in my
opinion, prayer is only a friendly intercourse in
which the soul converses alone with Him by whom
she knows that she is loved. . . .   Oh, my
Master, what an excellent friend Thou art in her
regard!   I have seen it clearly in my own case, and
I know not why every one would not aspire to draw
near to Thee by a friendship so intimate.   Those
who give up mental prayer I really pity, they serve
God at their own cost.   It is not so with those who
practise mental prayer.   This adorable master pays
all their expenses.   In exchange for a little trouble
He gives them consolations which enable them to
bear all crosses. . . .   God grants such sublime
graces, as He has given me, only to mental prayer.

If we close against Him this door, in vain would He seek to enter the soul to take his delight there and to flood her with joy, because He finds no way open." [1]   The demon seeks by every means to turn us away from prayer; " he well knows, the traitor, that a soul that perseveres in prayer is lost to him for ever; . . . you may believe me, she will arrive at the harbour of salvation." [2]   The saint relates that, during long years, " she was less absorbed by useful and holy reflexions than by the longing to hear the clock announcing the end of prayer-time "; she would have preferred the severest penance to the torment of having to recollect herself; " on entering the place of prayer, she was seized with a mortal sadness "; but " when she had conquered herself, she tasted more peace and delight than on certain other days when her inclination had led her to prayer." [3]   She relates also how the demon tried to persuade her that her imperfections rendered her unworthy of giving so much time to prayer, and that she ought, like the others, to be satisfied with the time allotted to that exercise by the rule.   " Where were my wits? What folly to fly the light, to stumble at every step in the dark !   What a proud humility the demon knew how to suggest in order to induce me to abandon mental prayer, that pillar, that staff," of which I had so great a need !   " In my opinion, it is the greatest danger I incurred in my whole life." [4]   Let those, then, who have begun to walk

---

[1] *Life*, viii.   [3] *Ibid.*, viii.
[2] *Ibid.*, xix.   [4] *Ibid.*, xix.

in this way "continue to advance always, no matter what obstacle presents itself, no matter what difficulty crops up, or what tribulation they must endure, however much they may be blamed and reviled, whatever faintheartedness they may feel on the road, whatever uncertainty they may experience as to their arriving at the goal, however apparent it may be in their case that they can never support so many labours; in fine, though they should die in consequence, though the whole world and all it contains were to perish with them, let them never stop advancing on this path." [1]

"Since mental prayer," says St. Francis of Sales," [2] "brings our intellect to the light of God, and keeps our will exposed to the flames of divine love, there is nothing which can better dispel the darkness with which ignorance and error have obscured our intelligence, nor better purify our hearts from all our depraved affections. It is the water of benediction which should serve to wash away the iniquities of our souls, to refresh our heart consumed by the thirst of our cupidity, and to nourish the first seeds which virtue has there planted, and which are good desires."

St. Philip Neri, with his uncompromising energy, says that "a religious without mental prayer is an animal without reason"; that is, that he ceases to live by faith, to walk by the spirit, in order to become the slave of his senses.

According to St. Liguori,[3] "as long as a person

[1] *Way*, xxii.
[2] *Devout Life*, 2nd part, c. i.
[3] *True Spouse*, xv. § 1.

gives herself to mental prayer you will behold her
a model of modesty, of humility, of devotion, and
of mortification; let her abandon mental prayer,
and soon the modesty of her looks disappears, her
pride will burst forth at the least word which
offends. . . . She will scarcely think any
longer of mortifying herself, on the contrary, you
will behold her in love with vanities, amusements,
and earthly pleasures. Why? The water of grace
flows into her soul no longer, she wants life; she
has abandoned mental prayer, the garden is parched
up, and the evil grows daily worse"! "We
see some," adds the holy doctor, "who recite the
rosary, the office of the Blessed Virgin, and give
themselves to other exterior practices of piety, and
nevertheless continue to live in sin; but when any
one constantly practises mental prayer it is impossible for him to continue to live in sin." He also
goes so far as to declare mental prayer to be
" morally necessary." It is especially indispensable
for those who are tending to perfection, all the saints
have arrived there by this way; it is the shortest
road to it, according to St. Ignatius of Loyola.

This moral necessity, however, is incumbent only
on souls that are not incapable of making mental
prayer. Should there be found minds for whom this
was really impossible, God would supply its place by
pious reading and vocal prayer well made, and this
would suffice to lead them even to perfection. But
we must be very careful not to take difficulty for an
impossibility, nor our own negligence for an ex-
cusing cause. When we know how to reflect upon

our work, our occupation, on a thousand temporal affairs, can it be possible that it is only on the things of heaven and our eternal interests that we cannot think ? There is no need of fine phrases nor of lofty conceptions. It suffices to reflect on the things of God in oneself and for oneself alone as simply as one pleases. Books to aid us are not wanting, and it is a science which is acquired by study and practice. It may seem troublesome at first, but experience will make it easy.

We beg, therefore, our brethren in religion to make well the meditations prescribed by the rule, but not to be satisfied with that. As the members of a community have not all the same tastes nor the same aptitude, our constitutions impose only a minimum accessible to every one, and this is the measure indicated by St. Liguori : " The confessor at first should not prescribe more than half an hour, afterwards he can more or less increase the time according to the soul's spiritual progress." [1] Our constitutions expect that " when the Work of God,[2] which takes precedence of everything, is ended, the monks, during the hours not assigned to manual labour, should occupy themselves in prayer or spiritual reading." They advise us, with our Holy Father St. Benedict, " to apply ourselves frequently to prayer," and they permit every one, " outside the time of the common exercises, to give himself to prayer, if drawn to it by the inspiration of divine grace.[3]

[1] St. Lig., *Praxis*, 123.
[2] So the Divine Office is called by St. Benedict.—*Trans.*
[3] Cons. O. C. R., 83, 84, 92.

Do you wish to know why our houses are no longer peopled with saints as they were in the heroic ages? We watch, we chant, we fast, we work pretty much as our Fathers did; but we are not to the same extent as they were, men of prayer; they trampled the world under foot because their "conversation was in heaven."[1]

The holy Abbot St. Antony spent the whole night in prayer, and complained that the day came too soon to interrupt his converse with God. St. Rose of Lima spent twelve hours in prayer daily. St. Francis Borgia used to spend eight hours in prayer, and to beg "as a favour yet another moment." St. Philip Neri passed whole nights in prayer. The Rev. Fr. Torres imposed on the religious whom he directed an hour's mental prayer in the morning, a second hour during the day, and half an hour in the evening, unless they were otherwise hindered. After quoting these examples, St. Liguori adds: "If this seems to you too much, I advise you to make at least one hour of mental prayer besides that made in common."[2] It is true we have many other pious exercises, but we are contemplatives by profession; "let us then allow no one to surpass us in the love of God since we more than others are obliged to love Him."[3] The world, too, needs our prayers so badly!

Let us conclude with a counsel of St. Peter of Alcantara: "The servant of God should reserve

[1] Phil. iii. 20.
[2] St. Lig., *The True Spouse*, xv. § 2.
[3] Id. *Serm. to Ordinandi.*

to himself certain moments, when, laying aside all occupations, even holy ones (the necessary permission being pre-supposed), he will devote himself exclusively to spiritual exercises, and give to his soul a more abundant spiritual nourishment which may repair the daily losses, and procure for him new strength to advance still more.   And if this be true of ordinary days, how much more so of great feasts and of times of tribulation and trial? It is also advisable to do this after long journeys and certain affairs which distract and dissipate the heart; this is the true means to regain recollection of spirit." [1]

[1] St. Peter of Alcant., *Prayer and Medit.*, 2nd p., v., 5th counsel.

CHAPTER IV

THE ELEMENTS OF SUCCESS IN MENTAL PRAYER

ALTHOUGH the non-mystical kinds of mental prayer are accessible to all, with perhaps some very rare exceptions, yet account must first of all be taken of the will of God, who distributes His gifts as He pleases. Still there are divers elements of success that depend on our own will. Some of these regard the dispositions of our soul, others our monastic observances, others in fine mental prayer itself.

§ I.—DISPOSITIONS OF THE SOUL.

Let us put in the first place the degree of purity to which the soul has attained. There will always be a rather strict proportion between holiness of life and the degree of mental prayer one has arrived at. These two things run parallel, and give each other mutual support; they progress together or they fall away together. Meditation, for instance, produces little by little purity of heart, and this latter predisposes the soul to contemplation.

It is, therefore, of supreme importance to acquire the fourfold purity of the conscience, of the heart, of the intellect, and of the will.

1°. Purity of conscience, which is a state of aversion for venial sin. Some slight faults still escape the soul, but she is not satisfied to live in the habit of these faults, and to permit them to take root. She is watchful over herself, combats sin, detaches herself from it, conceives a profound horror of it, and, "loving cleanness of heart, she has the king for her friend."[1] On the other hand, if she is entangled in any affection for sin, she has no longer the same relish for God, and God has no longer the same liking for her; all these multiplied, ill-combated faults, like a thick and icy cloud, dim the eye of faith, cool holy affections, benumb the will and paralyse its good resolutions. After our falls we must hasten to confess them with humility, and to blot them out by a prompt repentance.

Nevertheless, "even in and after our sorrow for our sins," says St. Francis of Sales, "we should keep our peace of mind. . . . Put aside then all that gloomy, restless, peevish, and therefore proud depression." In consequence of a repentance full of trust in God, our very weaknesses, by humbling us, become a part of our remedy; and, according to the same saint, to rise constantly without ever being discouraged, without losing anything of our firm resolution to belong wholly to God, is the effect of heroic virtue. Such a soul pleases Our Lord very much and draws Him to her by her humility.

2°. Purity of heart. Our heart is pure when we love only God, or according to God. We must,

[1] Prov. xxii. 11.

therefore, banish thence every culpable affection, sever every tie of which the Divine Master is not the beginning and the end, and which is not regulated according to His will.   As long as we are attached to anything created, we have no longer the same freedom to raise ourselves to God; the affections of the heart engross the thoughts and distract the mind; and then these thoughts and affections draw us far away from Our Lord towards the object of our love. If, on the contrary, the heart belongs to God alone, our thoughts and affections move at ease in prayer, as a fish does in water.   The heart carries the soul to God, and then everything else becomes to it insipid; and, whilst it is making and multiplying acts of love, it holds the mind captive and keeps it steadily fixed upon God, like to a mother who, passionately loving her child, finds no difficulty in thinking of him, in gazing upon him for whole days together; in fact, to look upon him and to love him is her very life; and to sacrifice herself for him is her happiness.

3°. Purity of mind.   This is the control we exercise over the working of our imagination, our memory, and our thoughts, in order to banish whatever sullies or endangers the soul, and even what merely dissipates or unduly engrosses it.

First, then, there are bad or dangerous thoughts, imaginations and memories; all, for instance, that is contrary to the holy virtue, to charity, to humility, &c.; all that recalls the real or imagined success, injuries, or praise we met with in the past; all that nourishes resentment, bitterness, or a too tender affection; whatever could attract and seduce

us, such as beauty and pleasure; in a word, whatever would stain the purity or trouble the peace of
the soul.

There are also useless thoughts which distract the
mind; idle at first, they soon become dangerous and
culpable.

Finally, there are thoughts good in themselves,
but which come at a wrong time, or absorb too
much of our attention; they regard, for instance,
our work, our office, our studies; but it is not now
the time to attend to them; or, if it be, instead
of admitting them only as far as duty requires,
we allow them to invade, pre-occupy, or even wholly
absorb us. Or they may be thoughts connected
with virtue, but in such a way as to cause
agitation and trouble, as happens in the case of
scruples.

If we wish to become men of prayer we must
regulate and discipline the mind; for whatever
sullies, troubles, or distracts it can only be harmful
to union with God. All this is an obstacle to
recollection and attention, stifles devotion, paralyses good resolutions, and causes a mutual coldness between God and the soul. God willingly
communicates Himself to hearts that are pure, to
minds that keep silence in order to listen to Him;
He loves not to raise His voice in the midst of
tumult; and an unmortified soul is exposed to the
turmoil and noise of a thousand various thoughts.
To abandon oneself habitually to every caprice of
one's mind, and to aspire at the same time to
become a man of prayer, is to desire the impos-

sible; you might just as reasonably select as your place of prayer the most crowded street of one of our great cities.

When our heart has been thoroughly purified, the disorder of our thoughts will cause us less trouble, it will hardly have any hold upon us. Meanwhile, we must ceaselessly watch and combat. St. Bernard [1] points out to us the means to gain the victory. "Place at the door of your memory a porter called the remembrance of your profession, and when your mind feels itself overwhelmed by weight of shameful thoughts, let it reproach itself in these terms: Come, now, ought you to think on such things, you who are a priest, you who are a cleric, you who are a monk? Does it become a servant of God, a friend of God, to dwell upon such thoughts were it only for an instant? So also at the door of your will, where carnal desires usually dwell like a family at home, place a sentinel named the memory of your heavenly country; for it has the power to expel evil desires *as one wedge drives out another.* . . . Finally, beside reason's couch you must post a guardian so inexorable that he spares no one, and this guardian is the remembrance of Hell." The memory of the Passion, and also that of benefits received are likewise excellent door-keepers; but the most vigilant will ever be the love of God.

4°. Purity of the will. Our will is pure when it no longer desires anything but the will of God. It is pure in its interior dispositions, when it is

[1] St. Bernard, *Serm.* 32 *de div.*

thoroughly resolved to submit to the laws of God and of His Church, to our rules, to the orders of superiors, to the guidance of Providence; in a word, when it is ready to do always what God wills, in the time and manner that He wills, and for the motives that please Him. God, thus being master of our will in its interior dispositions, will also be master of its external acts; the source will communicate its own purity to the stream.

We must, above all, take care to maintain our will in this habitual tendency, and when we must pass on to acts, especially if they flatter some passion, or if they are in harmony with some natural inclination, we must watch over our intentions to purify them and make them supernatural, and over our acts themselves lest they deviate from the straight path and end in self-love.

The purity of the will contributes to the success of mental prayer just as does purity of conscience, of which it is the source. Between the soul and God union of wills produces union of hearts and a holy familiarity; on the contrary, disagreement of wills breaks off this intimate union and replaces it by constraint and coldness. When the soul is ready to do whatever God wills she has no difficulty in understanding what her duty is and resolving to perform it; whilst any attachment to our own judgment and our own will blinds the eyes of the intellect, hinders good resolutions, and thus sterilizes mental prayer, which fails to attain its principal end if it does not break off this attachment.

To sum up, purity of conscience draws God to us; purity of mind contributes to recollection and attention; purity of heart to devotion; purity of will to efficacious resolutions. When a soul is thus purified she has God alone in the mind, God alone in the heart, God alone in the will; now that she has removed the obstacles she converses quite naturally with her Guest, and finds in her prayer great facility, real profit, and sometimes even delight.

We do not require this purification to be already accomplished, in order that the soul may enter upon the way of meditation and take its first steps with success; on the contrary, we are perfectly well aware that meditation is one of the great means to arrive at this purity. We merely mean to say that purity of life and mental prayer travel hand in hand, and lend each other a mutual support; and that the great preparation we must bring to mental prayer is steady progress in purifying our souls by prayer, by our penitential life, and other ordinary means. Happy we, should it please God to perfect this purification at some future day, in the crucible of passive purgation!

§ II.—OUR MONASTIC OBSERVANCES.

Enclosure cuts off the noises of the world, and favours solitude of heart and mind; our austerities, by detaching the soul from sensible pleasures, leave it free to raise itself to God; all our observances, when well kept, contribute to produce

that fourfold purity which is the sister of mental
prayer. St. Bernard[1] in particular says that fasting "imparts devotion and confidence to prayer.
And so we see how well fasting and prayer go
together, according to what is written : ' When a
brother is helped by a brother, both shall be consoled.'[2]   Prayer obtains the strength to fast, and
fasting merits the grace of prayer. Fasting
strengthens prayer, prayer sanctifies fasting and
offers it to the Lord." Two of our observances,
silence, namely, and the good use of our free
time, have a more intimate relation to mental
prayer.

How can a religious neglect to observe silence
and be also a man of prayer? Besides multiplying acts of disobedience, small scandals, and sins
of the tongue, he shows by his talkativeness that
God is not enough for him, that he knows not how
to abide with himself and watch over his interior;
by speaking, he is constantly labouring to empty
himself of God, to lose the perfume of piety, to
extinguish all devotion; by listening, to fill his
soul with dissipation and to deliver it up to the
demon of curiosity and levity. So St. John
Climacus says that "much speaking dries up the
tears of compunction, destroys the custody of the
heart, renders meditation distracted, cools and
freezes divine fervour, weakens or rather kills
prayer. But, on the contrary, silence is the
father of prayer, the master of contemplation,

---

[1] St. Bernard, *Serm.* 4, *on Lent.*
[2] Prov. xviii. 19.

. . . the guardian of divine fervour, the secret path by which the soul ascends to God, the lover of tears, etc." [1]

External silence of tongue and gesture is not sufficient, if the memory and imagination may prattle away and fill us with distractions. Our silence itself ought to be occupied with God, and, the more silent we are towards men, the more sustained ought to be our conversation with Him. Silence thus kept makes of our monasteries, in spite of numbers, a solitude as still as the desert, and of the heart of each religious a silent sanctuary, wherein is heard only the prayer which ascends to God and the voice of God lovingly answering the soul.

In like manner, the good use of our free time favours mental prayer. As soon as the bell announces the end of work, let us hasten, unless obedience withholds us, to the place of pious reading, as a hungry man betakes himself to a well-served table. For a fervent religious ought always to have a hunger for God, and during the free time to replenish himself with Him. Whether he prefers to pray or to employ the time in pious reading, he substitutes for the grosser thoughts of work thoughts more divine; if he had been somewhat dissipated, he now returns to God, and plunges once more into the supernatural, into holy thoughts and pious affections. By reading he learns, and acquires a treasure of safe and abundant spiritual knowledge, and thus, according to the

[1] *Ladder*, Degree 4 and 11.

expression attributed to St. Bernard,[1] he will have a substantial nourishment " to chew and ruminate, in order to extract its sap and penetrate with it even the inmost recesses of his heart. How, indeed, can we have holy thoughts, and how can we help making empty and useless meditations, if we be not first of all instructed by reading or sermons?" Thus pious reading is at once the great provider and the guide of our mental prayer.

§ III.—MENTAL PRAYER ITSELF.

Finally, there are elements of success which have reference to mental prayer itself.

1°. We must adopt that which suits our degree of progress.

It is the common teaching of the saints,[2] that to each of the three ways, purgative, illuminative, and unitive, corresponds a special kind of prayer. Beginners need meditation; those who have already made some progress will succeed better with affective prayer and derive more profit from it; to the most proficient the prayer of simplicity will be best suited, unless, indeed, God should raise them to mystical contemplation. Let us not conceive the silly ambition of rising at once to the higher kinds of prayer; we would resemble a child who would want to work with his father's tools although he can hardly lift them. David[3] was unable to move in the gigantic armour of Saul; if he had

---

[1] *Scala claustral.*

[2] Rodriguez, *On Prayer*, c. vi. Suarez, *De Devot.*, ix., 3.

[3] I Kings xvii. 38.

kept it on, it would only have encumbered him and led to his ruin; he took it off, relied upon his sling, and triumphed.   An opposite, and not less fatal mistake consists in wishing to confine oneself to meditation for one's whole life; for after some time it has produced its effect, and then becomes unprofitable; to persist in it, therefore, would mean to be perpetually recommencing a work already done, a path already traversed.   Let every one keep to the kind of prayer that suits him; and, of course, in such a delicate matter the advice of a wise director is especially necessary.

2°. We should choose a subject suitable to our needs.   To take up a book of meditations, even the very best, and to go through all its meditations one after another, whether they suit the state of our soul or not, is the very way often to make entirely useless meditations.   In a good meditation-book there are remedies for all ills; but no one in a pharmacy would think of taking the remedies in the order in which they are placed on the shelves— to-day the first bottle, to-morrow the second, then the third.   There are tools for fashioning all the virtues; the choice of them should be made according to the work and purpose we aim at accomplishing.

Now, (1), to every one it is profitable to foster or revive the general desire of perfection. (2). All again, except the most advanced, ought to come to a resolution which is particular and suited to their needs, as, for instance, the practical way to extirpate such a vice, to cultivate such a virtue.

These principles being laid down, beginners

having for their object to purge themselves from sin—*i.e.*, to repent, to atone, to correct themselves; and having to fight against temptations, passions, and evil inclinations; combat being their element, fear their main-spring, should, unless they be scrupulous, choose for their ordinary subjects of meditation the great truths of salvation, everything in fact which may excite this fear which is their motive power. The " *Maxims of Eternity* " [1] of St. Liguori, for instance, would be for them an excellent manual.

Those who are more advanced—the proficients—although they may not abandon the fight, have, however, for their principal object the acquisition of virtues, especially of faith and hope without forgetting obedience, humility, and self-denial. What sustains one in this long and rugged path is, first of all, the hope of eternal goods, and the example of Our Lord. These, then, should generally leave aside the great truths, unless, indeed, they meditate upon them under a new light, namely, in order to excite themselves to the practice of virtue, and should habitually choose such subjects as Heaven, divine grace, and glory, the value of efforts and sacrifices, the mysteries of Our Lord's life and death, the obligations of their state, vices, and virtues, &c.; then there will come a time when their attraction will be to meditate on the truths which are apt to inflame love. The greater number indeed of meditation-books seem written for proficients.

[1] More fully developed in his "*Preparation for Death.*" Centenary Ed. Vol. I.—*Trans.*

In the unitive way, God has been found, is
possessed, and at times is enjoyed with delight.
There remains still a struggle to be maintained,
and progress to be made; but the ordinary state of
the soul is that of a loving union with God. Fear
has become more filial; hope, on the side of self-
interest is often as it were unconscious; love it is
which now rules; it is it which now has most power
to move and most charm to occupy the soul. The
time of prayer is now passed in simple and but
little varied acts of loving union; the soul thinks
upon God with less reasoning, it looks upon Him
rather than reasons; and above all it makes acts
of love, praise, admiration, humble adoration,
devotion, self-abandonment, &c. The same love
which makes our prayer an effusion of the heart
before God, communicates at the same time to the
conscience more delicacy, to the will more generosity, to the hand more energy. It becomes the
main source whence spring affections and actions.
Souls arrived at this point will find hardly any
profit in meditation-books.

Jesus Christ being our all, the beginning, the
way, and the goal, it is only right that He should
be the chiefest object which occupies us in prayer.
Some will meditate on His childhood, others on
His hidden life, His divine Heart, the Holy
Eucharist . . . , &c. St. Liguori advises meditation especially on the Passion. The particular
mystery is of small consequence, provided that
there Our Lord is found. St. Francis of Sales [1]

---

[1] St. Francis of Sales, *The Devout Life*, 2nd p., c. i.

recommends " meditations made upon Our Lord's Life and Passion; looking upon Him by frequent meditations your whole soul will be filled with Him, you will learn His demeanour, and model your actions upon His; . . . you will learn, with the aid of His grace, to speak, act, and will like Him. . . . In all our prayers and actions the Saviour should be meditated, considered, sought after," that our soul may be nourished by the " bread which has come down from Heaven."

What we have just said is rather a direction than an invariable rule; there are certain feasts and certain circumstances which will determine differently the subject of our prayer.[1] Besides, account must be taken of our spiritual leanings; and, finally, according to St. Liguori,[2] " the good rule is to meditate by preference upon the truths and the mysteries which affect us more powerfully, and which procure for our soul the most abundant nourishment."

3°. Beginners especially are advised to prepare the subject of the morning meditation, " to consecrate to it the last thoughts of the evening before and the first thoughts of the next morning. . . . According to the most renowned masters who have treated of mental prayer, the subject should be determined upon from the evening before, at least in its general lines, and the less that is left to accident and to mental effort at the time itself of meditation the more secure will be our prayer. . . . Negligence in preparing the points is men-

---

[1] *Cf.*, 2nd part, c. i., § 1.   [2] St. Lig., *True Spouse*, c. xv.

tioned as one of the causes which commonly produce aridity." [1]

This preparation is indispensable when we have
to make our mental prayer in the dark, but may
still be fruitfully made, even when we are to use a
light, because we shall thus bring to our prayer
a mind full of the subject. It would, however, be
too much to exact it for every meditation which we
may make during free time. When treating of the
prayer of simplicity we will point out who those are
that may omit all preparation of this kind.

4°. Another element of success, upon which St.
Teresa strongly insists,[2] is a determined will to
persevere in prayer in spite of temptations,
troubles and aridity. For this the saint gives
three reasons : God, who heaps His favours upon us,
well deserves that we should give up to Him a little
of our time. The demon fears nothing so much as
strong and resolute souls; his cowardice prevents
his attacking those who are on their guard, the
more so as what he does to injure them turns to
their profit and his own discomfiture; but if he
finds a soul which has not a will determined to
persevere, he never leaves it at peace, he agitates
it by a thousand fears, and puts before its eyes
numberless difficulties. Finally, we combat much
more generously when we have a fixed resolution
never to yield. To become, therefore, men of
prayer, we must be armed with courage and constancy.

[1] Ribet, *Christian Asceticism*, p. xxxviii., 6.
[2] *Way*, c. xxiii.

CHAPTER V

CAUSES OF FAILURE IN MENTAL PRAYER

WE shall notice distractions, tepidity of the will, vagueness of resolutions, illusions, and indispositions.

§ I.—DISTRACTIONS.

Some there are which come from the enemy. Prayer is the great battle-field. "The war the enemy wages against us," says the holy Abbot Nilus, "has no other object than to make us abandon mental prayer; prayer is as odious and insupportable to Satan as it is salutary for us." He will let us apply ourselves to our fasts, our mortifications, to whatever may flatter pride, but he cannot endure mental prayer, whereby the soul, by humbling and transforming itself, glorifies God. He seeks to draw off elsewhere our thoughts and affections, to tire us out with a thousand frivolous memories, with dangerous or evil images, to overwhelm us with painful temptations; he disturbs, agitates us; then he will persuade us that we have no aptitude for mental prayer, that we are losing our time at it, that by it we offend God, and that it would be better to omit it entirely than to make it so ill. But to abandon it would be to fall completely into the snare; the channel of grace being once cut off, our soul could only wither and die.

Many of these distractions come from ourselves.

Distractions due to levity.—If I deliberately give full liberty to my eyes to look, to my tongue to speak, to my ears to hear, will not distractions in crowds enter through my ill-guarded senses as through so many open doors? How can we restrain the imagination in prayer, if everywhere else we yield to its caprices? If we have the unfortunate habit of allowing our memory to drift about after everything it recalls, and our light, fickle, and impressionable mind to flutter away like a butterfly in all directions, after its every caprice, how can we become suddenly attentive in prayer after being thus continually dissipated? Instead of that, we are sure to reap then the crop of distractions which we have been sowing all the day long.

Distractions due to passion.—The heart draws the mind after it, and our thoughts of themselves follow after our affections, antipathies and passions. In the agitations caused by anger, jealousy, animosities, and other irregular affections, the soul, like a skiff tossed upon a stormy sea, no longer obeys the helm.

Distractions due to employments.—Manual work, studies, public offices, especially if we abandon ourselves to them without measure and with passion, are wont to recur to our minds and besiege us in the quiet time of prayer, sometimes with a vividness and clearness which are not to be found in the noise of action.

Distractions due to weakness.—It costs a great effort to keep one's mind attentive for any length of time; the truths of faith are supernatural, they demand a thousand sacrifices, and they offer at times so little attraction. At such times, in order to fix one's thoughts, a very strong will to please God and to advance in perfection would be necessary; and the poor soul is so weak!

Every distraction, whatever its source, is culpable, when deliberately entertained, or when voluntary in its cause; not so, however, if you have posited the cause, even recognised as such, with a sufficient motive, and if, moreover, when you perceive your mind to be wandering, you make an effort to bring it back to the subject.

We ought, therefore, to strive earnestly to remove the causes of distractions; for instance, to restrain our imagination and memory, to regulate our affections according to God, to lay aside at the door or our oratory all thoughts of our office, business, &c. However voluntary may have been their original cause, from the moment we retract our consent to it, they cease to be imputable to us on that head.

As for distractions actually adverted to, the sole remedy is to combat them, and for this three things are very useful. 1. To humble ourselves in God's presence; for humility is the remedy for all our ills. 2. Gently to bring back our mind to the subject of our prayer, a thousand times if necessary, for the most part despising the temptation, or, calling fervently upon God, without, however, being disturbed or troubled; for trouble, stirring the soul to

its very depths, only raises more mud; and
besides, even though our whole prayer be passed in
repelling distractions as often at they attack us, we
shall nevertheless have pleased God, as did
Abraham when he drove away the birds from his
sacrifice.[1]   3. Not to expose ourselves to fresh
ramblings by examining too minutely whence these
distractions come, and whether we have consented
to them.   Generally speaking, it is better to defer
this examination to another time.

Every distraction, well combated, far from
injuring us, increases our merits and hastens our
progress; how many acts of humility, patience,
and resignation they make us practise! Every
effort we make to return to God is a preference we
give Him over the objects which draw away our
thoughts, a victory gained over the demon, and
new merit acquired for Heaven.

§ II.—Want of Sincere Devotion and of Strong Resolutions.

We are not here speaking of aridities, but of
lukewarmness of the *will,* of spiritual sloth in mental
prayer.

It costs an effort to establish one's soul in that
fourfold purity which agrees so well with a life of
prayer; it costs something to keep to regularity,
silence, recollection, serious reading; it costs something to keep one's mind fixed on God, in spite of
the distractions which beset us; it costs a great deal

[1] Gen. xv. 11.

to persevere in pious affections amidst the weariness of aridity, and to elicit from a heart plunged in desolation some dry and frigid acts and petitions; it costs a deal to submit oneself to God's will, and to form a resolution which lays the axe to the root of the evil. Hence it is that, like the sluggard, "we will and we will not."[1] A careless life has produced dissipation of mind, enervation of will, lukewarmness of heart. After having elicited some few affections in a half-hearted way, and without conviction, and formed some vague resolutions which aim at the cure of no evil, at the practice of no virtue, we make haste to quit prayer, to divert our mind in active work, and to forget our resolutions almost as soon as made. And we call that a prayer! Alas! how many such would be required to convert a soul! Or, to speak more correctly, the more we multiply such like prayers the more tepid we become; sloth sterilises piety, and converts the best of remedies into a dangerous poison.

Such persons have great need to shake off their torpor and to regain, with the help of prayer and spiritual direction, more courage, more energy, more soul and life. Above all, let them pray and pray again, let them, with loud cries, beg for this devotion, which no one can of himself attain to; for God makes "whomsoever He wills religious, and, if such had been His good pleasure, He could have made the ungodly Samaritans devout."[2] He

[1] Prov. xiii. 4.
[2] St. Amb., *in Luc.*, ix.

will listen willingly to a petition so well calculated
to please Him. These souls should, moreover, co-
operate with the divine action, and, with the aid
of divine grace, neglect nothing needful in order to
prepare themselves and to pray well; they have a
particular need of understanding thoroughly the
value of devotion, of appreciating the misery of
their carelessness, and of re-awakening their
fervour by means of fear, or hope, or love.

§ III.—Illusions in Mental Prayer.

We shall point out briefly some few of these
illusions in order to avoid having to repeat ourselves.

It is an illusion to pretend to become a man of
prayer with a lax conscience, a dissipated mind, a
heart full of attachments, and a will enslaved to
self.

It is an illusion for those who are employed in
absorbing duties, to wish to pass directly from the
tumult of business to the repose of mental prayer;
it is generally necessary to take some little time to
get rid of pre-occupations, to allow agitations to
subside, and to regain the presence of God. Oh,
how precious in our eyes should be the free time
between manual work and the Divine Office !

It is an illusion, at least for a beginner, *not to
choose his subject,* not to read it over attentively,
on the pretext that there will be light and he can
use a book. At the commencement of the spiritual

life, we have need of these precautions, and we are too hasty in thinking ourselves sufficiently advanced to leave them aside.

It is an illusion to want to enter at once on the body of our prayer, without first putting ourselves thoroughly in the presence of God, unless we are just after ending an exercise which has already made us recollected, or we belong to that class of persons who hardly ever lose the sense of the Divine Presence.

It is an illusion to quit too easily the subject we had prepared, not in obedience to the spirit of God who breatheth where He wills, but out of caprice and inconstancy.

It is an illusion to wish to leave off our method too soon, or to be a slave to it. Method is not perfection, it is not even prayer; it is a mere instrument to be used as long as it is serviceable, to be laid aside as soon as it ceases to be useful, much more so when it becomes harmful. Now, in the commencement method is at it were indispensable, a beginner is too much of a child to walk without leading strings; later on it will lose its usefulness; besides the Holy Ghost has His own word to say in the matter, and is under no obligation to regulate His inspirations according to our method. When the prayer of simplicity or mystical contemplation is reached method might be an impediment.

It is an illusion to give *too much* time to considerations. Prayer then becomes a mere speculative study, a labour of the intellect; affections, petitions, resolutions, which are the main point, are neglected; consequently, this exercise remains barren, and hardly any fault is corrected.

It is an illusion to give *too little* time to considerations, and to launch oneself at once wholly and solely into affections. In this way we run the risk of never having any well-grounded or thorough convictions, at least unless we supply this want by serious spiritual reading. And without reflections how long will our pious affections last? Let us, then, devote to considerations a suitable time; more is necessary in the beginning, less will be required in proportion as we advance, but it is only when we are sufficiently prepared for the prayer of simplicity, that they ought to be laid aside.

It is an illusion, when we have found devotion, to leave off too soon the acts which have procured it, and to pass on to others on the pretext of following out our method. " We must halt there as long as the pious affection lasts, even though it should occupy the whole time of our meditation; for, devotion being the end of this exercise, it would be an error to seek for elsewhere, with an uncertain hope, what we are certain of having already found."[1]

It is an illusion to confine our prayer to one small corner of the day, and afterwards to think no more about it. No doubt it produces at the very time it is made a part of its effect; the mind is enlightened, affections and petitions are made, all which has its own value; but this pious exercise does

[1] St. Peter of Alcant., *On Prayer and Meditation*, 1st part, c. xii., 1st counsel.

not yield us all its fruit, unless it results in a practical resolution which corresponds to our needs, and which dwells in the memory in order to be put in practice. A prayer, which does not result in this, is like a remedy that is never applied, an instrument that is never used, a sword that remains in the scabbard.

In fine, it is an illusion to take scrupulosity for delicacy of conscience and its futile pre-occupations for a good prayer. On the contrary, this is one of the greatest obstacles to union with God; an obstacle, because it hinders tranquility of mind and attention to God; an obstacle, because it contracts the heart with sadness, stifles confidence and love, paralyses the will, inclines us to fly from God. Besides, what prayer can there be in a heart tossed about by scruples? Instead of adoring, it is examining its conscience; instead of thanking, it is probing its sores, it asks no pardon, it is too busy investigating its guilt, it begs for no grace, it is too much occupied in self-inspection. It has not then made any prayer, it was too busy with self to have any time to speak to God; or, if it has done so, it was a prayer without confidence, without any expanding of the heart; fear has banished the familiar intercourse of prayer, anxieties have destroyed calm and peace. Scrupulosity is not repentance, it is merely trouble; it is not delicacy of conscience, but its unhealthy counterfeit. Therefore, we must drive it away, by avoiding such subjects for meditation as are calculated to augment a fear already too much developed, by choosing such truths as are most apt to strengthen our confidence, by leaving aside anxious, minute, and disquieting examinations, and especially by blind obedience to our superior or our director.

§ IV.—BODILY INDISPOSITIONS.

Sometimes, says St. Francis de Sales,[1] " disgust, sterility, dryness spring from bodily indisposition, as when through excessive watchings, labours and fasts, we are overwhelmed with drowsiness, lassitude, heaviness, and other such infirmities, which, although they depend on the body, do none the less inconvenience the mind on account of the close union which exists between body and soul. . . . The remedy, in this conjuncture, is to restore our corporal strength."

The saints, however, sought for the fervor and delights of prayer in the midst of their austerities. Far from listening to the demon, who, assuming the rôle of our medical adviser, . . . pleads our constitution, and dins loudly into our ears the infirmities which religious observance, if kept, may engender "[2]; we should, on the contrary, cling to our austerities as to the will of God, and keep our rules with a jealous care as our best inheritance and our true treasure. But as *indiscretion* in penitential exercises injures contemplation, if our body is exhausted and our mind inert, let us make known to our superiors our condition, and abide by what

[1] St. Frances de Sales, *The Devout Life*, 4th part, c. xv.
[2] Hug. of St. Victor, *De Claus*, l. i. c ii.

they tell us to do.   As to voluntary mortifications, let us subject them to the control of our superiors, and not undertake such as tend to ruin our health, to destroy our mental vigour, and render us heavy, inactive, without thought, or life in prayer. Voluntary austerities have their value, but prayer is a more desirable treasure; let us husband our strength in order to give ourselves up to the hard labour of a life of prayer, contemplation being our principal end.

CHAPTER VI

CONSOLATIONS AND DRYNESS

ONE of the most common and deplorable illusions consists in judging of our prayer by the consolation or dryness we meet with therein; in thinking it good because accompanied by consolation, bad, if chilled by desolation. No, no, such is not the case. The best prayer, were it ever so dry, is that which leaves us more humble, more disposed to renounce ourselves, to practise obedience, to live the life of dependence which our state requires, to bear with our brethren, and never to be a burthen to others; in a word, to do in all things the will of God. On the other hand, our prayer, were it an ocean of sweetness, is barren and even baneful when it leaves us more full of ourselves, more attached to our consolations; for our end is not enjoyment here below, but ever to tend to prefection.

Since consolations and aridities may serve or injure us according to the use we make of them, let us examine then what they are, whence they come, whither they tend, and how we are to make use of them. We will here speak chiefly of the consolations and aridities which are met with in ordinary prayer, as we mean to give later on an explanation of the passive purifications and the joys of mystical contemplation.

§ I.—THEIR NATURE.

Devotion is the promptitude with which the will tends to the service of God, to prayer as well as to other duties. The whole substance and marrow of devotion consists in this promptitude, quickness, agility, holy ardour, generosity, and devotedness of the will. With this disposition of soul we possess the essence of devotion; without it we have only its phantom; and this is why this readiness of will is called substantial devotion.

Generally speaking, it is seasoned with a certain charm and sweetness; we tend with love and keen relish to the things of God, we are well with Him; the soul is in peace, the heart joyful, and duty is easy. This sweetness is not devotion; for, without it, the will may be prompt in the service of God; but being superadded to devotion as accident to substance, it is called accidental devotion.

If it remains in the soul without passing into the senses, we have accidental spiritual devotion; if it spread from the soul to the senses like the overflow of a vessel which is too full, we then have accidental sensible devotion, or, to express it more concisely, sensible devotion. Then the heart is dilated with joy, and beats with more life, the eyes glisten and moisten with tears, the face is radiant, the voice full of emotion, all the senses filled with sweet impressions. And this sometimes reaches even to a kind of transport and of spiritual inebriation.

Sometimes, on the other hand, although the will

does its duty with generosity, the senses are not affected, the soul is not pervaded by this sweetness, it feels itself abandoned; the mind is empty and has no ideas, the heart is cold and conceives only affections without relish, and the will remains without energy. This is aridity, dryness, abandonment, desolation.

According to St. Liguori, says Fr. Desurmont,[1] "there are three kinds of ordinary mental prayer. The first is *easy prayer*, in which the soul, aided by grace, produces (at least with ease, and sometimes with sweetness) the various acts peculiar to conversation with God. The second is *dry prayer*, during which the soul can only make petitions, and humble and resign itself. The third is the *prayer of desolation*, in which the soul can hardly do more than utter a cry of alarm."

According to this teaching, then, consolations are not devotion; for the prompt will, which is the essence of devotion, may very well subsist without consolations, or be altogether wanting in spite of their presence.

St. Francis of Sales [2] gives as an example a child who weeps tenderly on seeing its mother bled, but none the less refuses to give her the apple it holds in its hand; so some souls experience great tenderness of heart, utter sighs, and shed tears when meditating on the Passion, but will not sacrifice to Our Lord some trifling affection, delight, or

---

[1] *The Divine Art of Mental Prayer.*
[2] St. Francis de Sales, *Devout Life*, part iv., c. xiii.

satisfaction, which He wishes to take from them."
Such persons have, indeed, some feelings, but
they have no devotedness; their sensibility alone is
touched, their will is not devoted to God. "Ah!
all that is only children's friendship, tender indeed,
but weak, fanciful and without effect. Devotion,
therefore, does not consist in these tender feelings
and sensible affections."

On the other hand, dryness does not always prove
a want of devotion. Certainly, if the will faces its
duty feebly, if it has become cowardly and without
energy with regard to obedience, mutual forbearance, humiliations, &c.; if in time of prayer it
makes hardly any effort against distractions, and
does itself no violence to keep united to God; the
soul has lost not only the sweetness of devotion but
devotion itself. But if the will remains prompt
and generous in fulfilling its duties, if, in prayer,
it does what it can to remain united to God, even
though it may hardly succeed in so doing, the soul
has lost only sensible devotion, but has preserved
substantial devotion, and has not ceased to belong
to God and to please Him.

§ II.—The Origin and Tendency of Consola-
tions and Desolations.

Consolations and desolations may come from
God, from nature, or from the demon.

1°. In order to attract the soul to spiritual goods,
God at first feeds it with the milk of interior con-

solations, with an abundance of happy tears. This is not a proof that the soul is strong and devout, but rather that it is weak, since God treats it as a child; it is God, who is good, and not ourselves. He lavishes upon us His consolations and caresses us to the end that those higher joys may banish from our minds the coarse delights of this earth, that our heart may be won by His goodness, and that we may lovingly embrace His will by our obedience and fidelity. But, alas! these bounties of God inspire us with a secret self-complacency, which is displeasing to Him, and we seize upon these spiritual sweets with a greediness which St. John of the Cross calls spiritual gluttony, so that "we seek the consolations of God as much and perhaps more than we do the God of consolations; and, if this sweetness were separable from love, we would abandon love to keep the sweetness." [1] Hence it is that, as soon as we are capable of supporting the withdrawal of these consolations, without abandoning virtue, God takes them from us, because we make a bad use of them.

He withdraws them, because we have failed to employ them in producing those fruits of virtue and self-sacrifice which He expected from our use of them.

He withdraws them, because we have been negligent in receiving them, and so when we get up to gather the manna, behold, it is melted away!

He withdraws them because we cannot at the

---

[1] St. Francis of Sales, *Love of God*, b. ix. c. x.

same time enjoy earthly and heavenly delights. The seeking of our own satisfaction, disorderly attachment to creatures, deliberate venial sin, and especially a habit of such sins, effectually dry up devotion.

He withdraws them, adds St. Bernard, on account of our pride; whether it be that we have already fallen into this vice, or that we should, without this withdrawal, fall into it. " The taking away of grace, is a proof of pride. . . . Pride, either already existing in the soul, or to be apprehended in the future, is always a cause of the withdrawal of grace." [1]

According to Fr. Faber, " the time of prayer is God's time for punishing us for our faults. Then it is that our venial sins, our slight infidelities, our inordinate friendships, our worldly attachments rise up against us, and we must pay the penalty of them." [2] It would perhaps be more exact to say that God awaits us there in order to admonish us of our faults, to correct us like a father, and to bring us back to our duty.

To resume then, by sending us dryness, God means to humble us, to detach us from creatures, to complete the purification of our soul, to lead us to a better appreciation of His gifts, to a more ardent desire of them, and to a greater readiness to make sacrifices in order to seek them. It is one of the ways, one of the artifices of God's love to make

[1] St. Bernard, *In cant. serm.*, 54, n° 10.
[2] Fr. Faber, *Growth in Holiness*, xv.

E

Himself loved, to unite Himself more closely with
a soul hungering and panting with the desire of
Him, and to make it, in the meantime, practise more
heroic and more meritorious acts of virtue.

2°. The demon has no power to enter directly into
our intellect and will, but he can exert a great
influence over the blood, the humours, the nerves,
the imagination, and the senses. Sometimes he
excites in us feelings of sweetness and consolation;
he thus urges the soul to indiscretion in austere
practices, in order to render it useless by ruining
its health, or to drive it later on into discouragement,
by the fatigue caused by a burden which is too
heavy; he entices it to take a secret complacence
in its own virtue, or to conceive an inordinate love of
these spiritual sweets. Whilst engaging her in this
treacherous game, he hides from the soul defects
and faults which stand in much need of correction;
he tries to persuade her that she is remarked and
admired; he urges her to desire supernatural favours
that may set her on a pedestal of honor; he seeks, in
a word, to throw her into pride and sentimentalism,
at the expense of true spiritual progress, which is
ever solidly based on humility and abnegation.

Sometimes again the demon creates dryness in
the soul to cause disunion between her and God,
and that too, in prayer itself, whose end is to foster
divine union. He fatigues the mind by a multitude of impertinent thoughts; he aggravates the
apparent sterility of her prayer by temptations of
all sorts; he overwhelms the sufferer with sleep,
sadness, vexation; he suggests abominable

thoughts; he hopes that the soul will be lost by consenting to evil, or at least be discouraged. Can God hear a prayer so ill made? Is it not a mockery to multiply acts of faith, love, and such like, when it seems to us that we believe in nothing, and that our heart is frozen? Instead of accepting our prayer shall not God be rather offended by it? Is it worth while taking so much trouble to arrive at nothing but committing sins even in prayer? Then, if God sends us neither light nor devotion, is it not because He is indifferent, irritated, implacable? We serve Him so ill! we don't know how even to pray! &c. In short, the demon wishes to make us abandon prayer, or to render it sterile; and for this object the attraction of pleasure, the fear of difficulties, presumption, or despair—anything at all will suit his purpose—provided only that he can separate the soul from God and make us partakers of his own lot, which is eternal torments and banishment from heaven.

Often the demon insinuates himself into the consolations given by God, in order to turn these latter from their end; and into the desolations sent by God, in order to drive us into discouragement. And in these cases we must co-operate with the divine action, and combat the diabolical temptation.

3°. Consolations and desolations may also come from our own nature.

When fatigue and pre-occupations are not overwhelming us, when our body is full of vigour and health, when we have the head clear and the heart content, prayer easily abounds in consolations.

There are also some sensitive and impressionable natures whose emotions are aroused by a mere nothing. When they consider the benefits, mercies, and perfections of God, or the mysteries of our Saviour's life and death, especially on feast days, their hearts are full of love and their tears flow readily.

On the other hand, there are days when nature is weighed down by fatigue, sufferings, and cares; when the mind is empty, the heart insensible, the eyes dry, and the whole soul without life; then prayer becomes a painful labour, if we try to undertake the task.

Given the corruption of nature, our soul, in these alternations of sadness and joy, is accessible at one time to the demon of vain complacence and spiritual gluttony, at another to the demon of discouragement; but God is there, and we can always resist and gain the victory.

By the above signs it may be seen whence come our consolations and desolations. To throw more light, however, on this subject let us add a few words from St. Francis of Sales.[1] " Since there are sensible consolations which are good, and come from God, and yet others which are useless, dangerous, and even pernicious, coming from nature, or even from the enemy, how can I distinguish them from each other, so as to know the bad or useless from the good? The general teaching, my dear Philothea, concerning our affections

---

[1] St. Francis of Sales. *Devout Life*, 4th part, c. xiv.

and passions is that we are to know them by their fruit. . . . If sweetness, tenderness, and consolations render us more humble, patient, tractable, charitable, and compassionate with regard to our neighbour, more fervent in mortifying our concupiscence and evil inclinations, more constant in our pious exercises, more manageable and pliable in the hands of those to whom we owe obedience, more simple in our conduct, there is no doubt, Philothea, but that they come from God. But if these sweets have sweetness only for ourselves, and if they render us curious, bitter, punctilious, impatient, obstinate, haughty, presumptuous, harsh towards our neighbour, and if, thinking ourselves already little saints, we are no longer willing to be subject to direction or correction, indubitably they are false and pernicious consolations. (And by these same principles we must also form our judgment of aridities.)   A good tree produces only good fruits.''

§ III.—Practical Conduct.

On the part of the intelligence.—1°. Let us commence by examining our conscience by the light of these principles, in order to see whence come our consolations and desolations, and especially what effects they produce in our souls. '' But remark, Philothea,'' says St. Francis of Sales,[1] '' that we must not make this examination with disquietude

----

[1] St. Francis of Sales, *Devout Life*, 4th part, c. xiv.

and too much curiosity. After having carefully considered our excesses in this respect, if we find the cause of the evil in ourselves, we ought to thank God for the discovery; for the evil is half cured when we have discovered its cause. If, on the contrary, you find nothing in particular which seems to have caused this aridity, don't amuse yourself seeking it out more curiously, but with all simplicity and without further examining into particulars, do what I will tell you."

2°. First of all, we must, if necessary, set right our ideas about consolations and desolations. Even though they should be the fruit of nature or an artifice of the demon, both may still be very useful to us if we only know how to make a right use of them; which is, to use consolations in order to unite ourselves with God, and desolations, to detach ourselves from everything, and especially from ourselves. Though they be the work of God, they will injure us, if we turn them away from their end; the former, in order to nourish our pride and spiritual greed, the latter so as to become discouraged, and to abandon God and prayer. Consolations are not substantial devotion, nor do desolations constitute the want of it; both are, in the designs of God, powerful means of sanctification. It is only through nature's depravity and Satan's malice that they become rocks on which we may founder.

On the part of the will.—There are three things to be done :—To resign ourselves with confidence; to avoid dangers; to correspond with the designs of God.

1°. Whether we are in consolation or in desolation, let us submit ourselves with confidence to God's treatment. According to an expression of St. Francis of Sales, we must accept everything without fear from the hand of God, whether from the right hand or from the left; from the right consolations, from the left desolations; for God, like a father, as loving as He is wise, always intends our greater good.

" Far from rejecting divine consolations," says St. Liguori,[1] " as some false mystics maintained we ought to do, let us receive them with gratitude, without, however, stopping to enjoy them or to take complacence in them. . . . These spiritual consolations are gifts far more precious than all the riches and honours of this world." If our sensitive nature itself is affected this perfects our devotion, since then our whole being tastes God and is united to Him; our sensitive nature is to be feared when it leads us away from our duty; but it is right well regulated when it aids us to accomplish better the Divine Will.

A person may pray for consolations, provided he do so with a right intention and humble submission; but, in our opinion, it is better to leave ourselves with confidence in the hands of God, who is love itself and wisdom impeccable, and to keep ourselves detached from those sweets, ready for sacrifice, and resolved to draw profit from every condition.

Likewise, in desolation, a person may ask with

[1] St. Liguori, *The Love of Jesus Christ*, xv.

humility and submission that this bitter chalice may
pass away; but, for our part, we prefer a trustful
and filial abandonment to divine Providence.
" Invoke God," says St. Francis of Sales,[1] " and
beg of Him to impart to you His gladness.   .   .   .
Away, then, O barren north wind, that driest up
my soul! and come ye sweet and gracious breezes
of consolation and breathe upon the garden of my
heart!   .   .   .   After all, in such dryness and
sterility nothing is so profitable, nothing so fruitful, as not to cling or be attached to our desire of
being delivered from it.   I do not say that we may
not wish for deliverance, but I do say that we ought
not to set our heart upon it; but rather to yield ourselves up to the pure mercy and special Providence
of God, that He may make use of us as long as He
pleases,   .   .   .   saying with our whole heart and
a profound resignation: ' The Lord gave me consolations, the Lord hath taken them away; blessed
be His holy Name.'[2]   For, if we persevere in this
humility, He will restore us His delightful favours
as He did to Job."

2°. *Let us avoid the dangers.*—In consolations
beware of pride.

God attracts us by His loving kindness, He
forgets all our past offences, our present weakness,
to see only our needs and His own love; this is why
we admire and praise His mercies, but let us not
forget our miseries, and let us abase ourselves all

---

[1] *Devout Life*, 4th part, c. xiv.
[2] Job i. 21.

the more in proportion as He caresses us; for the higher we are raised, the more fatal would be a fall. Let us avoid also becoming *attached* to consolations. To-day we have an abundance of them, to-morrow we may be in dire want; no matter, provided that we find God. Let us seek Him only, let us be attached to Him only, and let us beware of fixing our heart upon the consolations which help us on our way to Him; a traveller does not attach his heart to the carriage or boat which is conveying him.

Finally, let us, as far as depends on us, moderate our consolations when they go too far. St. Teresa compares the joys of contemplation to a heavenly water. " However abundant it may be," she says, " it can never be excessive, because there cannot be any excess in what comes from God, and when He gives this living water to a soul in great quantity, He also increases its capacity to drink abundantly of it. But, as the demon and nature may mingle their wiles with these consolations, and render them impetuous and violent even to indiscretion, the saint counsels us, whenever we feel that our bodily strength is beginning to fail, or that our head is aching, to moderate these emotions, whatever consolation we may be enjoying, either by a change of subject, or by abridging the time of our prayer (provided it be not prescribed by rule); for discretion is necessary in everything.[1] In dryness, avoid discouragement and pusillanimity.   However, profound and persis-

---

[1] St. Teresa, *Way of Perfection*, xix.

tent be the aridity, with whatever temptations it be aggravated, though all hell be let loose to harass the senses and imagination, let us never lose courage. God tries us in order to purify us, and does not wish our destruction; He is a father, not a judge; He is a director, whose object is to purge the soul, to strip it of all its attachments, in order to render it better. From the moment we make serious efforts to combat temptations, and, in spite of our aridities, to occupy ourselves with God with a good will, albeit without relish or enthusiasm, the temptations which agitate the imagination and disturb the senses are merely fears, torments inflicted on the soul, assaults of the demon, but are not voluntary acts nor sins. " If you wish to know," says St. Liguori,[1] " the true state of your soul ask it whether, in the height of its desolation, it would commit a single deliberate venial sin, and it will answer without hesitation that it is ready to suffer not one but a thousand deaths rather than offend the Lord." If you are thus disposed, bless God and remain in peace; you are doing all that He expects from you, although you feel it not; you possess the love of God and true devotion, you want only its sweetness. On the other hand, if you perceive that, in time of desolation, your will is prone to murmuring, to bitterness, to relaxation, that it avoids God and is slovenly in prayer, correct at once these and other such defects; for the evil is in your will, and the aridity is only its occasion.

[1] St. Liguori, *Love of Jesus Christ*, xvii.

Above all, do not abandon prayer; for you have
now more need of it than ever; to do so is the sure
way to fall into the snares of the enemy. Besides,
" during dryness we gain most merit," as St.
Alphonsus[1] says, provided only we persevere
courageously in prayer. "Happy," he repeats,
" happy he who, in spite of desolation, remains
faithful to mental prayer! God will load him
with His graces." But how must we employ
ourselves at such a time? "Let us humble ourselves, let us be resigned. Let us humble ourselves, I repeat, and make acts of resignation."
Humility and resignation; here, according to the
same saint, is the true prayer of the desert.   . . .
Sometimes, however, an humble and peaceable
resignation will be impossible, the soul is so
troubled, so distracted, so helpless; then is the time
to have recourse to the prayer of the drowning man,
who, struggling in the water, can only shout for
help."[2] So speaks Fr. Desurmont, and so he
acted himself, like a worthy disciple of St. Liguori.
" What kind of prayer do you make use of in your
troubles "? some one asked him one day.—" The
prayer *Kyrie eleison*," he answered.—He used to
present each of his troubles before God, saying at
the same time: *Kyrie eleison*. He used even to
name each of his miseries, repeating *Kyrie eleison*.
And is it not in truth the wisest method, when the
thought of our troubles and miseries pursues us, to

[1] St. Liguori, *Pious Reflections*, n° 15.
[2] Fr. Desurmont, *Divine Art of Prayer*, 7th max.

show them to God, and to make them the subject of our conversation with Him, and so to change into a prayer the very assault which threatens to stifle our prayer?

This is also the proper time to practise the prayer of patience. "But I am continually distracted," Fr. Crasset makes the soul say.[1] "If you are voluntarily so," he answers, "you are offending God, but if it is against your will, you are honouring, pleasing, loving Him; for everything is pleasing to God except sin, and there can be no sin where there is no will to sin. A meditation, passed in suffering, is better than one spent in consolation; it is a sweet-smelling perfume which ascends to heaven and delights Paradise. . . . Can you at present do any better than you are doing? If you can, why do you not do so? If you cannot, why are you troubled? In heaven we shall enjoy the embraces of a God of pleasure, but here below we must ourselves embrace a God of suffering. Our union with God in this life should resemble that of the holy Humanity with the Word; it was happy in the superior part, but suffering in the inferior; if any drop of consolation fell upon the sensible part it dried up immediately; His poor heart was continually immersed in an ocean of bitterness."

Let us conclude with St. Francis of Sales.[2] "Finally, Philothea, amidst all our dryness and barrenness let us not lose courage," but persevere

[1] Fr. Crasset, *On Prayer.*
[2] St. Francis of Sales, *Devout Life*, 4th part, c. xiv.

generously in mental prayer and the practice of virtue; " if we are not able to give our dear Spouse juicy preserves, let us offer Him dried fruits; it is all one to Him, provided that the heart which offers them is perfectly fixed in its resolution of loving Him. . . . Our actions are like roses, which, when fresh, have indeed more beauty, yet when dry have more strength and sweetness." According to the same saint, " an ounce of prayer, made in the midst of desolations, weighs more before God than a hundred pounds weight of it made in the midst of consolations." [1] Every one knows that delightful page, where the same saint compares the soul in the bitterness and quiet of aridity, to a statue, which its owner has placed in a niche, and which has no desire to see, nor to speak, nor to walk, but only to please its prince, and to obey its beloved Master.[2]

3°. Let us enter into God's views by profiting of our consolations and desolations to advance in the spiritual life.

" Having humbly received these consolations," says St. Francis of Sales,[3] " let us employ them carefully according to the intention of Him who gives them. Now, why, think you, does God give us these sweets? In order to render us meek towards every one and loving towards Himself. A mother gives her child a sugar-plum that he may give her a kiss in return; let us, then, embrace this loving Saviour who caresses us with His consola-

---

[1] Quoted by St. Liguori, *Praxis*, 125.
[2] St. Francis of Sales, *Love of God*, b. vi., c. xi.
[3] Ibid., *Devout Life*, 4th part. c. xiii.

tions. Now, to embrace our Saviour is to obey Him,
to keep His Commandments, to do His will, to
fly our own desires; in short, to follow Him lovingly
with obedience and fidelity. When, therefore, we
have received some spiritual consolation, we must
on that day be more diligent in well-doing and in
humbling ourselves.'' This is also the time to
accomplish the sacrifices which have hitherto dis-
mayed us; carried by grace, we shall have less
trouble in overcoming obstacles. Besides, sensible
graces are often the fore-runners of greater trials
and prepare us for them : we should try then to lay
up a store of courage and to hold ourselves in readiness for whatever God wills.

Desolations are the most favourable soil for the
growth of humility, detachment, and other solid
virtues :

Of humility. They force us to recognise our
helplessness, and the fund of miseries which is
within us; they are an evident and palpable proof
of this, and experience itself will completely convince us of this truth. Let us acknowledge with
sincerity that we have deserved these trials and even
more painful ones, and that we stand in need of
them in order to divest ourselves of self. Are they
not the remedy either to cure, or to prevent our pride
and other infirmities? Let us feel shame and
abhorence only for our spiritual maladies, and not
reject what is meant to be their cure.

Of detachment. We were accustomed to seek
ourselves even in the practice of piety; but if, for a
long time weaned from the sweets of consolation,

we have had nevertheless sufficient generosity to
persevere in prayer and the practice of virtue, we are
learning to dispense with enjoyment, to serve God
for His own sake, without self-interest, and at our
own expense.

Of all solid virtues. "Here is what enables
a soul to remain faithful and tranquil in its
various states of suffering and privation. It
believes in the presence of God whom it does
not see; it hopes in Him against all hope; it
abandons itself to Him, even when it seems to be
abandoned by Him; it continues to love Him
in the midst of disgust, sorrow, and bitterness;
it keeps itself in conformity with His severe and
crucifying decrees; it suffers a martyrdom of love;
it humbles itself in the knowledge of its miseries;
it remains content in its poverty, and blesses God
like Job upon his dunghill. . . . Oh! if a soul
did but know the honour it gives to God by this
prayer of patience! If it but knew the treasures of
merit that it gathers in at every moment, it would
never wish to change its state. . . . It is not in
the midst of light that supernatural faith is practised, but in darkness; it is not when God caresses
us that hope is divine, but when He afflicts us; it is
not in consolation that God is loved most purely,
but in desolation. Yes, believe me, never are you
doing more than when you think you are doing
nothing; never are you meriting more than when
you think you are meriting nothing. . . . Then
it is that a man pays honour to God with his own
substance, and immolates to Him his passions.

Why, then, be troubled? Why lose courage?
Why abandon mental prayer?" [1]

Alas! I know not how to think on God.—Be
satisfied, then, to love Him.—I have no heart.—Give
to God your will.—I have no consolation.—Is it in
order to have consolations that we betake ourselves
to mental prayer? .   .   .—I don't know whether I
love God or not.—Can it be that you do not love
Him when you are patiently suffering for Him?
Is it possible that you are not beloved by Him,
when, amidst so many sufferings, you abandon
yourself to His good pleasure, willing only what
He wills?

According to Fr. Faber, our " bad " meditations,
when we have no grounds to attribute them to our
own fault, " are generally the most fruitful. .   .   .
God often sends us back, as a master turns back a
boy, to re-examine our course and to discover little
forgotten infidelities, for which we have never done
penance. .   .   . It is no little thing to be able
to endure ourselves and our own imperfections.
On the contrary, it is a fine act of humility, and
draws us on towards perfection. In good truth,
we may make our bad meditations pay us an
usurious interest, if we choose " [2]

There is great need, in consolations as well as
in desolations, of being very open with an experienced director, and of allowing ourselves to be
guided. These paths are so complicated that it is

---

[1] Fr. Crasset, *On Mental Prayer*.
[2] Fr. Faber, *Growth in Holiness*, xv.

easy to go astray in them. Besides, we have need at one time of being humbled, at another of being encouraged; at one point of our journey of being restrained from launching forth into indiscreet fervour, at another of being urged forward lest we fall into discouragement and languor.

To sum up, then, the line of conduct to be pursued by the soul is the same in consolations and desolations. The same confiding submission to Divine Providence. The same shoals to be avoided—namely, satisfied pride, which takes complacence in self, or disappointed pride, which frets, murmurs, becomes discouraged; sensuality, which greedily seeks enjoyment, or the same sensuality, which complains of finding no satisfaction. The same zeal to enter into God's views by the practice of humility, detachment, and the other solid virtues, sometimes in abundance, sometimes in want; the same love of God, which we cultivate in consolation by loving ardently, in desolation by self-sacrifice. Circumstances may change, but the interior dispositions should remain the same.

We can, therefore, always derive profit. Consolations are sweeter, desolations more necessary, because we chiefly need to die to ourselves. Hence St. John of the Cross [1] teaches " that truly spiritual persons seek rather what is bitter than what is savoury; they incline to suffering more than to consolation, to be in want of everything for the love of God rather than to possess, to aridity and afflictions

---

[1] St. John of the Cross. *The Ascent of Carmel*, b. ii. c. vii.

rather than to the enjoyment of interior sweetness."
It is so easy to seek oneself when we wish to have
always these spiritual delights! For this reason
the wisest course is to abandon ourselves into the
hands of Divine Providence, ready alike for desolations or consolations, but firmly resolved to profit
of everything in order to advance in the way of
perfection.

SECOND PART

ON ORDINARY MENTAL PRAYER

OF ORDINARY MENTAL PRAYER

ORDINARY mental prayer includes meditation and its equivalents, affective prayer, and the prayer of simplicity.

These resemble each other inasmuch as they are in no way passive; the supernatural is latent in them. They differ in their ways of working. In meditation, considerations occupy more time, whereas they become fewer and shorter in the prayer of affections; and, in the prayer of simplicity, the work of the intellect is reduced to almost a simple look at God or the things of God. The affections, gaining all the ground lost by the considerations, follow an opposite course. In proportion as progress is made, they occupy more and more time, and end by occupying even the whole time of prayer. But, like the work of the understanding, that of the will also continues to become more and more simple; and the soul, which in the commencement had need of quite an equipment of considerations and verbose and complex affections,

83

advances gradually towards a kind of active prayer which is little more than a loving attention to God, and an affectionate conversation with Him.

We shall treat somewhat more at length of meditation, which, being the prayer of beginners, has a greater need of method and rules.

CHAPTER I

PRAYER OF MEDITATION—COMPENDIUM OF THE METHOD

§ I.—General Idea.

THE prayer of meditation is a mental prayer composed of considerations, affections, petitions, and resolutions.

It is called simply mental prayer, because it is the portion of a very great number,[1] and the first stage in the ways of mental prayer. It is called also meditation, discursive prayer, prayer of reasoning, on account of the important part which considerations have in it, and to indicate that the mind proceeds therein not by a simple look, but by the roundabout ways of reasoning.

Let us note, first,[2] that all the parts of mental prayer or meditation ought to converge to one single end, the destruction of a vice, the acquisition of a virtue, or some spiritual practice which may serve as a means to this. We should occupy our-

[1] St. Teresa (*Life* xii.) even says that it is the portion of the greater number; but she includes in her "first water," under the name of meditation, all kinds of non-mystical prayer. (*Cf.* 2nd part, c. viii.)

[2] 1st part, c. ii. § 3, p. 14.

selves chiefly about our predominant sin or vice, about some fundamental virtue, or some more essential practice.   Our subject, our considerations, our affections and petitions, should be chosen and regulated in view of this one object.

Let each one then accommodate his meditation to the state of his soul, the attractions of divine grace, and his own present needs.   A sinner, and even the greatest of sinners, can make his meditation, but let him treat with God of his sad state in order to become converted; the man of bad will can and should pray, but let him converse with God precisely about his bad will in order to be delivered from it.   The tepid soul should pray in order to abandon venial sin; the fervent should pray the prayer of the fervent, in order to love more and to persevere; the soul buffetted by trials the prayer of the tried soul, that humbles and subjects itself under the hand of God in order to recover peace.

This accommodating of our prayer to our present state renders it profitable and efficacious, sweet and easy; what can be more consoling and more easy than to converse with Our Lord about what we are and what we are at present experiencing?   On the other hand, if our prayer is not accommodated to the present state of our soul, does it not, by the very fact, lose the greater part of its attraction and utility?

It is better, at least for beginners, to prepare the morning meditation the evening before during the last free time.   Let them choose a subject, which they may divide into several points, each containing sufficient doctrine to enable them to elicit affections and to draw practical conclusions; let them foresee in each point the reflections to be made, the affections and resolutions to be drawn from it. Yet the same one resolution may last them for a considerable time. It is good to fall asleep with these thoughts, and to run over them again on awaking. In this way, when the time of prayer comes, the mind will already be full of them and the will on the alert.

We may add, that the most effective disposition for prayer is a hunger and thirst after holiness, a lively desire to profit by our prayer in order to advance in perfection. " Without this desire, the evening preparation will be languid, the morning waking without ardour, the prayer almost always fruitless." [1] " This desire to belong entirely to God and to advance in His love is a continual prayer," says St. Bernard. We ought always to be on the watch not to let it grow cold, but ever to inflame it more and more. It is the very soul of prayer, as indeed it is also of the whole spiritual life.

Thus the soul, prepared remotely by the fourfold purity already described,[2] and proximately by the choice of a subject and a spiritual hunger, will secure the success of her prayer. But how is she to employ herself therein ?

We shall explain further on, with abundance of detail, the essential acts of meditation, as well as some others which are rather optional. It will be a

[1] Fr. Chaignon, *Médit. rel.*, t. 1 p. 15.
[2] *Cf.* 1st part, c. iv. p. 34.

plentifully-served table, sufficient we hope for the various tastes and needs, and whence each one can pick and choose if he does not want to take all. But, for greater clearness, we shall begin by giving an abridgement of the method, which will include only the necessary acts; it will be short, simple, easy, yet full. We shall add a couple of brief explanations to convey a better understanding of the mechanism of the method; the details will come afterwards.

§ II.—COMPENDIUM OF THE METHOD.

Meditation comprises three parts, very unequal in importance and duration; the preparation, the body of the meditation, and the conclusion.

I. The preparation, or entrance into conversation, requires a few minutes at most. It essentially consists in placing oneself in God's presence, Who is looking upon us and listening to us. It is becoming to begin our conversation with a God so great and so holy, by acts of profound adoration of His Majesty, of true humility at the sight of our nothingness, and of sincere contrition for our sins. We then beg the grace of God, without which we cannot pray.

If the soul is already recollected; for instance, when we have just ended another pious exercise (as generally happens in the case of the meditations prescribed by our rule), the preparation is sufficiently made by the very fact, and we can enter at once into the body of the prayer, unless we prefer to employ a moment in reanimating our faith in the presence of God, and in asking His grace in order to pray well.

II. The body of the meditation is the chief part of this exercise, and it occupies almost its whole time. It consists of four acts, which form the essence of meditation; these are considerations, affections, petitions, and resolutions.

1°. We *reflect* on a given subject, we turn it over in our mind again and again on every side in order to grasp it well and to become thoroughly impressed by it; we draw the conclusions and make the practical applications which flow from it. This is the meditation properly so called. It is not a mere speculative study, stopping short at the knowledge of principle; its remote end is to strengthen our convictions in the course of time, and its immediate end is to call forth affections, petitions, and resolutions.

We then *examine* ourselves with regard to the subject on which we are meditating, to see whether our conduct is conformed to it, in what we fail, and what remedies we are to employ.

This work of the mind is not yet prayer, it is only *introductory*. Along with the preparation it ought not generally to occupy more than about half the time of the whole exercise; the other half is reserved for acts of the will which constitute the prayer proper; these are affections, petitions, and resolutions.

2°. Certain affections arise of their own accord from the reflections we have been just making;

thus, hell arouses repentance and aversion from
sin; heaven calls forth the contempt of this world
and the thirst after eternal goods; Our Saviour's
Passion excites love, gratitude, confidence, contrition, humility, &c. The examination of ourselves gives rise to regret for the past, confusion for
the present, strong resolutions for the future. We
may add at will many other affections, selected pre-
ferably from amongst those that are fundamental.
We shall mention in their own place those that are
most recommended.

3°. Petition is an important point, and we should
dwell upon it for a long time with faith and confidence, humility and perseverance, while, at the
same time, urging the reasons likely to move Our
Lord, and invoking the aid of the Holy Virgin and
the saints. We should first ask those graces which
the subject of our prayer suggests, and then it is
well to add petitions for divine love, final perseverance, the welfare of the Church, our country, our
order, our house, our relations, sinners, souls in
purgatory, &c.

4°. Resolutions end the body of the meditation.
One single resolution, precise and thoroughly practical, suffices, provided only that it be kept.

III. The conclusion consists in thanking God for
the graces He has granted us during our prayer,
in asking pardon for our faults and negligences.
Finally, we may again recommend to Him our
resolution, the coming day, our life, and our death.

To sum up then, after having placed ourselves in
the Divine presence, we reflect upon a pious subject,

examine ourselves, form suitable affections and petitions, make a resolution, and, having thanked God, we retire.

§ III.—Two Short Explanations.

Nothing can be simpler or more natural than the mechanism and working of this method.

I. Prayer is an audience with God.

No human motive should lead us to pray : neither routine, nor the habit of doing as others do, nor a thirst for spiritual consolations. No, we should go to prayer to render homage to God. It is not, however, a common-place visit of propriety, nor a conversation without any precise object; we want to obtain from Him some definite spiritual good, such or such progress in the uprooting of some vice, in the acquisition of some virtue. We have, there-fore, a purpose upon which we are bent, and all our considerations, affections, petitions, and resolutions should combine for its attainment.

God is there, surrounding us and penetrating us; but we were not, perhaps, thinking of this. We must, therefore, withdraw our powers from the things of earth, gather them together, and fix them upon God; thus it is we place ourselves in His presence. Naturally, we approach Him by salut-ing Him with a profound and humble act of adora-tion. In presence of so much greatness and holi-ness, the soul perceives herself to be little and miserable; she humbles herself, purifies herself by an act of sorrow; apologises for daring to approach a being of so lofty a majesty.   Powerless to pray as she should, she represents her incapacity to God, and begs the Holy Ghost to help her to pray well.

The preludes ought to be short, in order to come quickly to the proper object of the interview—that is, to the body of the meditation.

The work of the considerations is to show how desirable the spiritual good we have in view is, and that of the examination to show how much we stand in need of it.   They may be made as an internal soliloquy, a solitary meditation, in which we labour to convince ourselves in order to excite, along with repentance and confusion, ardent desires, fervent petitions, and strong resolutions.   It is more becoming, however, as we are in God's presence, not to be so intent on our own reflections as to neglect Him, but to make our considerations as though speaking with Him, and to mingle with them pious affections. In this way, our prayer will be a devout pleading, wherein the soul, whilst urging its reasons before God, becomes inflamed with a love for virtue, a horror of vice, understands the need it has of prayer, and begs with all the ardour of conviction the grace it wants, whilst at the same time it labours to persuade God, to touch His heart, to open his hand, by means of the most powerful motives it can think of.

We came to ask a definite spiritual favour, and we should urge this request in a pressing manner; but we should not forget that God, who is liberal almost to excess, loves to find empty vessels, into which He may pour His gifts, to meet with hands opening

wide to receive them; and the more he is asked for
the better pleased He is, such joy does it give Him
to bestow good gifts on His children! We should
profit, then, of this audience to expose our other
needs, to ask for all sorts of favours, general and
particular.

God has given His grace, we must now co-
operate with it. Hence we form a resolution which
will make that grace bear fruit.

The audience ended, we thank God for His goodness, apologise for our own awkwardness, ask a
final blessing, and withdraw.

II. According to the beautiful doctrine of M.
Olier, mental prayer is a *communion* with the
internal dispositions of Our Lord.

The well-beloved Master is, at the same time, both
the God who has a right to our homage and the
model whom we should imitate. It is impossible to
please the Father without resembling the Son; and
equally impossible to resemble the Son without
pleasing the Father. For a religious, who is seeking God and tending to perfection, all may be reduced to his adopting the interior sentiments of
Our Lord, following His teaching and copying His
example. A soul is perfect when it is an exact copy
of the divine model. Nothing, then, is so important as to keep Him continually before our eyes in
order to contemplate Him, in our hearts in order
to love Him, in our hands in order to imitate Him.
This is the whole economy of mental prayer,
according to M. Olier.

If I want to meditate upon humility, my object

in the *adoration* will be to honour the humility of
Our Lord, in the *communion* to attract it into my
heart, and by the *co-operation* to reproduce it in
my conduct.

I place myself, then, carefully, in presence of
my divine model; I contemplate His interior sentiments before the infinite greatness of His Father,
while bearing the shame of our sins; I listen to the
teachings, by which He preaches humility to us;
I follow Him for a moment throughout the mysteries, in which He most annihilated Himself.
This can be done rapidly.   I adore my infinitely
great God in His abasements, I admire and praise
His sublime annihilations, I thank Him for His
humiliations and His example, I love Him for so
much goodness, I rejoice in the glory which God
the Father receives, and in the grace which comes
to us in consequence, I compassionate the sufferings of our humiliated Lord.   These various
acts form the *adoration,* the primary duty of
prayer.

There is next question of *drawing into myself*
the interior sentiments and exterior life of humility
which I have just adored in Our Lord.   This is the
communion, and it is accomplished chiefly by
prayer.   I shall need an ardent desire, so that I
may open very wide the mouth of my soul, and a
prayer, based upon a deep conviction, so as to
receive into my heart not the body of Our Lord,
but His interior dispositions.   I shall hunger for
them and ask them as I ought, if I first understand
that these dispositions are for me sovereignly

desirable, and that I am in want of them. I shall make a prolonged consideration of my divine model, in order to engrave His features upon my mind and heart, in order to be smitten with esteem and love for Him; either by recalling, in general and by a simple view of faith, the motives which I have to imitate Him, or by leisurely running over in my mind these reasons one after another by a sort of examination, or, in fine, by striving to deepen my convictions by close and solid reasonings.

I may make such reflections as the following or similar ones:—Oh! my Jesus, how humility pleases me, when I contemplate it in Thee; Thou dost seek for humiliations with avidity, and dost communicate to them a surpassing virtue and sweetness; so that there is no longer anything in them which should repel me. I should be ashamed to be proud, mere nothingness that I am, when my God makes Himself so small. Thou wouldst blush for Thy disciple, and our common Father would not recognise me for Thy brother, if I resemble Thee not in humility and humiliations. My pride would harmonise badly with Thy annihilations, and would inspire Thee with horror. It is not possible to be Thy friend, Thy intimate, if I have not Thy sentiments, &c., &c. And yet how far I am from all this!

These considerations suggest reflections upon one's own conduct; I examine my thoughts, words, and deeds to see in what I resemble my divine model, in what I differ from Him. This

examination easily excites sorrow for having
imitated him so ill in the past, shame for my
miserable pride in the present, and a will to do
better for the future.

These considerations and this examination will
make me esteem, love, and desire the humble dispositions of Our Lord. It is chiefly prayer that
attracts them into my soul, it is by it that, properly
speaking, the *communion* is effected. I shall,
therefore, dwell upon it with special insistence,
striving to make my petition humble, confiding,
ardent, and persevering; I shall pray and implore
Our Lord to impart to me His dispositions; I shall
place before Him the reasons which seem to me
the most moving, and shall invoke in my favour
the intercession of His blessed Mother and of the
saints.

It now remains to transmit to my hands—*i.e.,* to
transmute into works, this spirit of Our Lord which
I have just drawn into my soul. For sentiments,
to be of any value, must lead to action. I take,
therefore, the resolution to correspond with the
lights and graces received in my prayer, by imitating Our Lord in such or such a practice of
humility; this is the *co-operation.* I then terminate my prayer as before.

§ IV.—Some Counsels.

1º. As we have already pointed out,[1] it is as
much an illusion to despise method as to be enslaved to it. Beginners, inexperienced in the

---

[1] *Cf.* 1st part, c. v. § 3, p. 55.

ways of mental prayer, have need of a guide to lead them by the hand. When we have become familiar with the divine art of conversing with God, and our heart desires to expand more freely, a method might be an obstacle; it would especially embarrass us in the prayer of simplicity, and be an impossibility in mystical contemplation. We must, therefore, have the courage to follow it as long as it is of service, and the wisdom to dispense with it when it becomes an obstacle.

2°. It is not necessary in the same meditation to go through all the acts of our method. Those which we have briefly indicated, and which we will now describe in detail, are sufficient to enable a soul with a turn for meditation, and who is not plunged in aridity, to occupy herself without much difficulty for hours in prayer, whereas the time assigned by our rule to each exercise is rather short. Are you penetrated with a lively feeling of the divine presence in your preparation? Receive it as a grace, and take care not to pass on so long as it is doing you good. A consideration touches you and excites pious affections, leave other reflections aside so long as this one is nourishing your soul; a pious act, say of divine love, of contrition, of gratitude, attracts and occupies you; do not leave it to pass on to others; you have found, cease to go on seeking. Nevertheless, it is always to affections, petitions and resolutions we should more particularly apply ourselves, as being the principal end of prayer.[1]

[1] *Cf. The Method of St. Sulpice.*

G

3°. For a stronger reason there is no necessity to make the acts in the *order* marked out above. We had, of course, to describe them in their logical sequence; but, if a movement of grace urges you to adopt a different order, follow then the guidance of the Holy Ghost; the method is meant to aid and not to embarrass us. St. Francis of Sales insists much on this advice[1] :— "Although, in the usual course of things, consideration ought to precede affections and resolutions, yet if the Holy Ghost grants you affections before consideration, you ought not to seek for consideration, since it is used only for the purpose of exciting the affections. In short, whenever affections present themselves to you, you should admit them and make room for them, whether they come to you before or after any consideration. . . . And this I say, not only with regard to other affections, but also with respect to thanksgiving, oblation and petition, which may be made amidst the considerations. . . . But as to resolutions, they should be made after the affections and near the end of the whole meditation."

4°. Let us apply our powers energetically to prayer, our mind by a firm and sustained attention, our will by animated and energetic acts. There is a vast difference between the prayer to which we wholly devote ourselves, and that to which we apply ourselves only languidly. But as we must

[1] *The Devout Life*, 2nd part, c. viii.

fear the laziness which will go to no pains, so we
must equally fly a too intense application, which
oppresses the head, strains the nerves, fatigues the
heart and chest, exhausts the strength, and may
end by repelling us altogether from an exercise
which has become too painful.

5°. Prayer *is more the work of the heart than of
the head;* it should, therefore, be simple, affective,
and sincere. Let not the mind, then, weary itself
in seeking for beautiful thoughts and sonorous
phrases; we meditate not to prepare a finished
sermon, nor to address God with fine rhetoric, but
to nourish our soul with reflections which may enlighten and move us, and excite holy and generous
resolutions; we make these reflections for ourselves alone, let them, then, be simple as well as
pious. In affections, likewise, we seek for the
practice of virtue, and not for the pleasures of a
refined egotism. Let us never confound our sensible feelings with our will, or mere emotion with
devotion. None of these acts need be made with
a feverish ardour, nor in a tone of enthusiastic
fervour. When protestations of friendship, gratitude, &c., are addressed to ourselves, the more
simple and natural they are, the more they please
us; the moment they appear forced, their sincerity
becomes suspected. Above all, our prayers should
be the faithful echo of our interior dispositions;
our affections should express the sentiments which
reign in our heart, or which we wish to form there;
our petitions should proceed from a real desire;
our every resolution should be a firm purpose of

the will, and thus our whole soul will be upright and sincere before God.

Imagination, sensibility, emotions are by no means required, nor are they sufficient for this work. It is the will that makes the prayer. Though our heart be in desolation and coldness, and devoid of all feeling, yet, as long as our prayer proceeds from an upright and resolute will, it is pleasing to God, who beholds our interior dispositions.

6°. Let us not prolong our prayer solely from the motive that it is consoling; this would be to seek ourselves rather than God. Away with vain complacence and spiritual gluttony! Let us receive sensible devotion with humility and detachment for the purpose of uniting ourselves more closely to God, and of being enabled to make for Him those sacrifices which we have hitherto refused Him. Let us make use of it and not be its slaves. In order to hide it beneath the veil of humility, and to preserve our health against its excessive ardour, let us moderate, if necessary, "those emotions of the heart and those not uncommon movements of devotion, which tend to break out into external manifestations, and seem as if they would suffocate the soul. [1] . . . Reason should hold the reins in order to guide these impetuous movements, because nature may have its share in them; and it is to be feared that there is a good deal of imperfection mingled with them, and that such

St. Teresa, *Life*, c. xxix.

movements are in great part the work of the senses, . . . whatever is merely exterior ought to be carefully avoided." " Tears, although good, are not always perfect. There is ever more security in acts of humility, mortification, detachment, and the other virtues." [1]

Let us never imitate those " indiscreet persons, who through the grace of devotion have ruined themselves, because they wished to do more than they could, not weighing the measure of their own littleness, but following the affections of their heart rather than the judgment of reason." [2]

7°. On the other hand, let us not shorten our prayer solely because it is full of desolation. A duty in which we find no pleasure is none the less a duty. To please God, to do good to our own soul, is the end of prayer; if consolation is withheld even till we reach heaven, the reward will be only all the greater. Hence, let us not yield to weariness, disgust, murmuring or discouragement; but let us begin by examining ourselves. Perhaps that fourfold purity, of which we spoke,[3] has been covered with some dust; perhaps we have been obstinate in our own opinion or yielded to self-will, offended charity by some antipathy, or entertained some inordinate attachment, broken silence, or given way to dissipation, committed more petty faults than usual, or multiplied our irregularities. The hand of God, as merciful as it

---

[1] St. Teresa, *Way*, xviii.
[2] *Imitation*, b. iii. c. vii. 2.
[3] *Cf.* 1st part, c. iv. p. 34.

is just, punishes our failings, and recalls us to our
duty; let us adore with submission His fatherly
severity, and not sulk with unrepenting pride.
Perhaps God wishes merely to preserve us in
detachment and humility, to test the solidity of our
faith, to try the constancy of our devotion, the
strength of our will, the disinterestedness of our
service. Or perhaps this desolation is but the
prelude to greater graces. However that may be,
let us never doubt the loving heart of our Father,
"Who chastises us because He loves us."[1] Far
from abandoning our prayer let us continue it
with courage. The soldier remains at his post in
spite of danger and fatigue; the ploughman bends
over his furrow despite the inclemency of the
weather. There is, in fact, nothing less troublesome than this powerlessness of the mind and this
desolation of heart, when the soul has the courage,
either to suppress what may be their voluntary
cause, or to embrace this cross with love, and to
persevere in prayer with patient energy. During
long years, St. Teresa sought in vain for a little
consolation in prayer. She persevered, however,
and, as a reward, God inundated her soul with His
favours, and raised her even to the heights of contemplation and of perfection. Our Lord deigned
one day to say to her with an accent of the most
tender affection: "Be not afflicted, my daughter;
in this life souls cannot always be in the same state;
sometimes you will be fervent, sometimes without
fervour; sometimes in peace, sometimes in trouble

[1] *Prov.* iii. 12.

and temptations; but hope in me and fear nothing."[1] God is very near the soul that generously does its duty in spite of dryness.

8°. Our prayer being ended, all is not yet done. It should, moreover, embalm with its divine perfume the Work of God, our free time, and the manual work which may follow it. We must strive, therefore, to preserve during our other exercises the recollection, the pious thoughts, and holy affections we experienced in our prayer. We are like a man who is carrying a priceless liquor in a fragile glass vessel; he will look now to his feet lest he make a false step, now to the glass lest it be tilted to one side and be spilt. No doubt we must pass from prayer to action, but, while abandoning ourselves for God and under His eyes to our various occupations, we must also " keep an eye upon our heart, that the liquor of holy prayer may be spilt as little as possible,"[2] through our natural activity, dissipation, routine, stress of business, or even the artifices of the demon.

9°. " You must especially bear in mind, after your meditation, the resolutions you have made . . . in order to put them in practice that very day. This is the great fruit of meditation, without which it is very often . . . almost useless. . . . You must then endeavour by every means to put them in practice, and to seek every occasion, great or small, of doing so. For instance, if I have resolved to win over by gentleness the minds of

---

[1] St. Teresa, *Life*, xl.
[2] St. Francis of Sales, *Devout Life*, 2nd part, c. viii.

those who offend me, I will seek on this very day
an opportunity of meeting them, and will kindly
salute them; " [1] I will render them some little
service, I will speak well of them, if permitted to
speak; I will pray for them and carefully avoid
causing them any pain.

[1] St. Francis of Sales, *Devout Life*, 2nd part, c. viii.

CHAPTER II

OF THE ENTRANCE INTO MEDITATION

§ I.—NECESSITY OF THE IMMEDIATE PREPARATION.

UNLESS the soul be already recollected, everything shows that it is a duty to make some immediate preparation for prayer:—1°. The majesty of God, Who claims our respect; to come before Him, without taking the means to arouse our attention and devotion, would be to insult Him. 2°. The importance of the matters of which we have to treat. Orators prepare their speeches; wise men, before a conversation of grave concern or a difficult negotiation, reflect seriously in order not to compromise its success. Now, what is greater, more noble, more important, than treating with God, the author of our being, and master of our destiny, about the affair of our eternal salvation? 3°. The difficulties which prayer itself offers. The human mind raises itself to God only with difficulty; it is not easy for it to enter the supernatural world and there treat about spiritual things with invisible beings; the demon hates prayer and does all he can to hinder it or to render it sterile; men for the most part, especially beginners, are habitually dissipated and full of profane thoughts and pre-occupations; often their heart is agitated by passion, their will bound to the earth by attachments; they have, therefore, much need to disentangle themselves from these trammels beforehand, and to bring themselves into a state of recollection, silence and peace, according to the precept of the Holy Ghost :—" Before prayer, prepare thy soul, and be not like a man that tempteth God." [1]

§ II.—First Manner of Making the Immediate Preparation.

The proximate preparation by which we begin meditation consists of three acts :—1°. To place oneself in the presence of God. 2°. To confess that we are unworthy of being allowed to appear before Him. 3°. To ask for grace, without which we cannot pray well.

1°. *To place ourselves in the presence of God.*— Meditation is not a solitary occupation, like study or reading, when the soul is alone with its books and its thoughts. It is a conversation with God or with Our Lord, sometimes also with our heavenly brethren. The moment we speak to the most Holy Virgin, to an angel or to a saint, those we address, all invisible as they are, hear us, and the conversation is as real as when we converse with an absent person by telephone. As to God, like to the deaf and the blind, we cannot here below either see or hear Him; but faith gives us the most perfect certitude that He is here present. It is we ourselves who are not present, when recollection is

---

[1] Eccli. xviii. 23.

wanting. The exterior senses, the imagination, the memory, the mind, the heart, and the will—all our faculties, stray away from us, and run in a vagabond fashion whithersoever our curiosity, our dreams, our memory, our every frivolous thought and foolish attachment or impulse of passion may lead them. We are everywhere, except at home. Before prayer, therefore, we must gather in our scattered faculties, summon them to prayer, place them in the presence of God Who is within us, but of Whose presence we were not thinking, saying in the words attributed to St. Bernard [1] :—" Intentions, thoughts, desires, affections, and my whole interior, come let us ascend the mountain, let us go to the place where the Lord sees or is seen. Cares, solicitudes, anxieties, labours, pains, and external duties wait here for my return."

This recollection of our whole soul is of supreme importance in mental prayer. A want of this is the reason why we sometimes lose our time or profit but little : we throw ourselves on our knees thoughtlessly and by routine, we enter right off into our meditation, instead of beginning by withdrawing our thoughts from the things of earth in order to fix them on God. There are, indeed, other elements of ill success, but this is not the least important of them. " On the other hand, when this beginning is well made, it penetrates the soul with a feeling of respect, which confers upon it stability for the whole time of the exercise ; for,

[1] St. Bernard, *De contempl. Deo.*, c. 1.

says St. John Climacus, he who, while praying, is filled with the thought of an ever-present God, remains in prayer like an immovable pillar." [1]

Should our mind wander during prayer, we must briefly recall it to the presence of God, by saying, for instance, with Jacob: "Truly the Lord is in this place, and I knew it not."

The way to place oneself in God's presence.—A *choice may be made* between several methods, some of which appeal to simple faith, others to the eyes, and to the imagination.

By simple faith.—St. Francis of Sales [2] points out divers considerations :—

1°. God's presence everywhere. He is in everything and in every place, nor is there any place or thing in this world wherein He is not by a most real presence, so that as the birds meet always with air whithersoever they fly, so we, whithersoever we may go, always and everywhere find God there. . . . This was David's thought when he exclaimed :—"If I ascend into heaven, Thou art there; if I descend into hell, Thou are present." [3]

Truly God "is not far from every one of us; for in Him we live and move and are." [4] He surrounds and envelops us on all sides, we are immersed in Him as fish in water.

2°. His presence in us.—"As the soul being diffused throughout the whole body is present in

[1] Fr. Chaignon, *Méd. rel.*, t. 1, p. 16.
[2] St. Francis of Sales, *Devout Life*, 2nd part, c. ii.
[3] *Ps.* cxxxviii. 8.
[4] *Act.* c. xvii. 27, 28.

all its parts," so God penetrates our whole being and dwells in its every part, imparting to us life and movement. And "as the soul . . . resides nevertheless in the heart in a more special manner, so God is in a most particular manner in your heart, and in the very centre of your spirit, which He vivifies and animates, being, as it were, the heart of your heart and the spirit of your spirit."[1] And if we are in the state of grace, our soul is a sanctuary wherein the Holy Trinity dwells, imparting to us a divine life, the power to do divine works, light and help to enable us to act after a divine manner. We have, then, no need to seek God very far away, since He fills our body and our soul with His most holy presence.

3°. The third means is to consider our Saviour, who, in His human nature, looks down from heaven upon all persons in this world, but particularly upon Christians who are His children, and more especially upon those who are engaged in prayer, whose actions and deportment He minutely observes. Now, this is no mere flight of the imagination but the very truth; for although we see Him not, yet from above He beholds us. It was thus St. Stephen saw Him at the moment of his martyrdom.[2]

By the eyes and the imagination.—" The fourth way consists in making use of simple imagination, representing to ourselves Our Saviour in His sacred humanity as though He were beside us just

[1] St. Francis of Sales, *Devout Life*, 2nd part, c. ii.
[2] *Ibid.*

as we are wont to represent to ourselves an absent friend."[1]   We may picture Him to ourselves as in the Crib, in His infancy, in His hidden or public life, on His cross, amidst the splendours of His glory, according as it does us more good, provided that this be done without any violent straining, and that we do not confound the realities of faith with the creations of our own imagination.   We may also makes use of a statue or any other pious image, to draw our soul away from the earth and fix it in God.

But when we are making our meditation before the Blessed Sacrament, the most natural manner to place ourselves in God's presence is to raise our eyes to the tabernacle.   For the more advanced this will suffice to fix their attention lovingly upon Him Who " standeth behind our wall, looking through the windows, looking through the lattices."[2]   He is their Well-Beloved, their God, their All; they will contemplate Him, they will love Him.   As for those who are beginning, or even have already made some progress, they may need to reanimate their faith by pious considerations. " He is there, I see Him not, but I am more certain of it than if I beheld Him with my eyes, for faith reveals Him to me.   He has His eyes upon me to observe all the movements of my soul, and to fathom the dispositions of my heart.   He beholds how I keep my body in a modest posture, my mind recollected, and my will devout.   He

---

[1] St. Francis of Sales, *Devout Life*, 2nd part, c. ii.
[2] *Cant. of Canticles* ii. 9.

knows me better than I do myself, and I can hide nothing from Him." Who, then, is He? Beginners will chiefly see in Him the master of their life and of their eternity, the judge who hates evil, who has created hell, purgatory, and the other punishments of sin, and they experience that saving fear, which is the main-spring of the purgative way. Those who are making progress will consider Him chiefly as the model they ought to resemble, the source of light and strength, the happiness which shall crown their virtues; and this view will reanimate the hope which is their support. The holy tabernacle, therefore, speaks to all, but accommodates its language to each one's special attraction. If in the course of our prayer our thoughts wander, a glance upon " Him who is in our midst " will bring them back.

"Make use, then, of some one of these four means to place yourself in the presence of God before mental prayer, but there is no need to employ them all at the same time, you need use only one, and that briefly and with simplicity." [1]

2°. *To confess that we are unworthy of being allowed to appear before God.*—Entering, then, into conversation with God, we begin by saluting Him. Struck with a sense of our own nothingness and of His greatness, kneeling if circumstances permit, let us prostrate ourselves in spirit before Him in profound adoration, let us make ourselves quite small before such lofty

---

[1] St. Francis of Sales, *Devout Life*, 2nd part, c. ii.

majesty, contrite and humbled by the memory of our sins in presence of so pure a sanctity. We may express this second point of our preparation in some such terms as these :—" I believe, O Lord, that Thou art here really present, that I, dust and ashes, am going to speak to my Lord and my God, that Thine eyes are upon me and that Thou deignest to listen to me. Thou art my God, I humbly adore Thee; Thou art my Sovereign Master, I submit myself to Thy absolute authority. Deign to look upon me mercifully and to bear with me indulgently, for I am most unworthy to appear in Thy presence; unworthy, because Thou art infinitely great, and I am but nothingness; unworthy, especially, because Thou art holiness itself, and I, poor sinner, have so often offended Thy Divine Majesty, especially by such or such a fault; even still, I have such or such a defect which I have not corrected, such or such a bad inclination which puts me to shame. To appear in Thy presence I ought to be as pure as an angel. Oh! how far from it am I! but Thou knowest that I love not my faults and spiritual miseries; I am ashamed of them before Thee, I beg Thy pardon for them, I will correct them with the aid of Thy Holy grace, and it is even for this purpose that I come to Thee, hoping that ' Thou wilt not despise a contrite and humble heart'; and, if I am not sufficiently penetrated with this salutary compunction, deign Thou to pour it into my soul and I shall have it. ' Purify my heart and my lips, O Omnipotent God, who didst purify the lips of Isaias with a burning coal,' and then I shall be less unworthy to converse with Thee."

You may say the *Confiteor*.

As Our Lord is our mediator it is good to unite ourselves with Him, in the following way, for example: "I do not deserve, O Lord God, that Thou shouldst pay any attention to me; but the prayer and the merits of Thy Son Thou canst not reject. Now, He prayed for me and still prays for me in heaven and in the holy tabernacle, He offers to Thee His homage, pleading for me with His lips and His heart, by His past labours, His tears and His blood. He adores Thee, He thanks Thee, He implores Thy mercy and begs graces for me. Whatever He says to Thee, I say the same; I make all His homage mine own by joining Him in intention. It is while invoking Him, holding Him by the hand, and sheltering myself under His merits, that I dare to present myself before Thee with a firm confidence of being heard."

3°. *We must acknowledge ourselves incapable of praying of ourselves, and invoke the Holy Ghost.*—O Lord, I am not capable of having a good thought of myself, but my sufficiency is from Thee.[1] I am not able to concentrate my thoughts if Thou dost not control them, nor to raise my heart to Thee, unless Thou dost attract it; nor to love Thee, if Thou dost not inflame me; nor to form a good resolution, still less to put it in practice, if Thou dost not give me " to will and to

---

[1] II. *Cor.* iii. 5.

H

accomplish.''[1]   I renounce, therefore, my own
thoughts, which are not capable of guiding me
aright as to what concerns my salvation, and my
own affections, which are wont to tend towards evil.
Come, then, O Divine Spirit, have compassion on
my indigence, I abandon myself to Thee, in order
that, illuminated, moved and guided by Thee, I
may make my meditation well; come, enlighten my
intelligence, inflame my heart and convert my will,
that my prayer may contribute to Thy glory and
to my own spiritual advancement.''

N.B.—The object of these last words is to remind
us of the purity of intention we should bring to
prayer, if we would seek God, and not ourselves.
Father Crasset[2] very justly remarks:—'' Be resigned to pass this time (of prayer) either in light
or in darkness, in consolation or in desolation,
without seeking any other satisfaction than that of
doing the will of God. This resignation is important, in order to receive His grace, and to
remain peacefully in whatever state He may place
you. If you leave off your prayer with a satisfied
mind, after having done what you could to make it
well, it is a sign that you entered upon it with a
pure intention; if you leave it off saddened and cast
down, it is a sign that you sought in it your own
satisfaction and not God's will.''

---

[1] *Phil.* ii. 13.   [2] Fr. Crasset, *Méd. prép.*

§ III.—SECOND WAY TO COMMENCE OUR PRAYER.
OF THE COMPOSITION OF PLACE AND OTHER
PRELUDES.

You may, *if you prefer it,* begin your meditation
in the following manner. Put yourself briefly in
the presence of God, and ask the grace to pray well.
Then make the *composition of place,* according to
the method of St. Ignatius and St. Francis of
Sales.

This consists " in placing before our imagination
the substance of the mystery we are about to meditate, as if it were really taking place before our
eyes." [1] If I want to meditate upon our crucified
Lord, I will transport myself in spirit to Calvary,
and will recall to mind all the scenes of the
Passion. I behold my Saviour covered with
bleeding wounds; I assist at the scourging, the
crowning with thorns; I hear the sarcasms and
blasphemies, &c. I may do the same when I meditate on death, on hell, or on any mystery where
there is question of visible and sensible things. It is
otherwise " with regard to such truths as the greatness of God, the excellence of virtue, the end for
which we were created, which are all invisible
things." However, if I am meditating upon some
saying of Our Lord, I may imagine myself as
present amongst His disciples, that it is to me He
addresses His words, or that He speaks to me from
the holy altar. But we should avoid subtle imagin-
ings, and act " so that our mind be not too much

[1] St. Francis of Sales, *Devout Life,* 2nd part, c. iv.

engrossed in the work of inventing images." [1] For,
if these representations do not occur to us as if of
themselves, and without effort, it is better to confine
ourselves to simply recalling our subject to mind.

With these restrictions, the composition of place
cannot fatigue the mind, it fixes the imagination
by confining it to an object which interests it, and
thus hinders it from wandering hither and thither;
or, if it does wander, to recall to mind this mental
picture suffices to bring it back.

To this prelude St. Ignatius always adds at least
one other by which " we ask the grace, not now in
general to make a good meditation, but a special
grace conformable to the fruit we wish to derive
from the meditation. We ask for light and
strength; light to know, strength to will and to
accomplish. Lastly, when our subject is some
historical fact, St. Ignatius would have us recall
briefly the fact in question, before the two preludes
of which we have just spoken, which makes a third
prelude." [2]

These preludes not being required by all the
methods, there is no objection to our not making
use of them if we find them embarrassing; we
thought it right to mention them for those who
might wish to employ them. In short, we may
limit the whole immediate preparation to placing
ourselves in the presence of God, adoring Him
humbly, and asking the grace to pray well. This
hardly requires five minutes. But should we be

[1] St. Francis of Sales, *Devout Life*, 2nd part, c. iv.
[2] Fr. Chaignon. *Méd rel.*, t. i. introduction.

strongly impressed by the thought of God's presence, by sorrow for our sins, by a feeling of the need we have in grace, &c., we should abandon the subject we have prepared and hold on to this thought which is doing us good; for, as we have already remarked,[1] it is unprofitable to continue searching when we have already found what we need.

[1] 2nd part, c. i. § 4, 2nd counsel, p. 97.

CHAPTER III

BODY OF THE MEDITATION

CONSIDERATIONS

§ I.—Optional Acts which may serve as an Introduction to the Body of the Meditation.—Of Adoration.

The method of St. Sulpice enters upon the body of the prayer by adoration, which Tronson thus defines:—"We call the first point *adoration*, because in it principally we discharge our duties towards Our Lord, we adore Him, we love Him, we thank Him, and fulfil our other obligations towards Him. As adoration is one of our first and principal duties, it gives its name to this first point. . . . This point consists in· contemplating the subject of our meditation as it is in Jesus Christ, and, under this aspect, which is necessarily a religious one, performing towards Him those acts which the virtue of religion requires us to perform. For instance, we want to meditate on humility: the first thing we must do is to consider humility in the person of Our Lord,

to contemplate Jesus Christ as humble and under
this respect to tender Him our worship. Two
things, therefore, are to be observed in this point.
. . . 1°. To contemplate Jesus Christ as
humble; now there are three things which we may
consider in Him; the disposition of His heart re-
specting humility, the words He spoke of it, and
the humble actions He performed; and these three
things we may consider in all kinds of subjects.
2°. To discharge towards Him our duties of
religion; now there are six principal ones upon
which we may usually dwell, adoration, admiration, praise, love, joy, gratitude. . . . These
are the six chief duties of a religious soul, not that
it is necessary to make all these acts in every
prayer, but we may dwell now on some of them
now on others, according as we are drawn thereto
by the Holy Spirit, or find ourselves impressed by
them. But if we are meditating upon some
sorrowful mystery, as the Passion of Our Lord,
then we may abandon ourselves to sentiments of
compassion instead of sentiments of joy." [1]

Nothing is more fitting than to refer to Our
Lord in everything, since He is the rule and model
of virtue. These numerous acts may seem complicated, but custom renders them easy; at the
most we mention them only as optional; it is for
each one to see whether they are a help or a
hindrance, whether he ought to make use of them
or to leave them aside.

[1] Tronson, *Manuel du Sém.*, entr. 7.

§ II.—Of Considerations—Their Role and Extent.

Now comes the meditation properly so called, in which we consider the subject in itself by means of considerations, and in ourselves by means of self-examination. Let us first see the part which considerations play and how far they are to be extended, we shall afterwards examine the practical manner of making them.

Their *rôle* is to strengthen in the course of time the spirit of faith, and to give rise in our present prayer to affections, petitions, and resolutions.

So long as a person has not begun to practise meditation or its equivalents, his faith may be all right, but it has little influence on his life, because it remains upon the surface of the soul, and does not penetrate into its depths. If he reflects upon the great truths of faith at distant intervals only, these will have only a passing influence upon him and, at other times, will be just as if they did not exist at all.

A long practice of meditation brings them constantly before the mind, fixes them in our memory, obliges us to turn them over and over in every sense, to examine them minutely in order to get a thorough grasp of them, and to penetrate our mind with them. Little by little our convictions thus become deeper and more vivid; they exert a continual and really effective influence on our thoughts, our words, our resolutions, our works, and our sufferings; faith becomes the spirit of faith which animates our whole life and gives it a supernatural character, as the soul communicates to the body natural life and action.

This first operation of meditation requires years, and brings forth its fruits only by degrees. The equivalents of meditation may, indeed, effect this, and supply for the want of meditation: spiritual reading for instance, well made, produces almost the same results; but meditation produces them with more vigour, because the affections and resolutions fertilise the reflections, by making the mind's convictions act effectively upon the will and whole conduct.

The immediate end of meditation is to call forth affections, petitions and resolutions; the work of the mind has for object to set the will in motion. Considerations in fact are not prayer,[1] which is by no means a mere study; we don't meditate to acquire knowledge as we study in order to learn. Although faith is enlightened and our convictions strengthened by meditation, our chief object is to inflame the will by ardent affections, and draw it to make generous resolutions, by bringing before it convincing arguments. In a word, meditation is not so much prayer as the agency which moves us to pray.[2]

Rodiguez makes use of a familiar comparison which well depicts the *rôle* meditation plays in prayer:—" In order to sew we have need of a needle; yet it is not the needle but the thread which

---

[1] See below, 2nd part, c. iv. § 1 p. 133.
[2] See 2nd part, c. i. § 2 p. 89.

sews; and a man who would spend his day in running a needle without any thread through a piece of cloth, would be doing a very unprofitable and ridiculous work. Yet this is almost what those do, who, when praying, meditate and reflect much, without ever applying themselves to make acts of the will and of charity. For meditation should be as it were the needle; it should go before, but only in order to draw after it the thread of love and the affective motions by which our will is united to God." [1]

This being so, what time must we give to our considerations? We must devote more or less time to them according as we have more or less need to strengthen our convictions, and especially to excite affections, petitions and resolutions.

I am making my mental prayer, for instance, on the shortness of life and the endless duration of eternity, on the nothingness of goods which pass away and the importance of those which are eternal, &c.; so long as I have as yet but little reflected upon this class of ideas, I shall require some time to get a grasp of them, I have need to turn them over and over in my mind, to examine them in all their aspects; and it is only with toilsome effort that they penetrate my mind and will. In the beginning, therefore, I shall need long considerations. Afterwards, when habit shall have rendered these thoughts familiar, a moment's reflection, perhaps even a mere remembrance, a rapid glance, will suffice to make these thoughts take

[1] *Christian Perfection*, On Prayer, c. xi.

hold of me, and revive their influence on my prayer
and my conduct.

So likewise, if there is question of exciting
prayerful acts, I ought to use the needle of meditation only in as far as it is needed to introduce the
thread of the affections. I shall, therefore, impose
silence on my reflections, as soon as they shall have
given rise to affections and petitions; and, since
prayer, properly speaking, consists in these acts of
the will, I shall occupy myself with them as long as
I can, and shall resume consideration only in as far
as it is needful in order to bring back, maintain,
and energize the affections.

All this varies much according to the state of the
soul. At first our convictions are weak, our
passions and our faults darken the mind, creatures
occupy and absorb it, things divine enter it with
difficulty; the heart is cold in God's regard, the
will difficult to move, countless attractions tie
it down to earth. Therefore a long and painful
labour of meditation is necessary, in order to make
the light shine amidst so much darkness, and to
enkindle holy affections in a heart as yet benumbed
by the glamour of the passions. But, in the course
of time, mental prayer produces that fourfold purity
of which we spoke; and that purity, as it increases,
has for effect that the mind is sooner convinced,
the heart is more quickly warmed, and the will is
more prompt to move. Hence considerations are
at first allowed a large place in our prayer; afterwards they are gradually allowed less space, and,
little by little, we progress towards that better state,

in which our prayer becomes more affective than meditative, when the soul, more fully purified, need do hardly more than keep its interior eye fixed lovingly upon God in order to converse with Him heart to heart.

It is quite natural that, in monasteries of our order, the soul should from the beginning have less need of considerations, and that it should attain to affective prayer sooner, because our frequent spiritual reading, the Divine Office, the hearing of the word of God, the habit of thinking on heavenly things, fill and saturate the mind with pious thoughts, whilst our austerities, by purifying the heart, facilitate its union with God.

We may say in a general way of those souls who are still at the stage of simple meditation, that something less than half the time of their prayer would be amply sufficient to devote to the preparation and the considerations. Even from the commencement, it is profitable to intermingle some pious affections and petitions with our considerations, so that these latter may be a beginning of conversation with God, and not degenerate into a mere study.

§ III.—Practical Way of making Considerations.

Considerations are differently made, according as there is question of a fact or sensible mystery, which appeals to the imagination, or of a purely spiritual truth.

I. If the subject of the meditation is a fact or

sensible mystery, such as death, judgment, heaven, or hell, the life and Passion of Our Lord, and such like, I shall try to represent to my mind the subject with its different circumstances, as if the fact was taking place before my eyes; taking care, however, not to fatigue my brain and nerves by too much intensity of thought, guarding also my imagination from vain dreaming and distractions, and not taking all its creations for realities. Whilst it reproduces in its entirety and its details the event or the mystery, my mind will strive to draw from them the lessons which they contain, and their practical application to my own case. I may run over in this way the different circumstances mentioned in the well-known Latin verse.—

" Quis ? Quid ? Ubi ? Quibus auxiliis ? Cur ? Quomodo ? Quando ? "

Who, what, where, by what means, why, how, when?

If, for instance, I am making my prayer upon the Passion, I may ask myself : *Quis?* Who is it who is suffering? It is the son of God.—*Quid?* What pains is He enduring? Here I may represent to my mind, the multitude and immensity of His sufferings.—*Ubi?* In what place? I transport myself in spirit to the different places where Our Lord suffered : to the garden, the pretorium, to Calvary, &c.—*Quibus auxiliis?* By what means? His abandonment by His Father, His Mother's desolation, the flight of His Apostles, the treason of Judas, the denial of St. Peter, the hatred and perfidy of the judges and witnesses, the

popular feeling, the weakness of Pilate, the rage of
the executioners, &c.—*Cur?* Why? Our Lord's
love for His Father's glory and our salvation, His
hatred of sin, our faults in fine, &c.—*Quomodo?*
How? He voluntarily abandons His body and
soul to suffering, He delivers Himself up to His
enemies of His own free will, and chooses the
most ignominious death, &c.—*Quando?* When?
At the Paschal time, when foreigners, the inhabi-
tants of Judea, those who had heard Our Lord,
and witnessed His miracles, were in crowds at
Jerusalem, &c.[1]

It is easy to see that this method of considering
the subject with its various circumstances furnishes
an inexhaustible fund of matter capable of occupying us for whole hours, and often requiring to be
divided into several meditations.

II. In the second case—*i.e., when the subject is
purely spiritual*—I make use of my imagination at
the most only to represent to myself that I see Our
Lord giving me the example, and that I hear Him
formulating the precept. I content myself, therefore, with recalling what faith and reason teach
upon this matter; I consider all its various aspects
in order to grasp its whole import; I endeavour to
engrave it in my mind, to apply it to my actual
needs, to draw from it practical conclusions, by
weighing the motives which urge me to it, by
examining what has been my past conduct in this
matter, and what should be my resolution for the
future.

[1] Abbé Saudreau, *Degrés de la vie spirituelle*, b. ii. c. iii. § 2.

For all prayer, we repeat, should aim at reforming ourselves with regard to some special point; for instance, such or such habitual sin to be corrected, such or such a virtue to be practised. Considerations, affections, petitions and resolutions, the details and the whole body of the exercise are like soldiers and an army manœuvring to attain this end. The strategy which regulates all these movements in mental prayer should never lose sight of this end.

Hence, "if we are meditating upon some virtue," says Father Crasset, "we must consider its nature, properties, beauty, utility, necessity, the means of acquiring it, and the occasions of practising it. If it is a vice we are meditating upon, we should realise to ourselves its malice, its bad effects, and find out the remedies to cure it."

As regards the motives for coming to such or such a practical resolution, they may be reduced to three :—1°. Duty; nothing is more just; the will of God, His rights, those of my neighbour, gratitude for favours received, &c., all urge me to it. —2°. Our interest; nothing is more advantageous for this life and for the life to come; it is the means to preserve and augment in myself and others the life of grace, virtues and merits, peace with God, with my conscience, and with my neighbour; then there is heaven, purgatory, the temporal punishment of sin, &c.—3°. The facility of it; so many others have succeeded with the aid of grace! Why should not I do as they have done ?[1]

[1] Abbé Saudreau, *Degrés de la vie spirituelle*, b. ii. c. iii. § 2.

It is easy to see to what a number of developments these motives may give rise; and it is profitable to dwell upon them and to penetrate one's mind with them. But nothing obliges us to consider them all; on the contrary, we must learn to confine our thoughts to one or two, so as to leave due space for the acts of the will. "If your mind," says St. Francis of Sales,[1] "finds sufficient relish, light and fruit in one of these considerations, you should rest there without passing on to others; acting in this like the bees which never leave a flower as long as they find on it any honey to gather. But should you find nothing to your taste in one of these considerations" (or when that point is exhausted), "after having made a few efforts and tried it, you should pass on to another point from which you may derive considerations and affections, and so on."

"Louis of Granada and St. Francis of Sales counsel those who have a difficulty in reasoning to make use of a book, especially in the beginning; to read the first point, and, if no good thought occurs to occupy their mind, to recommence and read over again some lines, and then to apply themselves to reflect a little, to produce affections of gratitude, grief, humility. When they find something which touches them, they should dwell upon it in order to draw from it all the fruit they can."[2] St. Teresa declares[3] "that she spent

---

[1] St. Francis of Sales, *Devout Life*, 2nd part, c. v.
[2] Fr. Chaignon, *Méd. rel.*, t. i. introduction.
[3] St. Teresa, *Way*, xvii. and *Life*, iv.

more than fourteen years before she could meditate otherwise than whilst reading." We must not, however, allow our meditation to degenerate into a mere spiritual reading, or curiosity in reading and slothfulness in reflecting to hinder the personal work of the mind. "God takes account of our good will and rewards it. Little by little reflections diminish and affections abound, the heart tastes, is nourished, is inflamed; sometimes a single word suffices to occupy it for a long time." But, when this is the case, we are entering upon affective prayer.

There are very few minds, excepting those who have passed beyond the prayer of meditation, who cannot, by means of this method, find enough matter to occupy them. We must sometimes shake off the torpor which benumbs our faculties and conquer their sluggishness; but whatever courage may then be necessary, we must always try to avoid overstraining our mind. "These reflections [1] should be neither subtle nor studied, but simple and natural." "Proceed quite gently and simply in this business without being in any hurry," says St. Francis of Sales.

"It is strongly recommended to make acts of faith on the subject we are meditating. It is in fact on the manner more or less clear with which the truth is grasped, on the more or less lively faith which is given to it, that the operations of the intellect and those of the will depend. This first exercise of faith well done sheds over the whole

[1] Fr. Chaignon, *Méd. rel.*, t. i. introduction.

I

matter of our meditation a certain glow of truth, which singularly facilitates considerations and affections." [1]

Such is the generally accepted method of making considerations.

The Redemptorists, following St. Liguori, recommend another more simple method, but which seems to us less suitable for beginners than for those who, after a long use of meditation, have arrived at affective prayer.

We take some pious thoughts from memory or from a good book; for our time of mental prayer which is so short, two or three will generally suffice. We repeat them over to ourselves—*i.e.*, we are satisfied with saying them over interiorly, but rather slowly, in order to give ourselves the time to grasp them fully; we avoid long and abstruse reasoning upon them, in order to confine ourselves to a kind of attentive look at them, a look steadied by many acts of faith, which fix the truth in the soul; and we ask of God the grace to be deeply impressed by them. For instance, if I am meditating on the Passion, I shall again and again say to myself with attention:—"What a prodigy of love! Jesus Christ died for all, for me; I believe it; O my God, make this belief penetrate my soul." These thoughts, acts of faith and prayers, may occupy about a third of the time of my prayer; and I should repeat them if needful as often as required; then I should pass on to the conversation with God properly so called.

[1] Fr. Chaignon, *Méd. rel.*, t. i. introduction.

Or rather, it is better still to make the meditation itself a conversation with God. With this object, after having read and whilst reading, we may thank Our Lord for the truth He teaches us, ask Him for the grace to call it frequently to mind, declare to Him that we believe it with all our heart, beg of Him an increase of faith and the full understanding of this truth, &c. In this way faith enlightens us, and the conviction it produces strongly influences our will.

Of these divers methods each one after trial may choose that which succeeds best with him and brings him most profit. All that we have just been saying will receive fresh elucidation in the chapter on the equivalents of meditation.

§ IV.—SELF-EXAMINATION.

After having considered the truth in itself, we examine it in ourselves. I have meditated on such a mystery: to what degree am I impressed by it? Upon such a virtue: how do I practise it in my thoughts, words and conduct? Upon such a vice: how do I preserve myself from it? I run over in my mind my days and my occupations; I examine my sentiments, language, manners; I probe my private conduct and my way of acting in my office or employment. I make this examination briefly and without anxiety, with the sincerity of a soul that desires only to discharge its duty, with that calm which confidence in God and a good will inspire. The end I propose to myself is rather to know my *dispositions* with regard to the object of my prayer, than to make out a list and enumeration of my faults; I have not in view sacramental confession, but the acquisition of a virtue, or the correction of a vice; it is sufficient, therefore, for me to see in what I fail, and what firm and definite resolutions I should take against the evil.

We have special need of this examination when we wish to excite certain affections, and it is more necessary still to aid us in making petitions and resolutions. I don't indeed need it in order to adore God, to praise, admire, love Him, &c.; but I shall pay Him a higher tribute of gratitude, if I first enter into myself to learn how little I have merited the favours which He has showered upon me. How can I conceive regret for the past, confusion for the present, and a true desire to live better for the future, if I have not recognised how wanting I am in that perfection which Our Lord requires of me, and how far I am from my Divine Model? That humble and suppliant prayer may spring forth from my heart and my lips, it is not sufficient that I understand the beauty and value of a virtue, the ugliness and evil consequences of such or such a fault; it is also above all things desirable, that I should fully realise the extent to which this virtue is wanting to me, or this vice reigns in my own heart.

Lastly, how can I take a firm, definite, and practical resolution, if I do not feel any need of it, if I do not know exactly the evil to be remedied?

We must, therefore, after having considered our subject in itself, apply it to our own case, and thus the meditation is completed by self-examination.

CHAPTER IV

BODY OF THE MEDITATION (*Continued*)

AFFECTIONS

§ I.—THEIR IMPORTANCE.

IN the considerations and examination we have
seen the principal work of the intellect. Now we
have to speak of the work of the will, which consists in affections, petitions and resolutions.

Here we come to the very heart of mental prayer,
and so to speak the whole of prayer. So long as I
am satisfied with reflecting and examining, I am
neither adoring, nor thanking, nor asking pardon
nor soliciting any grace; therefore, I have not been
praying; but still, as I make these considerations
in order to bring about affections, petitions and
resolutions, they are the introduction to prayer, the
needle which should draw after it the golden thread
of the affections. Hitherto I have merely understood the truth, now remains the most necessary
act—namely, to do what I know to be my duty.
The intellect does no more than make a rough
sketch of divine union, it is the heart and the will
which perfect it; to know God and what He wills
me to do is something; to love Him and attach
myself to Him is all.

We meet pious persons who misapprehend this elementary truth; they pass a whole half-hour in reflections without once speaking to God. No doubt the intellect has not been alone in its action, the heart has been warmed, the will has conceived some holy desires; but, if the soul has not unbosomed itself to God by affections and petitions, the union is very incomplete, there is only a beginning of prayer, and such meditations are almost sterile.

"No one," says St. Bernard,[1] "arrives at the highest point at one bound; it is by climbing, not by flying, that we reach the top of the ladder. Let us climb, then, as it were with two feet—viz., with meditation and prayer. Meditation shows us what we want, prayer obtains it. The former shows the way, the latter leads us along it. By meditation we learn the dangers which threaten us, by prayer we escape them."

We should, therefore, attach supreme importance to affections, petitions and resolutions. We should devote to them on an average not less than half of our prayer-time. In the beginning, however, we cannot rise to this point, because we feel more need of reflections, and later on the affections tend to pass beyond this limit, and they will end by occupying our whole time; we shall then have reached affective prayer.

---

[1] St. Bernard, *First Sermon on St. Andrew*, n. 10.

§ II.—Of the Affections which arise from the Subject of our Prayer.

" We call affections," says Father Crasset,[1] " certain movements of the soul, which arise from the consideration, or from the mere thought of some subject; such as are the acts of all the virtues of faith, hope, charity, adoration, admiration, praise, thanksgiving oblation of oneself, grief for one's sins, shame for one's past life, and such like." These affections constitute the first three functions of prayer; we have mentioned some of them on a former page.[2] We shall point out many more of them when speaking of affective prayer.[3]

Some of these arise naturally out of the considerations. After having meditated, for instance, on some one of the divine perfections, it is quite natural to adore God, to admire, praise, love Him, &c. . . . When we reflect upon Hell we shall be inclined rather to humble ourselves, to ask pardon, to repair the past, to fly sin.

Other affections spring from self-examination; if we find that we have been faithful, we must give the honour to God, and thank Him with humility. More frequently we shall find that we have been in fault; then we should, *for the past,* accuse ourselves before God, beg pardon, and willingly make atonement; *for the present* be ashamed of our misery and our poverty, blush to see ourselves so far from resembling our divine model, so opposed

[1] Fr. Crasset, *On Prayer.*   [2] 1st part, c. i. § 1 p. 2.
[3] C. viii. art. 2 p. 187.

to what Our Lord requires of us; *for the future,* desire ardently to get out of this state.

At other times, the affections are not excited either by the considerations or by the self-examination; it is the abundance of the heart, which overflows and pours itself forth; or it is the will, which deliberately selects such or such an affection which appears to it profitable.

It is quite natural to begin by making the acts which arise spontaneously from the meditation or examination. However, it is good to add one or more fundamental acts, to which Christian piety loves to have recourse every day; thus our affections will not be left to the impressions of the moment, but will proceed from a reasoned choice and a formed habit.

§ III.—AFFECTIONS FOREIGN TO THE SUBJECT.

We shall indicate the principal ones, following St. Liguori.[1] It is not profitable to make all these acts in one and the same prayer; it is better to take only a few of them, and to make them thoroughly, dwelling upon each of them until we are penetrated with it, and taking care not to pass on to another as long as the present act is doing us good. We may choose sometimes one, sometimes another, a single act or several, in such a way, however, that none of these fundamental acts is habitually omitted.

[1] See Fr. Desurmont, *Retour continuel à Dieu* and *Divine Art of Mental Prayer.*

I. First of all let us mention acts of true repentance, which others call "*spiritual confession*."

This means—1°. To beg for a contrite and humble heart, for in order to repent we have need of God.—2°. Humbly to confess our sins to Our Lord, Who knows and detests them; I mean not only the sins which relate to the subject of our prayer, but all the faults of our past life, and our present miseries, especially our principal failings and our predominant vice.—3°. To make a serious act of contrition, and of good resolution. According to St. Alphonsus, acts of contrition and of charity are the most excellent part of meditation. Let us excite ourselves then to repentance by fear or by hope; let us aspire especially to that sorrow which springs from the pure love of God; and let us never forget that, if it is necessary to wash away the past by tears of repentance, our principal care ought to be to make sure of the future by a firm and efficacious resolution.—4°. To offer to God in atonement some voluntary sacrifice; above all, to accept those penalties, which our rules and the dispositions of Providence may impose upon us; to renounce, for instance, such an irregularity, to resolve to bear with such a brother, to receive as from the hand of God such an infirmity, or such a pain of mind, because we have deserved a much greater chastisement. This secret and interior expiation excellently disposes the soul for the outward accomplishment of the sacrifice.—5°. To implore the grace of pardon and amendment. St. Alphonsus recommends nothing more frequently

than this petition; in this, imitating Our Lord,
Who, in the *Pater,* places it upon our lips, and the
Church, which makes us repeat it continually. For,
in fact, " there are sins which are pardoned and
not pardoned; pardoned, since absolution or contrition has blotted them out; not pardoned, because
God may still hold a reckoning with them," [1] either
by inflicting temporal punishment for them, or,
what is more to be feared, by withholding from us
the special graces He had destined as a reward for
our fidelity. Full of sorrow for having offended a
God so worthy of love, a good heart never wearies
of expressing its regret.

Such is the spiritual confession or act of repentance in prayer. We may at times confine ourselves
to one or more of these acts, at others, elicit them
all; it is very good to employ the whole time of
one's morning meditation, on the days we have to
approach the Sacrament of Penance, in this exercise of compunction; and, on all occasions, let us
be sincerely penitent in our relations with God.

This spiritual confession is particularly suitable
for beginners; it remains still profitable for proficients, and even for the perfect; these last, however, simplify it as they simplify everything. If it
be a great misfortune to have sinned, it is great
wisdom to draw good from evil, to spread, by means
of these penitential acts, the manure of our sins over
the field of our soul in order to fertilise the germs
of humility, mortification, generosity, hatred of
self, avoidance of everything which separates from

---

[1] Fr. Desurmont, *Retour*, 2ᵉ part, xii.

God, gratitude for His mercies, and repentant love. Whosoever has found compunction has found a treasure, and this is above all true in an Order which makes penance one of its special ends; the contrition which springs from love, gives in reality soul and life to our austerities. This is why St. Benedict makes this spiritual confession the 58th instrument of good works: " To confess every day in prayer to God with tears and groans one's past sins, and moreover to amend them for the time to come," and he repeats this with earnestness, especially in the chapter on the observance of Lent.

II. *Acts of humility, confidence, and thanksgiving.*—Prayer is the great means of transforming our life. Spiritual confession begins this conversion by cleansing the soul; trustful humility and humble confidence go to the root of the evil. Is not man's greatest infirmity since the fall pride, that strange compound of presumption and discouragement, of self-sufficiency and diffidence? Under various guises it is always the same evil, confident pride, discouraged pride, pride self-satisfied, pride soured and cross. Here, however, we have an easy means of remedying the evil.

It is of supreme importance to multiply acts of humility in order to develop this virtue which is the foundation of all others, on account of its removing their chief obstacle.

Let us multiply also acts of confidence in God's grace, which will sustain us, in His mercy, which is ever ready to pardon us; for, without confidence, the heart contracts, the will is paralysed and has no longer any energy, we dread God and avoid Him.

It is right to unite these two acts and but rarely to separate them. For they mutually poise, correct, and balance each other; if one becomes excessive the other brings it back to the golden mean. Confidence prevents humility from degenerating into discouragement and pusillanimity; humility hinders confidence from falling into presumption. The one is not a true virtue without the other. Humility, without confidence, rather insults than honours God; confidence, without humility, resembles self-confidence, rather than confidence in God.

It will be useful to dwell, sometimes on one of these acts, sometimes on the other, according as self-sufficiency or diffidence in God gives us more trouble.

All our motives for humility are reducible to two, viz., unworthiness and incapacity: unworthiness, on account of past sins, lost graces, good omitted, present faults and bad inclinations; radical incapacity, in the order of nature, without the divine concurrence, in the supernatural order, without grace. Reviewing these divers motives in detail, or taking them all in at a glance, we should sincerely recognise that we are nothing, we have nothing, we can do nothing without God; we should sincerely confess our misery, we should humbly accept the humiliation of our condition. Some of our miseries depend on our own will, and, because they offend God, we should hate them, labour to amend them, and in the meantime bear patiently with ourselves. Others depend in no way upon our will, but are a pure humiliation inherent to our condition as creatures and as men, and there is nothing for it but humbly to accept of them : thus accepted, they will glorify God.

Humility ought never to make us lose confidence, but ought rather lead us to transfer it from self and to place it in God. True confidence does not rely upon our worth, our virtues, our merits, or our capacity, but upon God alone; upon His goodness, which wishes our welfare; upon His power and wisdom, which are able to procure it; upon His patience, which bears with us; upon His mercy, which pardons us; upon His Grace, which aids us, and upon Our Saviour's merits and promises.

We shall often, then, make acts like the following :—" O Lord, I am a sinner unworthy to appear before Thee, a mere nothing, incapable of doing anything without Thee, Thou seest all my shameful deeds, and I confess them frankly; ' *I am the man that see my poverty* ';[1] it is a grace which Thou givest me, and I thank Thee for it. I love not, on the contrary, I detest my faults and miseries, which displease Thee, and I desire to become more humble, more meek, more patient. But I cannot without Thee. *Convert us to Thee, O Lord, and we shall be converted.*[2] Thou hast, O Lord, to say but one word; ' *Say it, and my soul shall be healed.*' As to my infirmities, which do not offend

[1] Jer., *Lam.*, iii. 1.
[2] *Ibid.*, v, 21.

Thee, such as want of health, dulness of mind, as
Thou dost will them, so do I, and I accept the
humiliation of them, since it glorifies Thee. I am
but nothingness and misery, O my God; but I trust
in Thy indulgent goodness, because for whom is
mercy, if not for the miserable? and on whom wilt
Thou have pity, if not on him who is destitute of
every good, and abounds in every evil? I am
nothing but weakness; but, if I can do nothing
without Thee, ' *I can do all things in Him Who
strengthens me,* ' " &c.

To humility and confidence we should join
gratitude. Humility gives rise to gratitude, whereas
pride begets ingratitude. How could a proud man
give thanks? It seems to him that he has nothing
which has not come from himself, or which is not
owing to his own merits. Humility, on the contrary, sees its own poverty and helplessness, and
hence refers all the good it receives to its author
with sincere thanksgiving. Enriched with the gifts
of God—gifts of nature, gifts of grace, general gifts
and special gifts, and especially the many graces
included in our religious vocation—let us admire
the divine liberality, and repay so many benefits by
a frequent tribute of thanksgiving; this is a need for
noble souls, and, moreover, gratitude charms the
heart of our Benefactor and opens His hand, whilst
ingratitude is an icy blast which blights His
friendship and dries up the stream of His benefits.

These different affections suit all souls without
exception. They may vary in their expression, and
will become more simple as time goes on, but they

should never entirely disappear from our prayer. It would even be well to spend sometimes the whole time of our prayer in acts of humility and confidence in God, or in the thanksgiving of a grateful heart.

III. *Acts of Affective and Effective Love.*—Since charity is the queen of virtues, and all the others either lead to it or spring from it, since it is "*the plenitude of the law and the bond of perfection,*" and since, by making us do God's will through a motive of love whenever it is made known to us, it alone suffices, whilst the total want of it spoils everything, we should, with special care, cultivate so sublime and so necessary a virtue. St. Liguori [1] wishes "that we should, in our prayer, reiterate with special frequency acts of contrition and of love. An act of love, as also an act of contrition, is a golden chain which attaches the soul to God. An act of perfect love is sufficient to obtain for us the remission of all our sins; . . . every act of love acquires for us a new degree of glory," &c.

In beginners charity is in its infancy, it is growing in the illuminative way, and reaches its full development and its sovereign power in the unitive way. Acts of this virtue, therefore, are most suited to souls who have passed beyond simple meditation; but those also who are as yet taking only their first steps in the ways of prayer, may and ought to make acts of love; for perfect charity, being of precept for all, is impossible for none. Souls more purified, more detached, more en-

[1] St. Liguori, *True Spouse of Jesus Christ*, xv. § 2.

riched with virtues, will succeed best in the exercise of holy love; nevertheless, the others may make trial of this way, and God will take into account their good desires, their efforts, and their regret for not being able to love Him better.

Affective love in which the heart pours itself forth into the heart of the Well-Beloved. At the sight of God's perfection, and especially of His beauty and His goodness, the soul is captivated by God; places Him in her esteem above all, admires Him and praises Him (the psalms are full of these divine praises); she looks upon Him with pleasure, sighs after Him, seeks Him lovingly, wants Him and Him only; she rejoices in His perfections, in the glory which He finds in Himself and in His creatures; is afflicted to behold Him misunderstood, forgotten, offended, hated and persecuted; and, fired with zeal, she would like to overwhelm His enemies and bring them to adore Him, who possesses her whole heart. Our Lord especially should be the object of these acts; His divine perfections render Him infinitely deserving of them; as Man-God, He is Our Saviour, our model, our happiness, our all.

The sacred humanity brings the divinity within our reach, and gives it an incomparable charm in our eyes. God, in fact, has become our brother, our friend, our spouse, the conqueror of hearts.

By these and similar acts the soul pours herself forth into the heart of her Well-Beloved. As they would be far too elevated for beginners, these may at first content themselves with the usual formula, and say to God in all simplicity that they love Him and would wish to love Him more and more.

Love in action, or, *effective love,* which tends to show itself in our conduct. The proof of true affection is to be found not in fine words or sweet emotions, but in deeds. This is the reason that, while pouring forth our soul into the heart of Our Lord, we should still more earnestly strive to bring our will into unison with His. Once we love God we aspire to please Him, to gain His friendship; and the true means to this is to will only what He wills and not to will what He does not will. We should strive, therefore, to say to God in all sincerity :—" O my God, I love Thee, I wish to please Thee and to gain Thy heart; and, for this reason, I will whatsoever Thou willest, and I hate whatsoever displeases Thee. Such a fault, such an imperfection, such an attachment, such a bad inclination still displeases Thee in me ; I desire, with Thy holy grace, to remove it from my soul, help me to do so ; Thou desirest of me such a sacrifice, I now resolve to make it, give me the strength."

Amidst the various prescriptions of the Divine Will, we should love above all our rules and the orders of our superiors, which are the duties of our state; we should generously resign ourselves to the dispositions of Providence imposing upon us sacrifices, such as sickness, infirmities, dryness, moral sufferings, &c. For all this is more intimately and personally the Divine Will for us. To say to God that we love Him entirely, and, at the same time, to resist His decrees is simply to lie to His face, and

K

to cherish an illusion.   No; such an affection is not unreserved, we love God only by measure, and we want to make a bargain with Him about our devotedness.   But if we will all that He wills, and as He wills, because we desire to rejoice and to please Our Lord, this love is a thousand times more really love than the most tender emotions of mere affection.

"Conformably to this doctrine," says Father Desurmont, "and to complete the conversion of the heart by prayer, our saint (St. Liguori) requires us to add to the act of love properly so called, other acts which more immediately attack the will—*i.e.*, renunciation, resignation, conformity and oblation; so that the soul may say:—O Lord, I love Thee, I renounce my own will, I resign myself to Thine, I will all that Thou willest, I offer myself entirely to Thee, dispose of me according to Thy good pleasure." [1]

Prayer thus made is *fundamental* prayer; the habit of spiritual confession removes sin; a long practice of trustful humility uproots self-sufficiency and diffidence; love and conformity will with time extirpate selfishness and self-will, and thus the source of evil shall be dried up.

Remarks :—1°. "Nothing can be more salutary than *to introduce into our prayer some practical case,* and to apply to this case the acts we have selected. If, for instance, you happen to meet with a humiliation, make in your prayer the act of humility which applies to this humiliation;

[1] Fr. Desurmont, *Art divine de l'or. mentale,* 5ᵉ max.

if some circumstance has occurred which tries your
confidence in God, apply your act of confidence to
this circumstance; if you have happened to commit
a fault, exercise yourself in acts of penance and
repentance for this fault; if, in fine, an occasion
presents itself in which there is greater difficulty in
adhering to God's will, or in sacrificing self-will,
profit of this occasion and of this difficulty to exercise yourself, in your prayer, in conquering yourself as to these points, . . . and little by little you
will come to be well grounded in solid virtue." [1]

2°. "As it is by acts," says Father Crasset,
"that the heart detaches itself from creatures and
unites itself to God, we should produce as many as
we can, without, however, making violent efforts.
If you cannot produce an act of charity, produce
one of humility; for, says St. Bernard, this virtue
supplies for the want of charity. Suffer, if you
cannot pray, pray the prayer of patience instead
of the prayer of consolation. . . . Above all,
remain in peace and be not troubled, being persuaded that the most excellent of all prayers is to
do the will of God, and to be content in whatsoever
state He may place you."

3°. Let us be especially watchful that our conversation with God be always a reality. He is here.
He is listening to us; let us, therefore, speak to
Him with faith and with respect, awakening in our
soul, if necessary, a lively sense of His presence.
But let this conversation be always very simple,
devoid of fine phrases, just as we would speak to

[1] Fr. Desurmont, *Retour continuel à Dieu*, 2° part. xiii.

our mother, or to our most intimate friend. " If you accustom yourself thus to a perfectly easy and quite ordinary tone, a great deal of the difficulty of mental prayer will be smoothed away. If, on the other hand, you remain the slave, like so many others, of a craving to experience lively emotions, you, like so many others also, will find this exercise very difficult, and run some risk of abandoning it altogether. Pray, therefore, much to God to grant you the gift of holy simplicity, for it is a great grace." [1]

[1] Fr. Desurmont, *Retour continuel à Dieu*, 2ᵉ part. ix.

CHAPTER V

BODY OF THE MEDITATION (*Continued*)

PETITIONS—RESOLUTIONS

§ I.—PETITIONS.

AFTER the affections come the petitions. At all events, this is their logical place in the analysis of the acts of mental prayer. Prayer springs from deeper convictions, desire is more keenly earnest, when the mind is enlightened by reflections and the heart warmed by affections. But nothing obliges us to follow this order in practice; it is even desirable that the considerations be already seasoned by pious affections, and that petitions be sprinkled over the whole course of our prayer; as breathing accompanies every one of our bodily actions.

The importance of petitions is thus signalised by St. Liguori:—" It is extremely useful, and perhaps preferable to everything else, by frequent petitions to beg of God His graces with humility and confidence. . . .

" The Venerable Father Paul Segneri relates that before he had studied theology he used in prayer to employ himself chiefly in making reflections and exciting affections; ' but, at length,' adds he, ' God opened my eyes, and, if there is in me any good, I

regard it as owing to the habit I adopted of implor-
ing God's help and protection.' " [1]

As to the soul's dispositions, these prayers of
petition require, above all, faith and confidence.
He, whose aid we implore, is not far away from us.
He is a being truly living and truly present, who
sees all our needs, who has the power to relieve
them, who has the will to do so, but who generally
waits for us to ask for His assistance. He is here
quite near us, looking lovingly upon us, attentive
to our supplications, more desirous of granting
than we are of receiving His favours. The moment
we ask good and profitable things, His word is
pledged. We have only to knock and He will
open for us. Our Saviour complains that we
have hitherto asked nothing: ask, therefore, and
you shall receive.[2] He seems to long for the joy
of giving.

Alas! our great misfortune in prayer is that we
know not how to treat with God, "*as seeing Him,
who is invisible,*" [3] nor how to "ask in faith,
nothing wavering ";[4] although Our Saviour has
solemnly promised:[5]! "If you shall have faith
and stagger not, . . . and if you shall say to
this mountain; take up and cast thyself into the
sea, it shall be done. And all things whatsoever
you shall ask in prayer, believing, you shall
receive."

[1] St. Liguori, *True Spouse of Jesus Christ*, xv. 2.
[2] St. John xvi. 24.
[3] Heb. xi. 27.
[4] St. James i. 6.
[5] Matth. xxi. 22.

No doubt we must also pray with a lively sense of our misery and unworthiness, for "the prayer of the humble pierceth the clouds."[1] "The Lord gives His grace to the humble and resists the proud."[2] Pride is hateful before God,[3] above all, "pride in poverty,"[4] But humility must not destroy confidence; if our misery is profound, let us have recourse to the "great mercy of God and the multitude of His mercies";[5] our weakness so often experienced, will bring into greater relief the power of grace, Our Lord will have the more glory in saving us; the gravity of our malady will show forth the wisdom of the divine physician; when a poor man has many misfortunes to plead his cause, it is then especially that he excites the compassion of the rich man and makes him open his hand. It is a great blessing to feel our weakness and powerlessness, provided that we say with the royal penitent: "For Thy name's sake, O Lord, Thou wilt pardon my sin; for it is great."[6] What closes the heart of God against us is not our miseries, but our attachment to them, our pride, which refuses to acknowledge our faults, our spirit of independence, which will neither ask pardon nor obey, our want of faith, which has not the courage to hope everything from infinite goodness.

Finally, our petitions must be persevering. "When God delays to grant our petitions, it is to make us value His gifts, and not that He means to

---

[1] Eccli. xxxv. 21.
[2] I. Pet. v. 5. Jac. iv. 6.
[3] Eccli. x. 7.
[4] Eccli. xxv. 4.
[5] Ps. l. 1 and 2.
[6] Ps. xxiv. 11.

refuse to give them. When long desired, they are received with greater pleasure; whereas if granted without delay, they are less esteemed. Ask, seek, persist in asking and seeking. By asking and seeking your desire to obtain grows greater. God withholds for a time what He does not wish to grant at once, in order that you may learn to desire His great gifts with a great desire." [1]

We must pray for ourselves and for our neighbour.

For ourselves it seems best to begin with the petitions which the subject of our prayer suggests; the increase in some virtue, the avoidance of some fault, the grace proper to some mystery, according to the considerations and affections, with which we have just been occupied.

As there are certain fundamental acts (trustful humility, contrition, and love), which it is well to make in every prayer, there are also fundamental petitions, which it is useful never to omit. This is why St. Liguori counsels us, every time we pray, to ask for final perseverance and for charity, because this is the end of our being.

" St. Francis of Sales used to say, that in obtaining Divine Love we obtain all graces; for a soul which truly loves God with its whole heart will of itself avoid whatever may displease Our Lord, and will strive to please Him in all things." [1] Charity is a queen in whose train follow all the other virtues, a super-eminent gift which is obtained only

---

[1] St. Augustine, *De Verbis Dom.*

[2] St. Liguori, *True Spouse of Jesus Christ*, xv.

as an alms, yet, of all celestial treasures, that which God gives most willingly; and we never have enough of it, since what we have can always be increased.

Final perseverance is also a grace, and even the gift of gifts. " I conjure the reader," says St. Liguori,[1] " not to grow weary, when he sees that I am unceasingly asking for love and perseverance. It is because these two gifts include all others; and when they are obtained all is obtained."

Sometimes these petitions are general, often they will apply to particular cases. For instance, if we are pursued by a troublesome temptation, we may say to God : Grant me to conquer in this combat, in order to make my perseverance secure; when we hesitate in the presence of some sacrifice, we may ask of God the grace to love Him so as generously to renounce this pleasure for His sake.

All these petitions are for ourselves, but we ought also to recommend to God, the Church, its Head, its priests and religious, our house, our country, our family, all those for whom we are in any way bound to pray, the just, sinners, the souls in Purgatory, &c. This universality in prayer is charity in action; nothing can be more agreeable to God or incline Him more efficaciously to grant our personal desires.

In order to persevere for a longer time in these petitions, nothing need prevent us from repeating them a great number of times, or from adding even some vocal prayers. These repetitions are very

[1] St. Liguori, *Preface to the Preparation for Death.*

frequent in the prayers of the Church, in the litanies, for instance, and the rosary.

The Sulpician method advises us to represent to God some reasons which may induce Him to grant our requests, and this will have the further effect of prolonging our petitions and rendering them more fervent. "Amongst other things we may humbly tell Him :—1°. That it is His Will. 2°. That it will be for His glory. 3°. That He should not allow a person to remain so imperfect a member in His Church which He loves so much. 4°. To consider our frequent communions, and that His Son, the beloved object of all His complacency, will be otherwise so little glorified in us, and so imperfectly received into our heart. 5°. Above all, the most effective arguments are to represent to Him His own goodness, His infinite liberality, the merits of His Son, His promises and pledged word in the Scriptures."

"It is also good to make use of the influence of the most Holy Virgin, of our Angel Guardian, of our Holy patrons and other saints. This will be very serviceable, and it ought to be frequently practised."

§ II.—Of Resolutions

Amongst all the acts of mental prayer resolutions hold the chief place.

They are in relation to this pious exercise what the terminus is to a journey, the end, towards which should converge the reflections, the examination, the affections and the petitions. We have said already [1] that meditation is a kind of spiritual strategy which has for object to conquer a vice or to acquire a virtue, and all its acts, like so many battalions, should march together towards the attainment of this object. Meditation, without a resolution, is an army manœuvring at random and without any object, that consequently cannot hope to gain the victory. But often also to make resolutions without praying is to attempt to fly without wings.[2]

It would, however, be an exaggeration to say that without a resolution meditation has no good result; for the mind is enlightened, the will inflamed, many affections and petitions are produced which are so many acts of virtue, so many fruits gathered in; but, if it does not result in firm and efficacious resolutions, it has failed to produce its most desirable effect,[3] pretty much like medical advice in the case of an invalid, who, contented with reasoning and talking about his illness, will take no remedy.

" We must not judge of the goodness of a meditation," says Father Crasset, " by the lively feelings of devotion which we may have experienced during it, but by the profit which we have derived from it. . . . When you leave off prayer, no matter how dry it may have been, with a resolution to correct your faults and to do God's will, you have not lost your time."

[1] 2nd part, c. iii. p. 127.
[2] Fr. Desurmont, *Art div. de l'or. ment.*, 8ᵉ max.
[3] 1st part, c. v. p. 57.

" The principal fruit of mental prayer," says St. Vincent de Paul, " consists in making a good resolution, and a strong one too, in grounding one's resolutions on a firm basis, in being thoroughly convinced of their necessity, in being ready to put them in practice, and in foreseeing obstacles in order to overcome them."

There are general resolutions, and particular resolutions. " General resolutions," says Father Crasset, " are, for instance, to love God with one's whole heart, to fly sin, to practise virtue, . . . to conform oneself to God's will in everything. Particular resolutions determine the place, the time, the circumstances; such as, to mortify oneself on such an occasion, to practise meekness and patience in such a conjuncture, to be resigned to God's will, in such or such a loss, humiliation, sickness."

Our resolutions should not be so general as to remain vague and indefinite; nor should they be to such a degree particular, as to make us forget the main lines of our sanctification through attention to mere details.

In our opinion we may avoid these extremes by taking every day two resolutions, one general and invariable, the other particular, but renewable for any length of time we may desire. The former should bring us face to face with our end, and the latter should lead us to it by precisely determined acts.

As religious our end is to tend to perfection, as Cistercians to work out this continual progress by contemplation and penance. Our general and invariable resolution might then be like this: "O my God, I have done so little up to this! To-day at all events I shall become better by striving to be more contemplative and penitent." Let it not be said that this resolution is too vague, for there is already something precise in it; and, in any case, a particular resolution is to be combined with it, in order to put before us something definite to be aimed at. Nothing has more power over the mind than this habitual return to our end. It is a daily awakening of the whole soul, a daily resuming of the business of our whole life, a resurrection of our good will.[1] The saints, not content with merely thinking on their end every morning, kept their eyes continually fixed upon it, in order to aim at it as the sole scope of all their actions. Let us then bring ourselves face to face with this object at least once a day, for it is very easy to lose sight of it, and, nevertheless, this desire of perfection is the very soul of our religious life.

Under this general resolution, a particular one should be made " chiefly concerning the vice to which we are most addicted, and which we must strive to ruin in all our meditations, directing, so to speak all our batteries against it. We may at other times form resolutions to perform during that day some acts of virtue, determining their number."[2]

---

[1] Fr. Desurmont, *Art div. de l'or. ment*, 8ᵉ max.
[2] Fr. Crasset.

These resolutions ought to be altogether particular. St. Francis of Sales[1] gives the following
samples of them :—" I shall not allow myself to be
irritated by such or such annoying words, which so
or so says about me, nor by such or such contempt
which so and so shows in my regard; on the contrary, I shall say or do such or such a thing in
order to soften and win him."

They ought to be suited to the present time, so
that we may have occasion of putting them in practice that same day.

They ought to be efficacious, so that they may be
capable of curing our spiritual miseries, and such
that the remedy will be applied to the sore and not
alongside it. If I am dissipated, through breaches
of silence, it is on my tongue I should put the
bridle; if through wanderings of the imagination,
of the memory, or of the heart, it is the imagination, the memory or the heart that should be
watched. Attacking thus the source of the
disorder, I should courageously apply to it the true
remedy, and not one of those penances which do
neither good nor harm. My examinations of conscience will show me my principal faults, the predominant fault which is their source, the virtue
which I most want, the practices which I most
need; my director can guide me in this important
investigation; and after having examined my soul
by auscultation, as the doctors say, and diagnosed
the malady, I should not refuse to take the remedy.

Our resolutions ought to be at once humble and

[1] St. Francis of Sales, *Devout Life* 2nd part, c. vi.

full of confidence : humble, because faith teaches us that without Our Lord we can do nothing, we cannot even think one good thought, still less can we conceive a good desire, or put such a desire into practice. This point it is most important to remember. Often our checks are the punishment of our pride; they should be its cure, but alas! they rather produce vexation and discouragement. And yet our resolutions should be full of confidence. Whatever may have been our failures and disillusions up to the present, let us take occasion from them to acknowledge our powerlessness and to count only upon grace, and our hope shall not any longer be confounded; for God lovingly inclines towards the soul that invokes Him humbly. We are conquered only when we abandon the fight; assuredly we are not so, as long as we persist in rising again and returning to the combat. Victory will crown perseverance; every effort is a step forward, every renewal of our resolutions brings us nearer to final success.

Finally they should be often repeated. Even when well chosen, they will not be efficacious, if we change them too often. It is not in a day, nor in a few weeks, that we can correct our predominant sin, or acquire the virtue we most need. Perseverance and constancy are needed. It is quite right, then, to take the same resolution for weeks, and for months, for even a much longer period, provided our making it has not become a mere matter of routine; and if we can make it the subject of our particular examination, our success is all the more secure on account of the concentration of our efforts.

Remarks.—It is very useful to confine oneself to a single particular resolution " well impressed upon our mind, just as the hunter does not pursue several hares at the same time, but fixes his attention upon one only." [1]

II. Since our resolutions ought to be efficacious, we must proportion the work to our strength, and begin by easy things before undertaking what is difficult; otherwise we shall be discouraged.

[1] Fr. Crasset, *De l'or.*

CHAPTER VI

CONCLUSION OF THE MEDITATION

THE conclusion of meditation is very simple. We must :

1°. Thank God for the honour He has done us in granting us so long an audience, as well as for the lights, pious affections, and good resolutions He has given us.

2°. Beg of Him to pardon the faults and negligences we have committed in so holy an exercise.

We may confine ourselves to this, unless we should prefer to add the following acts, which are, however, optional.

3°. To offer to Him our soul, our mind, our body, our heart, our life and our death, especially the present day, and above all our good resolutions; and to beseech Him once more to give us His blessing, and the grace to accomplish what He has inspired, representing to Him our weakness and inconstancy.

4°. To make a spiritual nosegay. "This," as St. Francis of Sales[1] says, "is to take one or two thoughts which have touched us in prayer, and which before God we believe to be more useful to us, in order to think often upon them during the

---

[1] St. Francis of Sales, *Devout Life*, 2nd part, c. vii.

day, and to make use of them as ejaculatory prayers to raise ourselves to God and to unite ourselves to Him; just as we see persons of the world, who, being in a beautiful garden, carpeted with flowers, do not leave without having in their hand one or two of its flowers, whose scent they inhale continually after leaving the garden." [1]

Finally, we may put all into the hands of the Blessed Virgin by saying the *Sub tuum præsidium*. When the meditation is finished, if we have time, we may employ a few moments " in examining in a general way how we got on. If we have reason to be satisfied we thank God, resolving to proceed in the same way the next time; if we have not succeeded we will seek for the cause, and resolve to correct the defects we have noted, without ever being discouraged." [2]

[1] Method of St. Sulpice.
[2] Fr. Chaignon, *Méd. rel.*, t. i. p. 24.

CHAPTER VII

EQUIVALENTS OF MEDITATION

THE equivalents of meditation have all the essential elements of discursive prayer: considerations, affections, petitions and resolutions. Having thus a common groundwork, the effects will be practically the same. These equivalents differ from meditation in their way of presenting the considerations, in their freer and less methodical course; they serve to vary or diminish the labour of the mind, and some are a help, because they leave the largest share of the work to the imagination. They may, therefore, be of use, and may replace meditation, especially when we cannot make our ordinary mental prayer, and when the soul is in dryness, or has need of variety.

We shall mention: 1°. what St. Ignatius calls *contemplation* (which must not be confounded with *mystical* contemplation); 2°. what he calls the *application of the senses;* 3°. *the examination* made after the manner of a meditation; 4°. *vocal prayer meditated;* 5° *meditative reading.*

I. *Contemplation.*—This is almost what we described when speaking of the composition of place and of the manner of considering sensible objects and facts. The subject-matter is commonly one of the mysteries of Our Lord, or of the Blessed Virgin; it is reflected upon by looking at it rather than by reasoning about it; hence the name of contemplation.

We may begin as usual. After a rapid glance at the mystery of historic fact, taken as a whole, we consider all the details one after another with more care and attention. "We contemplate in each point: 1°. The *persons*, visible or invisible, with all they represent in themselves of good or evil; 2°. the *words*, interior or exterior; 3° the *actions*, praiseworthy or blamable, ascending to the principles from which they spring. From all we see, from all we hear and consider, we strive to draw some spiritual fruit by applying it to our own case. We may also consider the end of the mysteries, their causes, their effects, their date, and any other circumstances which may contribute to make the subject of our contemplation more suggestive and its fruit more abundant." [1]

These directions are somewhat abstract, an example, however, will set them in a clearer light.

I want to contemplate the birth of Our Lord. After having taken in at a rapid glance the whole of the mystery, I make the composition of place by picturing to myself a dark grotto, a wretched stable near Bethlehem where all is still, the silence of the night and the winter's cold. In these surroundings, so much forgotten by men, I contemplate the visible persons; first, Our Lord Himself, the Divine Majesty, abased to our condition, the

---

[1] Fr. Chaignon, *Méd. rel.*, t. i. introduction.

Eternal who has just been born, the Infinite annihilated; my God and my Master, become my Saviour, my brother, my friend. Then, also, His most holy Mother, a youthful maiden, poor, and as yet unknown, illustrious by the nobility of her descent, henceforth incomparably more so by the divine maternity; I see her interiorly adorned with all the jewels of the most sublime virtues, exteriorly by an ideal grace and virginal modesty. Again, I behold Saint Joseph, the spouse of the Queen of Virgins, the lowly carpenter become the confidant of God's secrets, associated in the august mystery of the Redemption, the foster-father of his God, the guardian of the Saviour of mankind. I contemplate, also, the invisible persons : God the Father, who has begotten from all eternity the Son, whom Mary has just brought forth in time; the Holy Ghost, by whose power this mystery has been effected; multitudes of angels, dazzling in their glorious beauty, ranged around the crib of their infant King.

None of these personages is represented as expressing his thoughts by word of mouth, their hearts alone speak; hence, to understand this language, I contemplate their actions. God the Father enfolds His Well-Beloved Son in a long look of complacency, and I rejoice to say to Our Lord with Him; Thou art my Well-Beloved in whom I am entirely pleased. The angels adore, and I along with them; they admire the infinite beauties of God, the ravishing charms of the Infant; with them I admire, I praise, I love; and, above

all, I am confounded, as they are, in presence of
the merciful abasements, and what we might call
the almost foolish excess of God's love for His poor
creatures, for sinners, for myself.   The demon
seeks for the means to destroy the Child, he pursues
Him with his hatred adown the centuries; I ask
myself how can any one hate Him who is love
itself, how, alas! have I been so mad as to sadden
Him by my own sins.   Our Lord humbly prostrate
in spirit before His Father adores Him, admires
Him, praises Him, rejoices with Him, thanks Him,
prays to Him, and offers Him countless acts of
worship in His own name and in ours; I unite
myself to Him in intention; I try to imitate all Our
Lord's acts of religion, and I offer my own to God
in union with His.   Laden with my sins, and the
crimes of the whole world, Our Lord is ashamed
and humbles Himself, He asks pardon for all the
guilty ones, and offers Himself as a victim of atonement; with Him I am covered with shame and
humiliation, I ask pardon and willingly accept
whatever expiation God may require.   The happy
Mother on her knees before the infinite majesty of
this Child, humbly adores her God, and lovingly
cherishes His Son; she casts upon Him those
burning looks, in which her whole soul pours
itself forth; while she holds Him in her arms,
consoles Him with the sweetest words, and fulfils
her maternal duties, her heart is on fire with love,
gratitude, faith, and adoration; but already grief
shadows her joy, for her Son shall be the Man of
Sorrows.   Saint Joseph marvels at the high honour

which God has done him; whilst he contemplates
the adorable Infant, and exchanges with Him the
marks of the most confiding love, his heart overflows with a thousand sentiments of love and gratitude; he offers himself to his God, and willingly
accepts for His sake his own *rôle* of self-sacrifice and
suffering.   With Mary and Joseph I adore, marvel
at, praise, and love my sweet Jesus; if I dared, I
would cover His feet with my kisses and water them
with my tears; I accept for His sake labours and
sacrifices, and give myself wholly to Him who
gave Himself wholly to me.   I may also consider
the end of this mystery, its causes, its effects, its
date and circumstances, &c.

Its end.—Our Lord comes to us as a Saviour, in
order to repair the glory of His Father, to over-
throw the empire of the demon, to break the heavy
chain of our sins, to restore to us liberty and
peace along with the life of grace and our rights to
Heaven.   He veils His majesty, that we may cease
to be afraid of God; He makes Himself an infant,
in order to be loved; He clothes Himself with
innocence and simplicity, to conquer our will
by ravishing our heart; He embraces poverty,
humiliations, sufferings, obedience, to render them
amiable in His own person, and to make of them
the remedy for our triple concupiscence.

Its causes.—They are the ineffable mercy and
love of God the Father, who delivers up His Son,
of Our Lord, who sacrifices Himself to save the
guilty.

Its effects.—God's justice appeased, the world

saved, childhood rendered sacred; poverty, suffering and obedience restored to honour; the nations, on their knees before a crib; God, formerly so dreaded, now ardently beloved, yet without losing anything of the reverence due to Him. . . . &c.

Its date.—It is after four thousand years of expectation, during which all hearts desired Him, the prophets announced Him, events pre-figured Him, and prepared His coming, &c., &c.

We see how capable a subject, thus contemplated by the heart and by faith rather than by complex reasonings, is of exciting love, gratitude, admiration, joy, praise, and countless other pious sentiments; the will is drawn to make more generous resolutions, whilst the heart pours itself forth in affectionate colloquies with God the Father, with Our Lord and His holy Mother.

II. *Application of the senses.*—" By the imagination an object is rendered present to us; we see it, so to speak, hear it, touch it, taste it. . . . Now, to apply this faculty and our senses to some truth of faith, as far as this truth is susceptible of such application, or to some mystery of Our Lord Jesus Christ, is to make what is called the *application of the senses*. This exercise consists, then, in this, that the soul, by means of the imagination, conceives itself to hear words, to touch objects; for instance, to kiss the feet of Our Lord. . . . which, however, must be done only with great respect. The sense of smell is applied to the perfume which such or such a virtue exhales, the taste to relish its sweetness. . . . This process will be quite the opposite if there is question of a vice. How many things the soul can represent to itself as having a sweet or a bitter taste, an agreeable or repellent odour! This application of the senses ought not, however, to be devoid of every kind of reflection, but it is merely the principal means " [1] by which we consider the mystery.

If we thus apply the senses to spiritual things, such as vices or virtues, is it necessary to say that we should carefully avoid whatever is subtle or forced?

If we apply them to facts or sensible mysteries, the application of the sight and hearing differs very little from what we have above described when speaking of contemplation; this latter, however, is satisfied with looking upon the persons and their actions and listening to their words, or to what they may be supposed to be saying. In the application of the senses we, moreover, bring the smell and the taste and the touch into action.

Thus, in the birth of Our Lord, I may touch the crib, the straw, the poor swaddling clothes, kiss the sacred feet and the little hands of Jesus; and breathe the cold icy air, the bad odour of the stable. I may also spiritually inhale the perfume of the virtues which Jesus, Mary, and Joseph practise in the grotto; and in the same way taste the joy of Mary and Joseph, the humiliations of Jesus, His suffer-ings, His tears, His self-sacrifice, in order to arouse my faith and to excite affections and resolutions.

" There is a well-marked difference between this

[1] Fr. Chaignon, *Méd. rel.*, t. i. introduction.

exercise and meditation. This latter belongs more to the province of the intellect, reasoning being more frequently employed in it. It reasons both upon the causes and effects of the mysteries; it carefully considers in them the attributes of God, as His goodness, His wisdom, His charity. The application of the senses, on the contrary, hardly reasons at all; it stops short at the sensible objects, at what can be seen, touched, heard, . . . the soul applying itself to draw from all this the fruit it desires.

" The application of the senses has two advantages; sometimes by making the soul, when it finds itself powerless to penetrate the depths of a mystery, dwell on the contemplation of sensible objects, it predisposes it to something more elevated; at other times, when the soul is already on fire with devotion through the contemplation of some sublime truth, by descending to these sensible objects, it finds therein an abundance of food and consolation. The smallest things then, the least details, become for it objects of inestimable value."

" This exercise is prepared for and concluded in the same way as the preceding, to which it is often joined by way of repetition, in order to render the impressions the former has made more deep and lasting." [1]

III. *Examination made after the manner of a meditation.*—St. Ignatius recommends this to those who are not used to meditation, and who

[1] Fr. Chaignon, *Méd. rel.*, pp. 26 and 27.

desire to set their life in order; and also to those
who are accustomed to mental prayer, when they
find themselves plunged in aridity.

It is a sort of examination intermingled with
affections, of contrition especially, and with
petitions and resolutions.

This examination may be made on the vows, on
the Christian and religious virtues. It is begun
as an ordinary meditation. After the preparation, we
consider briefly, for instance, obedience, in order
to see what it commands or forbids, and how just,
useful, easy, reasonable all that is. Then we
examine ourselves for a few moments, not as it
were for confession, but by way of a manifestation
of conscience made to oneself in God's presence;
for example, what have I to reproach myself with
on the subject of obedience of the intellect and of
the will, or with regard to exterior obedience
towards superiors and the rules, especially in such
or such a particular? We then make acts of
sorrow for the past, of shame for the present, of
good resolution for the future. We add to these
some very simple affections and petitions which
may be frequently repeated. After examining
obedience we may pass on to the other religious
duties. When the time we wish to devote to this
exercise is nearly expired, we form a particular
resolution and end our prayer in the usual manner.

We may perform this same exercise upon the
capital sins, the use we make of our senses, faults
against religious life, &c., in order to find out our
failings, consider their malice, excite a great sorrow

for them, and to rouse ourselves to a firm purpose of amendment.

We may examine especially our predominant sin or vice, seek out its causes and bad effects, conceive a horror of it, note its remedies, and, if we end our prayer resolved to labour at the destruction of this sin, we ought to rest satisfied that we have made an excellent prayer.

This exercise, recommended by St. Ignatius, is almost the same as what Father Desurmont calls "*Spiritual confession*," in making which he advises us sometimes to employ the whole time of our prayer.

"There are others who find much profit and consolation in thinking upon the graces God has bestowed upon them, and on the dangers from which He has delivered them. Those who have already made much progress in prayer may make use of this consideration to excite themselves to the love of God and to sorrow for their sins, contrasting all the benefits they have received with their own cowardice, treasons, infidelities and ingratitude. Here you have quite matter enough to pass half-an-hour's time."[1]

IV. *Vocal prayer meditated.*—This manner of praying, partly vocal, partly mental, is both easy and fruitful. St. Ignatius teaches it in his "Exercises"; St. Teresa extolls it, especially in her "Way of Perfection," and describes in very great detail the means to succeed in it.

It consists in taking any vocal prayer, the *Pater*,

[1] Fr. Crasset.

Ave, Salve Regina, a psalm, a litany, &c., and in
meditating upon the words of this prayer, quitting
the first word to pass on to the second, only when
the former ceases to afford us any more thoughts
or affections. We may profitably make use of
some comparisons and similitudes which help to
develop the subject. When the meditation of one
or more words suffices to occupy the whole time of
prayer, we may recite then the rest of the prayer
rapidly, and resume the meditation of the following words the day after.

" Thus when you have said : *Our Father,* stop a
a little time to relish the sweetness of this name so
suggestive of love and affection. Make an act of
faith that God is your father. Consider by how
many titles you are His child, to wit, by creation,
preservation, redemption and justification. Then
say to your soul : O my soul, if God is thy father,
why is it that thou lovest Him not? Whence
comes it that thou dost not obey Him ? If God is
thy father, why dost thou not hope in Him ? Why
dost thou not ask Him to supply all thy needs?
God is thy father and thou fearest to die of hunger !
He, a God, has given His blood for thee, and thou
thinkest He will refuse thee a morsel of bread ! *O
my God and my father! I hope in thee! O best of
all fathers! what a bad child Thou hast! Oh! how
afflicted I am for having offended, persecuted, dis-
honoured Thee as I have done since I first came into
this world! Oh my father, I have sinned, I am no
longer worthy to be called Thy child; but let me be
called Thy servant. Oh! never again shall I offend*

Thee, but from this time forward I shall love only Thee.

" If this simple word gives you enough occupation, you must not pass beyond it. When you have extracted its honey pass on to the next, *who art in heaven;* and consider how great and powerful God is who dwells in such a beautiful place; that there above is your true inheritance, and that consequently you ought not to attach yourself to earth. Dig diligently in this evangelical field, and you will find a treasure of grace that will enrich you, and a spring of living water that will quench your thirst.

" After the *Pater,* you may pass on to the *Ave,* to the *Credo,* or to any psalm, which you may recite and examine in the same way; you may also recite the litany of the Holy Name of Jesus, dwelling upon all the titles which are there given to the Son of God, and making acts of faith, hope, of love, contrition, thanksgiving, and such like others. When, for instance, you say : *Jesus, the God of Peace, have mercy on me,* stop for a little and reflect that Jesus is a God of peace, and that it is He alone who can impart peace to your heart. *Why, then, O my soul, you will say, dost thou seek peace in creatures? O God of peace, tranquilize my poor heart, for it is often troubled and restless. Oh! when shall I repose in Thy heart, which is the centre of my peace. O sweet Jesus! give me Thy peace, Thy love, and Thy blessing, speak and command the sea to be still, calm this storm that troubles Thy repose and mine. O my soul, love*

Jesus only, since He alone it is who can give thee peace and satisfy all thy desires.

" This mode of mental prayer may bring you far upon your way, and may also serve after communion to arouse your devotion. Amongst so many beautiful characteristics that are there given to the Son of God, there must be some one which will touch your heart, and suit your present mood. When you find it, fix your mind upon it as a bee alights upon a flower, and do not leave it till you have drawn from it the honey of devotion.

" You might also read with respect and attention words of love taken from Holy Scripture, or from the " Imitation of Christ "; there will assuredly be some of them which will touch your heart and inspire you with devotion, whether during meditation or after communion." [1]

V. *Meditative reading.*—St. Teresa [2] relates that during more than fourteen years, elsewhere she says eighteen years, she could not pray at all without a book, except after Holy Communion. She used to read more or less according to the grace God gave her; and sometimes merely to open the book sufficed to make her soul recollected and her mind tranquil.

You take, then, some spiritual work, and read over a few lines or even more of it, as much in fact as is required to furnish matter for reflections and affections. You meditate a little upon what you

---

[1] *Le secret de la sainteté . . . De l'oraison,* par le P. Crasset, c. ix. p. 225.
[2] St. Teresa, *Life,* iv ; *Way,* xvii.

have read, trying to penetrate its sense, to impress it on your mind, and to apply to yourself whatever is practical in it.—You draw from it holy affections, such as, of contrition, love, faith, confidence, humility, or of some other virtue; and if you meet with some good counsel which strikes home, you make a good resolution invoking the help of God's grace.

You continue making these acts of the will, as long as the sentiment which has touched you lasts; then you pursue your reading until it furnishes matter for new reflections and affections.

"Let us always act thus," says St. Liguori,[1] "after the example of the bee, which does not pass on from one flower to another until it has gathered all the honey it finds on the first. It does not matter in such a case that the time for reading is passing and is nearly at an end; for it has been thus employed in a manner more profitable for our spiritual welfare : the reading of a single line sometimes does us more good than that of a whole page."

This exercise thus performed comprises all the elements of a true meditation; it is even mental prayer rather than reading. At other times, especially in time of dryness, the work of the mind may be limited to reading attentively with a short self-examination; it will then be much more a lecture than a prayer, and the affections will be short, the petitions rapidly made. These, however, will suffice to season this exercise with prayer and love, and to enlighten the mind, while inflaming the will.

[1] St. Liguori, *True Spouse of Jesus Christ*, xvii.

There is no one, it would seem, who cannot do at least that much, when dryness is so great as to render meditation impossible.

Remark : Doubtless it is because they include in one view meditation and its equivalents, that certain authors [1] go so far as to represent mental prayer as absolutely necessary for perfection, and morally so for salvation; a total want of Christian reflection being the worst of plagues, and desolation by excellence.   In spite of all that, their opinion seems to us too severe.   All authors agree that the higher forms of prayer are a supremely desirable help, but not an absolute necessity.   But not even is methodical meditation indispensable for perfection; certain souls can attain to it by means of vocal prayer alone well made.[2]

[1] V. gr. Guilloré, *Conf. Spir.*, b. ii. c. iii.
[2] See 1st part, c. iii. p. 30.

CHAPTER VIII

OF AFFECTIVE PRAYER

§ I.—Description of this Prayer.[1]

To be acquainted with meditation alone, whose method we have just explained, would be regrettable. As time goes on, and we make progress, we shall feel drawn to a more simple form of prayer, in which the mind begins to be silent in order to let the heart speak.

St. John of the Cross and St. Francis of Sales, it is true, mention only meditation and contemplation; while St. Teresa includes, under what she calls "the First Water," all kinds of non-mystical prayer. Meditation, in their idea, comprises all kinds of active prayer, whether it consist in much reasoning, or in only a slight amount, or be content with almost a simple look. Hence it is, that, when the soul is no longer sufficiently occupied in contemplation, these masters of the contemplative life invite it to return to meditation—*i.e.*, to some

[1] Throughout the rest of this work we have by preference followed, amongst the older writers, St. Teresa, St. John of the Cross, St. Francis of Sales and St. Bernard; amongst the moderns, Fr. Poulain (*Grâces d'oraison*, Retaux, Paris), and M. l'abbé Saudreau (*Degrés de la Vie Spirituelle, Vie d'union à Dieu, État Mystique*, Amat, Paris).—The first two works have been translated into English.—*Trans.*

of the forms of active prayer—in order that it may not remain idle.

But the general practice is to admit, between these two extremes, at least one intermediate degree—namely, affective prayer. This latter, at first, allows a rather large space to considerations; in the sequel, it diminishes more and more the work of the mind, and ends by being reduced to hardly more than a simple look. In the beginning, it is merely a simplified and more rapid sort of meditation, later on it becomes an active contemplation. It passes, therefore, through somewhat different phases, which require different rules for their direction. On this account we shall follow those authors who make two subdivisions of it—namely, into affective prayer and the prayer of simplicity.

Affective prayer, as we understand it, is that which allows less space than meditation does *to considerations and more to the affections.* It notably diminishes the work of the mind, without, however, suppressing it. If formerly we gave a quarter of an hour to reasoning and a quarter of an hour to acts of the will, we are now satisfied with five minutes thinking, for example, and the rest of the time is a conversation of the heart with God. Our reflections will be at once more rapid, more affective, and less varied.

Nothing is more natural, or better founded on common sense, than this kind of prayer. In the beginning of the spiritual life, the soul was not perfectly instructed, still less penetrated with the things of faith; it required long and patient con-

sideration to understand and retain truths which
were not familiar to her, to imprint them deeply on
the mind, to assimilate them, and make them the
guiding star of her conduct. The heart, at first,
imperfectly detached from sin, solicited by rebel-
lious inclinations, tossed about by stormy passions,
found it difficult to leave the earth and attach itself
to God, to get rid of its carnal tendencies in order
to form spiritual affections, it remained inert and
frigid in the presence of God, slow to be touched,
hard to be inflamed. After a time, the habit of
meditation has formed profound convictions, the
will has become detached from evil, the heart has
acquired a taste for virtue. There is consequently
no longer the same need for considerations, a few
moments' reflection suffices to awaken conviction in
the mind, and to put the heart in motion.

It is not, however, inability which makes us
diminish our considerations, neither is it slothfulness, or deliberate choice, but the natural prompt-
ing of reason; for the light comes quickly, and, as
the mind is saturated with pious reading, instruction, and meditations, we must ruminate and digest
all this spiritual food, in conversation of the heart
with God. Nothing can be more legitimate than
this attraction, it is, in fact, almost a necessity.

We have already pointed out [1] the reason why in
our cloisters affective prayer is quickly reached.
There are even souls who could never conform to
methodical rules; reasonings embarrass them,
speaking with God is a rest for their heart, reading

[1] 2nd part, c. iii. § 2 p. 124.

affords them sufficient food for their colloquies with heaven : it would be a mistake to interfere with them.

To resume, then, we should remain faithful to the practice of consideration as long as it does us more good; we give less time to it in proportion as it affords us less profit.

§ II.—PRACTICAL RULES.

I. *Choice of a subject.*—This kind of prayer is especially suited to the illuminative way. The subjects, which tend to detach the soul from sin and guide her first steps in the way of virtue, would now no longer make upon her the same impression. She now wants to reanimate her desire of perfection, to draw down upon it the grace of God, to avow humbly her faults, to bless the divine mercy, to pour forth thanksgiving, to begin to speak the language of love and of confidence. Hence the subjects quite suited to her needs are heaven, the shortness of this life, the endless duration of the reward, the treasures of virtue, the value of sufferings, the example of Our Lord and of the saints, and everything that may help to inflame her desires of eternal goods.

Likewise, the fundamental duties of Christian and religious life; the spirit of faith which seeks God in everything, the recollection which enables the soul to be ever attentive to this her one only business, the humility and abnegation which are the conditions of success, and especially that super-natural obedience which makes the religious.

According to Father Surin,[1] the soul should return frequently to these fundamental subjects, dive deeply into them, penetrate herself with their necessity, reflect upon the means, upon the obstacles, desire and beg grace with much earnestness, make fervent resolutions, and not abandon any of these subjects without being fully satisfied, and having made marked progress. If the Holy Ghost should show her the attachment she cherishes for her honour, her comforts, her offices, or for persons, &c., she will make a hundred acts of renunciation, will think of the means to get rid altogether of such attachments, and will declare so often that she will no longer entertain them, that at last she will find herself freed from them. Here you have the right method of making your mental prayer. Those who every day take a different subject, now taking a fancy for one, and then for another, do not gain the same impor-tant advantages, as those who attach themselves to these foundations of the spiritual life, weighing and relishing them during several months and years, till by this means they at last find themselves possessed of solid virtues.

As Our Lord is at once our model and our re-ward, nothing is more profitable than to consider in Him each of these subjects; His lips formulate the precept, His conduct presents to us the example, and Himself will be the recompense of our fidelity.

[1] Fr. Surin, *Cat. Spir.*, t. ii. 7ᵉ part, c. i.

Thus, St. Teresa[1] wishes that "we should often revert to this source of all blessings, I mean to the Life and Passion of Our Lord Jesus Christ."—It is to the Passion especially that she continually refers us: so also St. Liguori. But we have already pointed out[2] that it matters little whether we be attracted by the Holy Childhood, the Hidden or Public Life, the Passion, the Divine Eucharist, or the Sacred Heart; for little or great, humbled or glorious, it is always Our Lord, and the essential point is to conceive an affection for Him, to strive to resemble and to please Him. Each one is free to seek for Him there where he may easily find Him.

St. Teresa[3] also wishes that we never lay aside " the knowledge of ourselves, . . . were we even giants in the spiritual life. . . . This consideration of one's sins, and this knowledge of oneself are the bread with which every other food, however delicate, must be eaten; without this bread we cannot live. Nevertheless, it should be used with moderation."

We may add, in fine, that every soul has its own needs and its own attractions, and that there are also subjects which are called for by our peculiar circumstances.

II. *Placing oneself in the presence of God.* We have already treated of this point when speaking of vocal prayer and of the commencement of mental prayer. Here we merely wish to mention certain

---

[1] St. Teresa, *Life*, c. xiii.   [2] 1st part, c. iv. § iii. p. 46.
[3] St. Teresa, *Life*, c. xiii.

pious thoughts of St. Teresa [1] which will complete what we have said on this subject.

" St. Augustine tells us that, after having for a long time sought God in the objects which surrounded him, he at last found Him within himself. Meditate deeply on this saying; for it is supremely useful to any soul that finds it difficult to be recollected, . . . to know that she has no need to raise herself to heaven in order to converse with her Divine Father and to find her delight in Him, or to raise her voice in order to be heard by Him. He is so near us that He hears the least movement of our lips, even the most secret and internal expression of our thoughts. We have no need of wings to pursue our search after Him; let us but place ourselves in solitude and look into ourselves, there it is that He dwells." [2]   Let the soul then enter with her God into this paradise of her own heart, and close the door after her to all the things of this world.[3]   If this appears difficult at first, " we ought, little by little, to accustom ourselves to converse sweetly with Him, without raising our voice, for this God of goodness will of Himself make us feel that He is present in our soul." [4]

Nevertheless, it is to attend to the presence of Our Lord that the Saint chiefly invites us. " This practice of having Our Lord ever present to our mind is useful in all states of prayer. It is the sure means of profiting in the first degree, of arriving in a short time at the second (she means the prayer of

---

[1] See also "*St. Teresa's Own Words*" already referred to.—*Trans.*   [2] *Way*, xxix.   [3] *Ibid.*, xxx.   [4] *Ibid.*

quiet), and of guarding against the illusions of the demon in the later stages." [1] " A means, which will help you to keep in the presence of Our Lord, is to have a picture, according to your taste, of this adorable Master . . . and to keep it continually before your eyes, in order that the sight of it may stir you up to converse with your Spouse." [2]

In church, we have the holy tabernacle; almost everywhere, statutes and pious pictures. Besides, nothing is easier than to represent Our Lord to ourselves as near us in that condition in which we prefer to contemplate Him, provided that we do so simply and without fatiguing the head. " Remain thus in your heart and thought near the divine Master. . . . and reflect that, as He said to the spouse in the Canticles, He waits only for a glance from us, a glance which He values highly. . . . But, when about to speak to Him, and whilst you are speaking to Him, remember, I conjure you, that you can never show Him enough reverence and love. . . . A thousand lives like ours could never enable you to understand how He deserves to be treated, He, before whom the angels tremble, whose word all things obey. . . . Behold (however) in Jesus Christ a father, a brother, a master, a spouse, and treat with Him according to these various characters." [3]

III.—*Considerations.*—" Do not think that I ask of you long meditations upon this divine Saviour,

---

[1] *Life*, xii.　　　　[2] *Way*, xxvii.
[3] *Way*, xxv.-xxvii. *passim.*

nor many reasonings, nor deep and subtle considerations; no, merely look at Him steadily.   If
you can do no more, keep the eyes of your soul, for
a few moments at least, intently fixed upon this
adorable Spouse."[1]

The same saint says elsewhere, speaking " of the
mystery of Jesus Christ at the pillar, It will be well,
no doubt, to reason during a little time, to consider
who it is that suffers, the greatness and the causes
of His torments, and, in fine, the love with which
He endures them.   But we ought not to weary ourselves by trying to fathom these divers points.   It
will be excellent to remain in peace, without reasoning, near the divine Master.   The soul should then
be occupied according to her ability, in reflecting
that He is looking at her; she will keep Him company and will address her petitions to Him."[2]

" We should vary this occupation according to
the season, lest by using the same food for too long
a time we may lose all relish for it."[3]

" Are you in tribulation or in grief, follow Our
Lord to the Garden of Gethsemani, . . . consider Him bound to the pillar, . . . or laden
with His cross and ascending the hill of Calvary."[4]
If we are too sensitive " to dwell constantly on such
great torments, well then ! behold Him risen from
the dead, full of glory, arousing some, encouraging
others, before He ascends to heaven; behold Him
our companion in the most Holy Sacrament; for
He has not been able, it would seem, to separate

---

[1] *Way*, xxvii.   [3] *Life*, xiii.
[2] *Life*, xii.   [4] *Way*, xxvii. ; *Life*, xii.

Himself from us even for a moment." Thus then, He will ever be for our souls a substantial, delightful, and varied nourishment.

According as we advance in this state of affective prayer, our considerations will become shorter and less numerous; it will then, perhaps, be more profitable for us to go through the mysteries of Our Lord by merely glancing at them, rather than by meditating upon them, and to make use of their different circumstances to excite in our soul acts of love, gratitude, humility, or similar affections.

IV. *Affections.*—" If His majesty confounds us, let His goodness reassure us. Let us speak to Him with great humility, indeed, but also with love, as children to their father, exposing our needs to Him with confidence, telling Him of our troubles, begging of Him to remedy them, and above all acknowledging that we are not worthy to be called His children." [1]

" You are not embarrassed when you are speaking to His creatures." Has not God infinitely more goodness? Is He not a father, and a Saviour, a physician, and the best of friends? " If you have not the habit of making these colloquies with Our Lord, small wonder is it that you can find nothing to say; but, if you once have acquired this habit, such a thing, in my opinion, cannot happen." [2]

" As long as prayer is merely affective, we have a facility for all kind of pious acts; we may, therefore, choose those which appear most in accordance

---

[1] *Way*, xxix.   [2] *Ibid.*, xxvii.

with our present needs and the state of our soul.
Let us again give some examples. Sometimes, for
instance, we may briefly review the faults of our life,
and employ the whole time of our prayer, and even
the whole day, in making acts of humility, and of
contrition, or in forming good resolutions, we may
accept in the spirit of penance the austerities of the
Rule, and the crosses sent by Providence; or again,
we may admire the divine mercies, which are infinitely greater than our miseries, praise, thank, and
love Him who has been so good to us.—At other
times, after having briefly recapitulated the graces
of God: such as creation, redemption, faith, Christian education, religious vocation, &c., we may,
during our prayer, or even during the whole day,
pour forth humble acts of thanksgiving, and try to
perform each one of our duties with all possible perfection, in order to make some return to God for all
He has done for us. Sometimes, if we are beset
by temptations, or overwhelmed by trials, we may
multiply our humble supplications and our protestations of loyalty to God; we may make countless acts,
accepting our sufferings, until our will has got back
its peace and a spirit of submission; we shall be
filled with confusion, that we are so easily troubled,
and have so little humility, so little of true mortification. We may also remember that our sufferings come from God, that, in His wisdom and
goodness, He has imposed them for the greater
good of our soul, and we shall make thereupon acts
of faith in His providence, of confiding and filial
abandonment to His Holy Will.—At other times,

we may lay before God our desires of perfection, our resolution to advance in such a virtue, to correct such a fault; we shall humble ourselves, be sorry, promise amendment, and beg for grace.—Again, after a moment's reflection upon God's goodness, His love and His perfections, we may abandon our heart to love, to praise, to confidence, &c.—We shall dwell upon those acts which best suit our tastes and our needs, repeating the same a hundred times over, with or without variations, or intermingling with them acts of various other virtues.

V. *Resolutions.*—There is nothing to hinder a soul, which is engaged in affective prayer, from taking good resolutions, just as in meditation. We should select such as best meet our actual needs and our special attraction. It is well, however, to keep to the same resolution for a rather long time, in order to cultivate with more steadiness and success one point at a time of the spiritual life.

CHAPTER IX

PRAYER OF SIMPLICITY

§ I.—What the Prayer of Simplicity is.

THE name prayer of simplicity clearly indicates its nature. The preceding form of prayer had much diminished considerations; this lessens still more the work of the intellect, and gradually comes to be contented with almost a thought, a memory, a glance; with contemplating, rather than meditating.

It likewise simplifies the affections. Previously, our acts were complicated, lengthy and wordy. We used to say, for instance : I love Thee with all my heart, Thou, who hast created, preserved, redeemed me, Thou, who hast loaded me with graces, and testified so much love for me, &c. The soul had need of strengthening her acts by their motives, in order to maintain herself in affections and to persevere in them. Now these various helps, far from being necessary to her, have become an embarrassment, a fatigue, a check. She prefers to say : My Jesus, I love Thee; and thus, by abridging her affections, she makes them in greater number.

The soul, in the beginning, used to vary her affections : such as acts of humility, contrition, faith, hope, love, &c.; employing the time of prayer sometimes in one of these acts, sometimes in another, or mingling them together in order to spend it more profitably. Now, many of these acts no longer correspond with her state nor with her attractions; having made more progress in perfection, she experiences a need, as it were, of loving God, of being united with Him, of enjoying Him; she feels no pleasure except in pouring forth her heart before Him who charms her; she delights now in acts of love, confidence, abandonment, gratitude, yet without ever forgetting humility.

She has even a tendency to become more simple as to her chief object, which ends by becoming almost unique, so that she is satisfied to think of God in a confused and general way; it is, for instance, an affectionate remembrance of God, a simple, loving look at God, at Our Lord, or at such or such a mystery of Our Lord, but ever the same.[1]

The prayer of simplicity passes through different degrees. It is the second phase of affective prayer, which is getting to be more and more simple, even so as to become a simple loving look. It is well not to forget this remark, in order to understand the developments about to follow.

This prayer got its clear and expressive name from Bossuet. When it has reached its most simplified form, others call it the prayer of simple look, simple settling down in God, active recollection,

---

[1] Read on this subject Fr. Poulain, *Grâces d'oraison*, 5th ed. c. ii.

active repose, active quiet, active or acquired contemplation. This last name is the only one we shall here explain.

§ II.—ACTIVE CONTEMPLATION.

Contemplation, in a wide sense, is a prayer consisting of a simple, loving look upon God or upon the things of God; it is not occupied in seeking for the truth, like meditation, it possesses it and rests in it with love.

It would be a great exaggeration to say that it always implies that lively admiration, which keeps the intelligence in raptures of astonishment,—that fire of love, which throws the will into transports,—and that joy, which overwhelms the soul and the senses. The stupor of admiration, the inebriation of love and the transports of joy are a very high degree of intensity, which is seldom attained; most frequently, contemplation remains devoid of these great emotions, or even is nothing more than one long exercise of aridity and desolation. Like discursive prayer, contemplation has its vivid lights, its sweet consolations, its calm and its fatigues; but it has not fixed its tent permanently upon Thabor.

In our opinion, the whole essence of active contemplation is contained in these two words: *it looks and it loves*.

It is no longer the toilsome work of the imagination, the memory, and the understanding, though these facilities are actually occupied, but in a more simple manner. Instead of seeking for the truth by the long, painful and roundabout ways of reasoning, they have already completed their journey and have reached its term. The mind, possessing the truth, contemplates it by a direct act, and enjoys it without effort.[1] It is a simple attention, a memory, a look, an intuition. The light has come, the convictions are well founded, the evidence is such, that the things of God are perceived almost as we perceive first principles; we remember, we look, we attend, and this is enough. This does not hinder this view from being sometimes more luminous, sometimes weaker and more veiled. By its very nature it is somewhat obscure and confused, because it proceeds mostly by way of general views, not stopping at details, pretty much as we take in at a single glance a whole landscape.

This simple look is always accompanied with love—a love, it may be, almost imperceptible or all on fire, calm or impetuous, bitter or savoury. This love is even that which is the chief thing in contemplation; it is at once the source whence this latter flows, the term towards which it tends, the fruit which it bears; we look because we love, we look in order to love, and our love is fed and inflamed by looking.

Love is always accompanied by knowledge. We cannot love God, if we do not know that He is lovable, and do not think on this truth; and this knowledge, being something general and indistinct, love also is somewhat obscure and con-

---

[1] St. Francis of Sales, *Love of God*, b. vi. c. vi.

N

fused.   Sometimes light dominates, and our contemplation is then *cherubic;* more frequently it is
love that prevails, and then it is called *seraphic.*
Certain authors give more prominence to the light,
others to the love ;   in reality, both elements are
indispensable.

The object of contemplation is God in Himself
or in His works; God is the primary object; the
things of God are its secondary object.   That
which charms us in God is His *beauty,* His *goodness,* His *love.*   Our Lord has an especial attraction for the contemplative soul.   Is He not God,
God nearer to us, God brought within our reach,
God loving our souls and adorned with charms
we can better understand?   Why should we not
be able to take hold of Him by means of that
simple, loving look which constitutes contemplation?   And, if God wishes to raise us to a still
higher degree, what can hinder Him from pouring
into our soul light and love, in order to give us a
share in that complacency which He takes in His
Well-Beloved?   Saint Teresa,[1] having read some-
where that the holy Humanity was an obstacle to
perfect contemplation, believed this for a time, and
wished to avoid it as a subject for her prayer.   She
complains bitterly of her error, which she calls a
great treason : " Oh ! what a bad road I was following, my good Lord ! or rather, I had lost every
road. . . . A hundred and a hundred times
have I learned this by experience, and heard it from

---

[1] St. Teresa, *Life,* xxii. the whole chap. ; *Castle,* iv° mans.
c. viii. *passim.*   St. John of the Cross, *Ascent,* b. iii. c. i. and xiv.

the very mouth of Our Lord Himself." His holy
Humanity is, in fact, the support of our thoughts,
His love calls forth our love, He is the gate by
which we enter into the secrets of the divinity.
" Seek, then, no other road, even though you be
elevated to the very highest degree of contemplation. On this road you travel in security." The
saint then mentions " some great contemplatives
who travelled by no other road. St. Francis proves
this by his stigmata; Saint Antony of Padua by
his love for the Infant Jesus; St. Bernard found his
delight in the sacred Humanity; Saint Catherine
of Sienna and many others did the same." [1] Elsewhere [2] she relates how our Lord was promised
and given to her " as a living book, who left im-
printed on her soul what she ought to read and to
do."

Thus the soul, ceasing " to meditate—that is, to
produce acts *by dint of reasoning,*" thinks simply
upon God, " by an attention, loving, simple, and
fixed solely upon its object, almost like that of one
who opens his eyes to give a loving look." [3]
Whilst the interior eye remains fixed upon God
alone, the will is borne towards Him by a movement of love or by acts: sometimes the soul remains silent in this admiring look and this disposition of love; sometimes it pours itself forth *in
a holy colloquy,* of love, confidence, abandonment,
humility, &c. But always at the end of this prayer

[1] *Life,* xxii.
[2] *Ibid.,* xxvi.
[3] St. John of the Cross. *Living Flame,* stanza iii. verse iii. § 6.

of contemplation the soul's union with God is more and more intimate.

There are two kinds of contemplation—the acquired and the infused [1], or, if you prefer it, the active and the passive. Authors differ considerably in explaining these terms. Some writers, in fact, require so many conditions for active contemplation that the difference between it and infused contemplation is hardly more than nominal.

In our opinion, *acquired* contemplation is that to which a person may raise himself by his own industry with the help of the ordinary graces of prayer.—Sometimes it is *transitory;* vividly struck by the force of conviction, the mind keeps silent and rests in the truth possessed; the will is silent in order to love, just as a mother enfolds her child in a long, silent look, replete with love; unless, indeed, the soul should give vent to its love by various tender acts. Sometimes, this contemplation *becomes a habit;* the convictions are formed, no need, then, to call upon reason for them; the soul, enlightened and purified, has only to look in order to love; her prayers are hardly anything more than a look of

---

[1] Although the older writers did not make this distinction, we have thought it right to adopt it, because it has become classical for more than two centuries. Some good authors, however, continue to reject it, maintaining that, *as a matter of fact*, every prayer of simple look is a mystical prayer, weak indeed and hidden at first, but which afterwards becomes more intense and manifestly mystical. In the system which we have thought proper to adopt, contemplation is called mystical only when the divine action is manifest. This difference of opinion is purely speculative, and in no way affects the practical advice given in our treatise.

love, or rather a series of mute but expressive looks, if, indeed, they be not a continual intercourse of heart with heart.

We shall later on treat of mystical contemplation; for the moment, it suffices to say that it also is a prayer of simple, loving look, but in it the soul is manifestly more or less passive, she realizes beyond the possibility of doubt that the light and love comes not from her own activity, that she receives them from God, who operates in her and makes her, generally speaking, feel His presence after an ineffable manner.

§ III.—THE PRAYER OF SIMPLICITY IS NOT A SPECIES OF MYSTICAL CONTEMPLATION.

As long as our prayer is merely in process of being simplified, and is only imperfectly freed from reasonings and the multiplicity of acts, it does not deserve the name of contemplation. It is otherwise, however, when, leaving aside reasoning, it goes straight to God by a simple look, when it has reached the state of being nothing more than a loving thought, of being content to look and to love.

Does God then begin to pour secretly His light and His love into the soul? It is hard to understand how, without this, one could persevere in a form of prayer so little calculated to captivate the mind. But this mystical element, if it exists, remains so hidden that the soul is not conscious of it. So, too, the difficulty of meditating, of producing multiple and developed acts is strongly marked in the night of the senses; here, however, it is but slight, and easily overcome. Everything then takes place just as if the soul were entering upon the prayer of simplicity of its own free choice, as if it were leaving aside reasoning and simplifying its affections, just because it so pleased and willed to do so. Here, then, we are as yet very far removed from that passive contemplation, in which the soul realizes, beyond all doubt, that God is operating in her and that she herself is merely passive. As to feeling the presence of God, as it were by an intimate and ineffable possession, she hardly knows what that means, because she has not yet experienced it.

The prayer of simplicity, such as we have described it, seems to us, therefore, to be active prayer arrived at its final development, rather than passive prayer in a nascent condition. We willingly grant that whilst the soul is still in this degree of prayer, some isolated mystical phenomena may already appear; and that, when she is journeying along the boundary line between active prayer and mystical contemplation, it is, in practice, very difficult to say whether the soul is still engaged in the common ways, or has already made some excursions into a new country. But, in theory, the prayer of simplicity seems to us to be the frontier line, along which active prayer touches upon passive contemplation.

§ IV.—Advantages of this kind of Prayer.

1°. *As regards the intellect.*—The mind is more enlightened than in meditation, and that without any trouble. I lay aside the fatiguing labour of reasonings, and cease striking the flint, because I already possess both light and fire; I am satisfied with opening my eyes and taking in my subject at a glance, and that suffices to reanimate my convictions, and to set the heart in motion. Meditation resembles the action of the student who needs much time and labour to study in detail, to understand and retain a theological thesis; the prayer of simplicity is like that of the master, who, with one rapid glance, takes in the whole lesson and has mastered it; the former has need to learn, the latter has only to remember; meditation is the way, the other prayer the term; the first suits beginners, the second proficients and the perfect.

This is the reason why Father Balthasar Alvarez used to say " that beginners would tempt God were they to attempt to pray by affections alone without using their reasoning faculty, unless indeed, they did so through a special impulse of the Holy Ghost; because this manner of praying is the perfection of this exercise." [1] The rule recognised by spiritual authors is this: meditation for beginners, affective prayer for proficients, active or passive contemplation for more advanced souls. Should it please God to dispense with these stages, the soul ought to abandon herself to the divine

[1] *Life of Fr. Balth. Alvarez*, c. xli. 2nd and 7th diffic.

action, after having submitted her attraction to the
control of her director; the lights, which meditation would have furnished, can then be supplied
for by good spiritual reading.

2°. *As regards the heart.*—The prayer of simplicity is superior to meditation on the score of the
affections. It enters upon them at the very start,
without the necessity of making its way to them by
a process of reasoning; all therein is prayer, for the
soul ceases not to adore God, to thank Him, to ask
pardon, and to beg for grace; pious colloquies
naturally flow from a heart where love is already
burning, from a will practised in virtues. Prayer
is no longer a laborious conversation, it is an affectionate and familiar outpouring of the soul into the
bosom of her Well-Beloved; if dryness makes itself
felt, the acts become short and more frequent;
hence there is all the more prayer.

Let not, then, this prayer of simplicity, in so far
as it regards the understanding and the will, be
regarded as mere idleness. Assuredly the soul is
not idle, when it ceases not to discharge its duties
towards God; no time is more fruitful, since by
multiplying pious affections, grace, virtue, and
merits increase in a continuous flow. With less
fatigue and bustle more work has been done than
before.

3°. *This kind of prayer has its own consolations
and its own pains.*—At certain moments it is full of
sweetness, the more so as the soul is loving, and
already purified in a remarkable degree. At such
times, we must, if necessary, moderate any excess of
sensible feelings and not so fan the flame, as by

indiscreet efforts to fatigue the head, the heart, and
the nerves.   Most frequently, this prayer is calm
and devoid of strong emotions; sometimes dryness
plunges the will into desolation, and it finds with
difficulty only some few affections without relish,
whilst the mind is assailed by distractions.   " With
regard to this torment of importunate thoughts,"
St. Teresa [1] makes the following very just observation, the import of which must not, however, be exaggerated.   " A special character of this kind of
prayer wherein the understanding is not occupied
in reasoning, is that the soul therein is either deeply
recollected, or cruelly wearied by distractions."
Yet this is no reason either to avoid it or to cling to
it with attachment.   We go to prayer to give ourselves to God rather than to enjoy pleasure; the
best prayer is not that whence we issue intoxicated
with delight and full of ourselves, but that which
leaves us more humble, more detached from everything, and better armed for the combat.

4°. There is nothing to hinder this prayer from
being *fruitful for the practice of virtues*. We see, as
it were by intuition, but in a most vivid, real way,
the resolutions to be taken, we attach ourselves to
them by the acts we make, we draw down floods of
grace upon them by incessant petitions. Our rules,
our spiritual reading, the exhortations of superiors,
spiritual direction, divine inspiration, had enlightened the mind as to our duty in general and in
detail; here the heart grows warm, the will draws
to itself the omnipotence of grace, and gives itself
up with courage to all that God wills.   It is by this

[1] St. Teresa, *Life*, ix.

result that we can know whether or not a soul is deriving profit from this kind of prayer. Most certainly, to pour oneself forth in effusions of love is an occupation always excellent and sometimes delightful; but who does not know that sincere love is proved by deeds, that it is built upon the ruins of self-love, that it lives upon devotedness and self-sacrifice, and that sentimentality is a wretched counterfeit of true love? There can be no doubt, however, that the effusions of your heart in prayer have been sincere and fruitful, if they have left you zealous in the discharge of all your duties.

§ V.—When should the Soul pass on to this form of Prayer?

The will of God should be our rule in this as in everything else. There are three rocks to be avoided.[1]

1°. The first of these is to decide for ourselves by a *fixed determination* to remain in the former kinds of prayer, under the pretext of humility, or through a dread of less beaten paths. God is my master, I am His servant, and it belongs to Him to determine my post, and appoint me my work. As the success depends on Him, I have some chance of succeeding, where He wills me to be, I am certain to fail where He does not wish me to be. The humility, which distrusts the designs of God and prefers to them our own thoughts and our own will, is a very false humility. When God has spoken, there is no longer anything to be feared, except our

[1] Courbon, *Instructions famil. sur. l'or. ment.*, 2ᵉ part 2ᵉʳ instr.

disobeying Him. If the paths into which He leads us are less beaten, His hand who led us into them will guide us therein. Besides, this prayer of simplicity has nothing in it mysterious or formidable.

2°. The second rock is to quit the former kinds of prayer *too late*. To delay, after the will of God has been sufficiently made known to me, is to remain where God does not will me to be; I disobey and cannot succeed. I imitate the scholar whose master has nothing more to teach him, and who obstinately refuses to place himself under another. I necessarily lose my time and my trouble.[1]

3°. The third rock is to abandon the former kinds of prayer *too soon*. So long as my convictions are not as yet deep, nor my detachment sufficiently marked, I have need that the patient and persevering action of considerations should make the light shine forth in my soul, should disengage my heart from created things, and excite it to acts of divine love and generous resolutions. When badly prepared for this prayer of simplicity, I cannot succeed in it; I am then like a schoolboy advanced to a class that is too high for him.

I ought not to abandon considerations through caprice, through love of change, to avoid the fatigue and dulness of a labour that is always the same, or through a foolish ambition to raise myself to a kind of prayer that is beyond my reach. In taking this step I ought to consult the will of God alone. What, then, are the indications of this will?

---

[1] St. John of the Cross, *Ascent*, b. ii. c. xii.-xiii. ; *Night*, c. x.

The mere *attraction* would not be a sufficient guarantee, we must see whether this attraction comes from God. Two signs will show that we can and ought to follow it : *success* and *profit;* success in the prayer, profit in the whole of our conduct. It is necessary that the prayer of simplicity should come easy to me, and that it should help me to practise virtue, at least as much as the preceding kinds of prayer. To ascertain whether this be so there is but one means—namely, to make the trial of it. If then my prayer goes on well in that way, and if progress in virtue is maintained or more marked, this success and profit will show that I have acted under the impulse of God, who alone could crown my efforts. This proof would be of itself sufficient. It will be singularly strengthened, if, on the one hand, this more simple form of prayer inspires me with a persistent attraction, and consideration, on the other, with an ever-increasing difficulty and disgust.

But should we find in the prayer of simplicity only dryness and distractions, must we return to the former kinds of prayer? Yes, if we succeed better with them; no, if we find too great a difficulty and disgust in this return. Be satisfied, then, with combating the distractions and uniting yourself to God by dry affections as well as you can produce them.[1] It would be well also in this case to examine whether we be not already in that night of the senses of which we shall speak further on.[2]

In order not to go astray in these rather intricate

[1] Fr. Poulain, *Grâces d'or.,* c. ii. § 4.
[2] See 3rd part, c. iii. p. 246.

paths, we should consult the superior or director whom God has given us for guide, and abandon ourselves to his direction.

To sum up, beginners require to devote more time to considerations; they should, however, give less time to them, in proportion as they appear to be less helpful whether to produce light or deepen our convictions, or to influence the affections and excite generous resolutions; but they should not be abandoned as long as they are doing us good, unless, indeed, a more affective prayer should do us still more.—On the other hand, let us not hesitate to abandon ourselves to the prayer of simplicity, when the success and the profit show that our attraction for it comes from God. But, if, from time to time, it appears to us useful to return to meditation, let us do so without any scruple. In a word, the different kinds of prayer are so many various tools, which we take up or lay aside according to our need and advantage; if one serves us we make use of it; if it should prove rather a hindrance than a help, we should lay it aside for one more useful.[1]

This simplification of prayer is not the work of time and years. God bestows attractions as He pleases, He harmonises them, however, with our interior dispositions, and the variety of our circumstances; He invites some sooner, others later. Should He call a soul from its very first steps in the spiritual life, His will being duly ascertained, no one has the right to hesitate to obey. In sick-

[1] St. Liguori, *Praxis*, 127.

ness, also, and in certain states of fatigue, meditation would be often impossible, and the prayer of
affections becomes as it were a necessity.[1] Generally, it is only after a long habit of meditation
that the soul feels itself drawn to diminish its considerations, and afterwards even to suppress them
almost entirely and to be satisfied, or nearly so,
with a simple look. The prayer of simplicity, therefore, means, ordinarily speaking, that a long journey has already been traversed; it is the normal
term, at which discursive prayer ends, and there is
no one who may not hope to arrive there in the
course of time, by a generous practice of mental
prayer and the other exercises of the spiritual life.

We have already pointed out, that *in contemplative orders* this prayer of simplicity is speedily
and, as it were, naturally reached. There, souls
easily become pure and hearts are drawn to love
God. By dint of meditating, reading, and hearing the word of God, they feel the need of pious
colloquies to assimilate it; the mind is full and the
heart wants to speak in its turn. The length of
the liturgical offices, during which it is difficult to
follow up a continuous meditation, the holy habit
of ejaculatory prayers during work and almost
everywhere, insensibly accustoms the soul to prefer
affectionate converse with God to mere meditation.

---

[1] "For the soul that loves," says St. Teresa, "the true
prayer in sickness, or in the midst of obstacles, consists in
offering to God what she suffers, in remembering Him and
conforming herself to His divine will, and in a thousand acts of
this kind which will occur to her; behold the exercise of her
love." *Life*, vii.

" Prayer was practised during long centuries, before persons gave themselves up methodically to meditation as is done to-day. Nay, more, the rules of the more ancient religious orders do not appear to have considered mental prayer as a distinct exercise." [1] The religious of those days were penetrated with the thoughts expressed in the Divine Office or the Scripture, and they ruminated upon them quietly during their free moments. In choir, pauses were made between the psalms, during which each one prayed in private; and, in a time so limited, this could not be a meditation. Ejaculatory prayers were in great favour; many fathers used to make some hundreds of them daily; their very number shows what they must have been. St. Benedict counsels us to employ ourselves frequently in private prayer; but he does not prescribe any set time for it, because, perhaps, his monks at all times and in every place used to occupy their thoughts with heavenly things. His life, however, shows that at Subiaco each one gave himself up to this exercise after the Psalmody.[2] In any case, he lays down no method for it; he merely disapproves of a multitude of words, and recommends purity of heart and the compunction of tears.[3] From all these facts we may perhaps safely conclude that the Ancient Fathers gave themselves up chiefly to affective prayer.

Loving souls will soon attain to a form of prayer in which the heart is more active than the mind.

[1] Abbé Saudreau, *I. Degrés*, b. iii. 3rd part, c. iii.
[2] St. Gregory, *II. Dial.* iv.
[3] *Holy Rule*, xx.

It is love which makes the prayer of simplicity, nourishing itself sometimes with a silent look, at other times overflowing in affectionate sentiments and generous resolutions. Let us love, and we shall easily find enough to occupy us; and, though our whole prayer should be spent in reiterating, with or without variations, the expression of our love and devotedness, it is a theme of which a loving heart hardly ever wearies.

Simple souls, and those who have little imagination, memory, or knowledge, have neither the relish nor the means to seek for coherent ideas and well-connected reasonings; they are reduced, almost of necessity, if they wish to make mental prayer, to think very simply on God, to look rather than to meditate. The case is quite different for quick and cultivated minds: memories, images, thoughts come in crowds; variety captivates them; a look, always the same, would appear to them a dispiriting monotony. They are tempted to make their prayer rather a study or a discourse, and to allow their mind to say so much that their heart has hardly time to pour itself forth before God.[1]

§ VI.—Rules of Conduct.

I. *Before prayer.*—It cannot be expected that all our conversations with God should be prepared beforehand and turn upon a subject precisely determined. But with regard to our regular meditations, and those we make during the free time, it

[1] Fr. Poulain, *Grâces d'or.*, c. ii. § 2 n° 25 and *ff.*

will be well for us to choose a subject, to have some ideas always ready, if needs be to use a book, especially at the beginning of prayer, in order to facilitate our loving attention to God and to afford food for affectionate colloquies; at least, until our experience has shown us that these means are no longer of any use. A soul arrived at this degree of prayer prefers short, pious, affective subjects, conformable to its tendencies towards love and union, such as are found everywhere in the " Imitation of Christ," in " The Visits to the Blessed Sacrament," and other works of St. Alphonsus. The soul knows by experience what kind of thoughts do her most good; by dint of ruminating them she makes them so familiar that she is always prepared.[1]

II. *During the prayer.*—There are two rocks to be avoided :

1°. Deliberately to suppress considerations and affections as the Quietists used to do. St. Teresa,[2] following St. Peter of Alcantara, rightly teaches that we ought never to do ourselves violence, in order to suppress reasoning and suspend the action of the mind. " The effort we make not to think will perhaps make us think the more "; it will render " the imagination more restless "; and " there we shall remain stupidly inactive ; the soul remains in a desert, a prey to great dryness, frigid as a being deprived of reason ; . . . we lose mental prayer, and we do not attain to contemplation."

---

[1] Fr Poulain, *Grâces d'or.*, c. ii. §4 n° 64.

[2] St. Teresa, *Life*, xii. *Castle*, 4th mans. c. iii. See Fr. Surin, *Cat. Spir.*, 1st part, c. iii. Courbon, *Inst. fam. or. ment.*, 2nd part 2nd inst., and 3rd part 2nd inst. *Life of Fr. Balth. Alvarez*, xli. St. John of the Cross, *First Night*, x.

O

We must, therefore, meditate until God, by raising the soul to a higher kind of prayer, keeps it united to Him by love."

The same motives exist for not deliberately suppressing the affections we might easily elicit. In doing so there would be a risk of remaining idle during the time of prayer, of being negligent afterwards in the practice of virtues, and of inflicting on ourselves an intolerable fatigue and a mortal weariness to end only in tepidity. Before abandoning distinct acts and contenting ourselves with almost a simple look, we must wait until God invites us to do so; we shall then meet with success and profit, because God will be with us. If we attempt to outrun our grace, we shall, to our misfortune, find only our own will.

2°. An opposite peril would be to do oneself violence in order to persist, with or without liking, in logical reflections, complex affections, too particular petitions, in an excessive number of private vocal prayers, and in other acts for which we have neither relish nor facility. Remain satisfied with the prayer of simplicity from the moment you find in it success and advantage, and do not imitate those who, "as soon as their understanding ceases to act, imagine they are doing nothing, are afflicted and cannot endure it." [1] You may limit yourself to those acts for which you have more attraction : such as love, confidence, abandonment, humility, &c. " If the soul can reach

---

[1] St. Teresa, *Life*, xi. and xiii. Fr. Poulain, *Graces of Prayer*, c. ii. §4.

this point even from the beginning of her prayer she will derive from it great profit. Such a method is the source of great good, at least it has been so for my own soul," says St. Teresa.[1]

But how are we to be occupied in this prayer of simplicity?

As to our mind,—if we can without much trouble make some short and affective reflections, if some well-chosen book revives in us the loving thought of God, it will be well to make use of them. Acts *combined with their formal motives* can supply the place of considerations. For instance: I love Thee with my whole heart, O my Jesus, because Thou art sanctity and perfection itself, Thou hast shed all Thy blood to redeem me, and hast so often pardoned me with so much mercy, &c. These motives, without being formal considerations, replace them and produce the same effects.— More simply still, a word or two may take the place of considerations: "O Jesus, so beautiful and so good, I love Thee with my whole soul: O my God, this nothingness adores Thy infinite majesty: O my Jesus, I trust in Thee who art so good, and lovest me so much; Thou art my King, I am resolved to obey Thee; Thou art my Shepherd, whom I am determined to follow: my Teacher, whose word I believe; I adore Thee as my God, and love Thee as my Friend, &c." Thus a few pregnant words, a mere title which we give Our Lord suffice to awaken attention and inflame the affections.

Often, too, the senses and imagination may help

---

[1] St. Teresa, *Life*, xi. and xiii. Fr. Poulain, *Grâces d'or.*, c. ii. § 4.

the mind.   We fix our eyes lovingly upon the Holy
Tabernacle, upon a picture which speaks to
our heart, upon a statue which we like, and this is
enough to keep our thoughts and affections raised
to God.   St. Teresa " wished to have always before
her eyes a portrait or picture of Our Lord, not being
able to have it as deeply engraved upon her heart
as she desired."   She exhorts her daughters to do
the same, and pities those who, by their own fault,
deprive themselves of so great a good, and declares
that, if they really loved the Divine Master " they
would feel joy at the sight of His portrait." 1   We
may also gently fix our imagination upon Him, in
some mystery of His life or death, which has more
attraction for us; it would only do us more harm
than good to try to picture to ourselves complicated
and too varied scenes; but our imagination itself
will in the end simplify its own action, and produce
for us a somewhat confused picture which, often
recurring, will facilitate that simple look of the mind
of which we are now treating.

Besides, in all this, every one has his own special
attraction and his own method begotten of experience; we merely indicate examples, and have no
pretensions to lay down a line of conduct.

As to the will,—we may, according to the state of
our soul, our attraction, and our needs, select and
vary our affections, or even confine ourselves to some
few for which we have a facility, and not trouble
ourselves about those to which we are not inclined.
As the soul advances the affections are simplified,

---

1 *Life*, ix. xxii.   *Way*, xxvii.

and become generalised just as do the thoughts; a single word, an outburst of the heart, may signify a world of things. How many virtues may be expressed in these two words: *My Jesus!* They express love, adoration, confidence, gratitude, repentance, supplication, &c. It is not necessary that the soul should analyse and determine in detail all its acts : God well knows how to recognise all it wants to say, and to estimate all that a single word, a single glance, a single gesture, implies.

Our attraction and advancement will also indicate whether we should prolong our acts, or simplify and multiply them. Some even count them for their own encouragement, and this practice is praiseworthy, provided that it does not give rise to vain complacence or feverish ardour.

On the other hand, one may, according to his attraction and profit, keep his looks fixed upon God, remain in a disposition of love, or tend towards Him as if by affectionate movements of the soul, without formulating any distinct act, or while making only a few acts, just as many as suffice to sustain this loving union. This silence tells God of all my love; it is not idleness, inasmuch as I am fully occupied in looking at Him and loving Him.

III. *After prayer.*—This prayer tends, like the preceding kinds, to render us better; hence it should reanimate our ardour for perfection, our vigilance and generosity in correcting our faults and advancing in virtue. But as it loves general views and simplifies thoughts, in order to reduce them little by little to a silent look, it also tends to simplify our affections and resolutions, to include them all in a general desire of perfection, *in a loving quest of God*. As long as we do not find too much difficulty in particularizing our resolutions, it will be better to do so, and to say with beginners : I am determined to avoid such a sin, such an irregularity, to eschew dissipation, to renounce my own will, to reform myself in such a matter, &c. But should it become too difficult to think on particular and detailed resolutions, we should not trouble ourselves about them ; the following general formula : O my God, I desire Thee and only Thee ; or any other similar one includes everything for a soul arrived at this degree. What we formerly resolved upon in detail, we now will in general ; but we will it so really, that this general resolution can, if needs be, descend to particular cases and produce the actions necessary to correct a defect or develop a virtue.

§ VII.—EMPLOYMENT OF AFFECTIVE PRAYER.

The two phases of affective prayer are suitable not only for the times assigned by our rules for mental prayer, spiritual reading and private devotion ; but they are quite adapted to the Divine Office also. A formal meditation would be here very difficult, but nothing is easier than to keep oneself united to God by pious affections. The sight of the Holy Tabernacle so eloquently speaks to the heart ; the words of the Office lend themselves to such numerous and varied acts ; and where these would not suffice to occupy us, it is so easy to find in ourselves wherewith to supply the deficiency, that we can always render our homage to God, thank Him for so many benefits, bewail our faults, and ask blessings for the Church and for all mankind.

So, also, during manual work a continuous meditation would fatigue us; but the smallest details of our work, the beauties of nature, our interior dispositions, may easily suggest a great number of pious affections.

The examination of our conscience is simplified, and becomes more rapid and as it were intuitive; we see our faults as they occur, and we arise promptly.

This loving union with God, these pious effusions of our heart into His, these unstudied colloquies full of affection, will be a fruitful and delightful occupation while saying the Rosary and other vocal prayers, at our meals and everywhere. The celebration of the holy mysteries, the reception of the Sacraments, in a word, all our exercises, if God attracts us this way, will derive from this source a sap as sweet as it is vivifying. Affective prayers, therefore, are an easy and powerful means of passing whole days in a continual intercourse with God, of attaining to that life of prayer, wherein prayer springs up in our hearts almost as naturally as the breath from our lungs, mingles with all our actions, supernaturalizes our intentions, stimulates generosity, sanctifies sufferings, raises the soul above earth, and keeps her sweetly united to her

Well-Beloved in an intimacy as delightful as it is strengthening and fruitful.

It was thus Father Balthasar Alvarez acted, having continually recourse to God in all his actions in order to take counsel with Him, to implore His aid, and to follow His guidance. "To pray mentally," he used to say, "is to raise our mind to God, to communicate familiarly, but in a respectful manner, with Him about all our affairs, to confide in Him more than a child confides in its mother, however good she may be; to offer to Him all we possess, all that we hope for, without reserving anything; to speak to Him of our labours, of our sins, of our desires, of our projects, of everything that occupies our mind; in fine, to seek in Him our consolation, our repose, as does a friend with regard to his friend whom he knows to be worthy of all his confidence." [1]

[1] *Life of Fr. Balth. Alvarez*, by the Ven. Louis Dupont, c. xv.

THIRD PART

ON MYSTICAL PRAYER

CHAPTER I

UTILITY OF THIS STUDY. FREQUENCY OF THIS PRAYER.

THE kinds of mental prayer hitherto described have nothing transcendental in them; there is no one who may not practise them by his own sole energy, aided by the ordinary graces of prayer. It remains for us now to supply some guidance to our brethren in ways less known; that is, with regard to mystical contemplation, for which a man can and ought to dispose himself, but into which God alone can introduce him. Amongst all the exercises of Christian piety, we have here without contradiction the most efficacious means to detach souls from earth and to unite them to God. It is the school of high virtue, " the short-cut," [1] to perfection, and the most rapid conveyance to this goal, a pearl of

[1] St. Teresa, *Castle*, v. mans. c. iii.

217

priceless value, a treasure so desirable that a pru-
dent merchant will not hesitate to sell all his goods
in order to obtain it.

God, Who distributes His graces " as He wills,
and according as each one disposes himself thereto
and co-operates therewith," [1] " bestows, likewise,
His favours when He pleases, after the manner He
pleases, and on whom He pleases; being master of
His goods, He can bestow them thus without
wronging any one." [2]—" He is not bound to grant
us in this world graces, without which we can be
saved." [3]—If the gift of mystical contemplation is
not granted to us, there may be reasons on the part
of God, who means, perhaps, to guide us to perfection by another road.   Nevertheless, " there is
nothing He so much desires as to find some one on
whom to bestow these gifts, nor do these gifts in
any way lessen His riches." [4]—The reasons of this
refusal will, therefore, be most frequently found on
the part of man, who neglects to prepare himself
for, and to co-operate with, these gifts.   We
should seek a director, obey him with docility,
generously embrace humility, obedience, self-renunciation, and all that there is of sacrifice and
prayer in our holy state, because in these consists
the active purification of the soul.   Now all this
costs our weakness no small effort, and very soon
wearies our inconstancy.   A thousand prejudices,
perhaps, make us dread mystical prayer as a veri-

[1] *Conc. Trid. de Justif.*, sess. vi. c. vii.
[2] *Castle*, 4th mans. c. i.
[3] *Ibid.*, c. ii.   *Way* xviii.
[4] *Ibid.*, 6th mans. c. iv.

table bugbear, and hinder us from forming a right estimate of its value. Now God wishes His gifts to be appreciated; will He, then, ever give them to one who despises them ? Hardly ever is this way entered upon save through the desert of passive purifications. In the midst of these disheartening trials a soul, that is not guided and sustained by a good director, may easily misunderstand the action of God in her regard, believe herself lost, and draw back discouraged. Those whose mission it is to guide her, if they have no knowledge of these ways by study or experience, exaggerating the dangers and illusions to be met with, and taking for miraculous operations the graces of prayer, will be tempted, through a false prudence and an apparent humility, which in reality are opposed to God's designs, to shut the door of mystical prayer against her.

Every soul belongs to Him; He has the right to lead her by what way He pleases; no one would be so rash as to venture to set right the Divine Wisdom, or to hinder Him from leading His friends by the way that seems good to Him. The Holy Ghost is the supreme director of souls. What is to be feared when following a guide infinitely wise? The part of His ministers is to recognise and to second the divine action; hence, once that action is manifest, we have never the right to thwart it or to regard it with suspicion.

Mystical contemplation has its perils, which must not be exaggerated; ordinary mental prayer has dangers of its own, which should not be for-

gotten. The dread of these dangers does not prevent us from applying ourselves to meditation
because of its advantages; neither, therefore, is it
a sufficient reason for placing contemplation on
the index, for systematically debarring from its
ways a soul to whom God is throwing them open,
for keeping souls imprisoned against His will in
the ordinary kinds of prayer, wherein God no
longer wishes them to remain. What progress
could they make thereby in opposition to His Will?
Is it not the greatest danger for a director to be in
conflict with the Holy Ghost; and for the soul he
directs to be placed outside the divine will, outside
the graces of predilection; to enjoy no longer the
advantages of meditation, and to lose the treasures
of contemplation? The forms of mystical prayer
are a golden mine, let us work it; they present certain dangers, let us be on our guard against them;
let us follow with docility the divine attraction,
avoiding at the same time the snares of the enemy.
After all, experience will soon teach us that if contemplatives must dread the fumes of pride and the
seduction of delights, far more must they fear discouragement. They have need of being tried, of
being humbled, and, above all, of being comforted
and strengthened; they will share more frequently
in the crucifixion of Calvary than in the glory and
joys of Thabor.

These are the reasons why we have deemed it well
to call our readers' attention to the ways of mystical
contemplation. Those who do not know these ways
and have but little time to spare, will perhaps

appreciate a short and substantial account of them. Those, too, who have spent much time in the study of these arduous matters, have been dazed, perhaps, by such divergence and confusion of opinions! God grant that our modest summary may furnish accurate and precise notions, clear up some points hitherto obscure, and dissipate prejudices! " It is a great happiness for a soul," says St. Teresa, " to find a description of what she experiences, she clearly recognises the path in which God has placed her. I say more, it is an immense advantage, in order to make progress in the various states of prayer, to know the line of conduct to be followed in each of them. As for myself, through the want of this knowledge, I have suffered much, and lost much precious time."[1]

Is it well to put this work in the hands of a whole community? Ignorance is the evil most to be dreaded. Without some study of this kind, many persons' knowledge of mystical ways would be limited to vague, inaccurate, and dangerous conjectures, perhaps even to one-sided criticism and blind prejudices. Amongst those, who would like to explore this science, so interesting, but so laborious, many would be quickly discouraged by the difficulties of the task, whereas it will be easy for them to read over a few pages, in which the whole subject is to be found precisely stated and condensed. There are, besides, many souls who need a knowledge of these states of prayer. If the more

[1] St. Teresa, *Life.* xiv. Dupont, *Life of Fr. Balth. Alvarez,* c. xiv.

elevated degrees are as rare as they are surprising, the passive purifications and the first degrees are much less so; these ought to be frequent in religion, especially in contemplative orders. Even in the world God has His privileged ones. However, these graces of prayer require purified souls, and are not, generally speaking, granted till after serious progress in virtue has been attained. Our monasteries, being schools of holiness, it is chiefly in them that God ought to find subjects prepared for this way. Would it, in fact, be anything strange that there should be a little mystical contemplation in an order essentially contemplative and entirely devoted to prayer and penance? Is it not rather the contrary that should fill us with astonishment?

Mystical contemplation, says St. Teresa, "is a general banquet, to which Our Lord *invites us all*. . . . . As He sets no limit to His invitation nor to His promise, I hold it for certain that *all those who will not stop on the way* will drink of this living water." [1] Contemplation, then, is offered, and, as it were, promised to souls of good will. The saint declares that the prayer of quiet "is that by which, she believes, the greatest number of souls enter upon this way." [2] She had already said in her *Life* [3]: "There is a *very great number* of souls who arrive at this state; but those who pass beyond it are few." "Some only," amongst you "are in the habitual enjoyment" of

---

[1] St. Teresa, *Way*, xx. end.
[2] *Castle*, 4th mans. c. iii.
[3] *Life*, xv. at the beginning.

the prayer of union; "still there are very few," who do not share in it more or less.[1] "In every one of our houses there is hardly one religious to be found, whom the Divine Master guides by the way of ordinary meditation alone; all the others have been raised to perfect contemplation. Some of the still more advanced are favoured with raptures," &c.[2]

St. John of the Cross also says many things in the same strain. According to him the beginners meditate; the proficients are already contemplatives; the perfect live in union of love with God.[3] Persons engaged in the religious state arrive more quickly at contemplation, and, generally speaking, hardly any considerable time passes without their entering into the blessed state of the night of the senses. Nevertheless, "God does not lead on to perfect contemplation all who walk resolutely in the spiritual way; He alone knows the reason of this."[4] St. Teresa has said likewise that we can be saved without these graces of prayer, and "that, without them, we may not fail to be very perfect and even to surpass contemplative souls in merit," provided we are more faithful than they to all our duties.[5]

St. Francs of Sales would not have composed his *Treatise on the love of God* for his Sisters of the

[1] *Castle*, 5th mans. c. i. at the beginning.
[2] *Foundations*, iv.
[3] *Night of the Senses*, c. i.
[4] *First Night*, viii. *Living Flame*, 3rd stanza, 3rd verse n° 5.
[5] *Way*, xviii.

Visitation if mystical prayer, which occupies so considerable a space in that book, was not very frequent in their convents.

Scaramelli begins his *Mystical Directory* by declaring, after thirty years of missionary life, " that in almost every place he met with some soul whom God was leading by these ways . . . to a high perfection." [1]

But what need is there to seek for arguments outside of our own order? In a thousand places, St. Bernard, our illustrious doctor, describes contemplation, arouses the desire of it, points out the conduct to be observed in it, indicating it sometimes by its name, sometimes by symbolic imagery. We should be very far from having grasped the sense of his works, and especially of his *Sermons on the Canticle of Canticles,* if we found in them nothing but asceticism. Certain parts of his works treat of contemplation in general, others can be understood only of mystical contemplation. He speaks of it because it is his own way, he preaches it assiduously to his brethren, no doubt because his community needed to hear about it, and were capable of understanding it. His disciples, whose writings are, so to speak, a continuation of his own, use the same language. However cursorily we may read both the Little and the Great Exordiums of Citeaux and our Menology, we shall soon be convinced that mysticism attained a splendid development in our Order, during its heroic ages, and that,

[1] Fr. Saudreau (*Degrés,* vol. ii. c. vii.) cites a number of other grave authors in support of our thesis.

even after its decline, that feature had not entirely disappeared.

In our own day, as in the ages past, experience shows that God has ever the same loving heart and liberal hand, and that He has reserved to Himself amongst us souls, whom He is pleased to favour with his choicest gifts. Happy are those who are understood, tried, encouraged and wisely directed! Happy, too, the directors who know how to discern the action of God, and to make it bring forth all the fruits of holiness that it promises!

We may add that these graces would be lavished with a more royal profusion upon souls who have left all for God, if they only knew better how to appreciate them and to dispose themselves for receiving them. Let us employ all our care and courage to cleanse perfectly our interior house, to adorn it with virtues, especially with a lively faith and ardent love, to desire " the Kingdom of God which is within us," to seek it alone in silence, solitude and peace of soul, in prayer and habitual union with God; and, although the Divine Master does not owe to any one these graces of predilection, He will not allow Himself to be outdone in generosity.

Souls who walk in these ways, those who seem to be called to them, and directors who have the formidable charge of leading them by these paths to the heights of a perfection which is by no means common, should not forget that mystical graces carry with them an obligation to live more entirely for God alone, and point to a more strict account

P

that must be given one day of graces so great ; they
are a way, not the term ; a marvellous instrument, not holiness itself ; prayer so elevated aspires
to something higher than merely ordinary virtue ;
whatever be the way, we must arrive at dying to
self in order to be filled with God alone.   Beginners and all those who are imperfectly purified and
little enriched by virtues, above all, those who go
back instead of advancing, are not prepared for
these celestial favours ; should such read these pages
they can, at least admire the riches of the divine
goodness, but let them beware " of blaspheming
what they know not,' and let them not take it ill,
that God leads other souls by ways different from
theirs.   Pure and generous souls, who may belong
entirely to God without, however, enjoying the gifts
of contemplation, will not disturb Mary seated at
Our Lord's feet, and " will esteem it their happiness to serve Him along with Martha."   Mary was
more praised by Our Saviour Himself, yet Martha
was a saint and her merit was great.   Nevertheless,
let them listen to this advice of St. Teresa : " Do
all that depends on yourself ; prepare yourself by
the practice of the other virtues, to merit this
precious gift of contemplation ; and I feel assured
the Divine Master will grant it to you." [1]

We shall treat more fully of the entrance into,
and the first steps in these paths ; and only briefly
indicate the more elevated degrees, which are hardly
ever met with.   We hope to put forward nothing
which might unduly excite imaginative souls, or

[1] St. Teresa, *Way*, xviii.

induce them to abandon humility. We shall describe the joys and advantages of the mystical states of prayer; but we shall also set in strong relief the painful labour of the active preparation, the severe crucible of passive purifications, and the sufferings which result from contemplation itself. It will be easily perceived that these kinds of prayer are suitable only for generous souls, who are ready to endure everything for union with God, and not for such as are merely thirsting for spiritual pleasures or a high degree in the spiritual life.

CHAPTER II

THE PASSAGE FROM ORDINARY PRAYER TO MYSTICAL CONTEMPLATION

ACTIVE PREPARATION.

GOD alone can lead a soul into mystical contemplation. Generally speaking, He waits till souls are sufficiently purified and already rich in virtues, and He always exacts from them a generous correspondence with His favours.[1] Very numerous are they who view the promised land from a distance, but never enter it on account of their infidelities. Let us beware of accusing God in order to excuse our own failings. With regard to the graces of prayer, almost the same thing takes place as with regard to those of the sacraments; let us open wide the door of our soul, and they rush in in copious streams; they flow less abundantly if the door is but half opened. It is not necessary that a soul should be already perfect before she takes her first steps in these mystical ways; on the contrary, the union of love and passive purifications are most powerful agents to purge the soul and perfect her virtues; but the budding forth of contemplation, its blossoming and its fruits, depend altogether on the divine pleasure. and on the zeal the soul shows in prepar-

[1] *Life of Fr. Balth. Alvarez*, xv.

ing herself and in co-operating with grace. Progress in interior purity and in virtue will give the measure of progress in contemplation; in proportion as the soul is purified and her positive holiness increases, her prayer becomes more elevated; union with God, having become more intense, hastens in its turn the purification of the soul and its further progress.[1]

We should cleanse our interior house, empty it out, give more room to God in it, by increasing our life of penance. We ought also to seek God with more ardour in the practice of virtue, especially of a *lively faith* and *generous love,* and of a life of *silence, recollection and prayer.* The more our soul is emptied of profane things and becomes a holy sanctuary, the more will it attract the Divine Guest. Penance will suppress whatever repels infinite purity; the virtues will adorn in a worthy manner the temple of so lofty a Majesty; the calm and peace of the sanctuary and the incense of prayer will invite God to honour us with His presence and with His intimate friendship. This beginning of a preparation, which leads the soul to the threshold of mystical contemplation, does not exceed the power of our own efforts aided by grace; perhaps God, some day, by putting us through special purifications, will deign to complete our preparation, and so open to us the gates of contemplation.

In order, therefore, to attain to these precious graces of prayer, an active preparation and also passive purifications are required.

[1] St. John of the Cross, *Ascent,* b. ii. c. v.

The active preparation consists in two things : in removing obstacles, and in positively disposing the soul for the visits of Our Lord.

§ 1.—Negative Preparation.

We must first remove the obstacles, and this is the fruit of our life of penance.

We have already said[1] that the fourfold purity of the conscience, of the mind, of the heart, and of the will, is at the same time the fruit of mental prayer well made and the condition of its progress. In order that nothing may hinder God from raising us to infused contemplation, we must increase this fourfold purity and bring it to its full perfection.

1º. We must redouble our zeal to *purify* and *pacify* our conscience; for " Wisdom will not enter into a malicious soul, nor dwell in a body subject to sins."[2] " The God of peace "[3] cannot take His delight in a troubled soul. We should, therefore, use more vigilance in guarding our thoughts and our affections, more generosity in combating our vicious inclinations, in governing our passions, in seeking less eagerly our own satisfaction; we should avoid with the greatest care the imperfections and the venial sins, which we commit through *habit* and with *attachment*. We may, doubtless, commit many imperfections and faults of frailty, and experience first movements of the sensitive

---

[1] 1st part, c. iv. § 1 p. 34.   [2] *Wisd.*, i. 4.
[3] St. Paul, *passim.*

appetite, which the will can neither anticipate nor repress; but this does not hinder divine union. "Often even, during the very act of this union, when the will elevated in God enjoys a salutary repose, these first movements may agitate the inferior and sensible part, but without affecting the superior whose prayer they in no way disturb."[1] Passions ill combated, irregular affections, habits of venial sin, voluntary attachments, these it is that "render divine union impossible and check progress, . . in proportion to the tepidity and remissness they introduce into the soul. . . . Although certain disorders of a passing nature might be more considerable, yet they would have less injurious consequences than a *habit* of these small faults, or than a persistent *attachment* to any object."[2] Thus speaks St. John of the Cross, and he gives as examples: the habit of much speaking, a slight attachment to anything whatsoever if it be not given up, an inordinate affection for any person, or common object, curiosity to hear news, to see, &c."[3] It is but a thread, yet as long as it remains unbroken, the soul is held and cannot fly towards God.[4]

According to this holy doctor, "a single irregular appetite, even in a venial matter,[5] . . . an imperfect desire of the will, no matter how trifling,[6] . . . one single human desire,"[7] to

---

[1] St. John of the Cross, *Ascent*, b. i. c. xi.-xii.

[2] *Ibid.* c. xi.   [5] *Ascent*, c. ix.

[3] *Ibid.*   [6] *Ibid.*

[4] *Ascent*, b. i. c. xi.   [7] *Ibid.*, c. xi.

which the soul is inordinately attached, is enough
to prevent her from being raised to divine union.
" It is sad to see certain souls, richly freighted with
merits and good works, who, because they have not
the courage to break with certain tastes, attachments, or affections, never reach the haven of divine
union, although God gave them strength to burst
the bonds of pride and sensuality, and of many
other vices and gross vanities, so that they are no
longer held but by a single thread.[1] . . .
There is, likewise, reason to deplore the ignorance
of some, who, *neglecting to mortify their real
passions*, think they can dispose themselves for
divine union by indiscreetly undertaking a number
of penances and other extraordinary practices; these
are simply on the wrong road." [2]

This is the teaching of a great saint and
eminent mystic. If it is felt to be somewhat severe,
at least every one must agree with him that the
passions "fatigue, torment, darken, defile and
weaken the soul." [3] It is of the highest importance to discipline them, if we would advance in
virtue and in prayer; " the greater or less purity of
the soul determines the degree of illumination and
union of which it is capable." [4] The best, surest
and most meritorious means to pacify the soul is to
strive always, not after that which is most easy, but
after that which is most difficult; not after that
which is most pleasant, but after that which is most
unpleasant; not after that what is more agreeable,

---

[1] *Ascent*, c. xi.   [3] *Ibid.*, b. i. c. vi. and ff.
[2] *Ibid.*, c. viii.   [4] *Ibid.*, b. ii. c. v.

but after what is less agreeable; not after what is more consoling, but after what is afflicting," &c.[1]

It is not enough to purify the conscience, it must be *pacified.* " Remorse, . . . when excessive, . . . produces in the soul restlessness, depression, discouragement and weakness, which render it unfit for any good exercise. It is the same with regard to *scruples,* for a similar reason; these are thorns which prick the conscience, agitate it, and deprive it of tranquility, repose in God and the enjoyment of true peace." [2]

Let us, then, watch over the purity of our soul, without being too concentrated upon ourselves. Exaggerated examinations, minute inquiries, scruples, continual fears narrow the heart, hinder it from dilating with love, and are a great obstacle to divine union.

2°. It is impossible to be a contemplative without *purity of mind.* Our Well-Beloved loves only the silence of solitude and the religious calm of the sanctuary; He does not select the tumult of public places to speak to souls and enter into familiar converse with them. " He shall not cry out," says Isaias, . . . " neither shall His voice be heard abroad." [3] Neither the violence of the storm, nor the earthquake, nor the fire revealed Him to Elias, but the breath of a gentle breeze." [4] It was in soli-

---

[1] *Ascent,* b. i. c. xiii.
[2] St. Peter of Alcantara, *Prayer and Meditation,* 2nd part, c. iii.
[3] *Isaiah,* xlii. 2.
[4] *III. Kings,* xix. 2.

tude far from the noisy crowd, and in mysterious converse with Moses and Elias, that Our Lord was transfigured before the eyes of His three chosen ones on Thabor.[3]

"Contemplation," says St. Peter of Alcantara,[2] "cannot endure curiosity, whether of the senses or of the mind. . . . All this takes up time, disturbs the senses, disquiets and dissipates the soul, and scatters it in all directions."

"Nor does contemplation agree any better with immoderate work; this deprives us of all leisure and wearies the mind. Thus we remain in want of time and courage for the service of God.

"It likes not excessive cares, veritable gnats of Egypt, which worry the soul and will not allow it to sleep the spiritual sleep of prayer; indeed, it is rather during that very time, they by preference torment the soul and distract it from its object."

We should, therefore, adopt the habit, as far as duty permits, of keeping the windows of the senses closed, of imposing silence upon the lips, the imagination and the memory, of banishing human thoughts, and entertaining only those which are divine. For this purpose, we should expel without pity from our minds all images, thoughts, memories, which defile, trouble, or dissipate the soul; and when the proper time has come, we should lend a docile ear to the counsels addressed by St. John of the Cross, in his "Ascent of Carmel," *to souls*

[1] *Matthew*, xvii. 1.
[2] *Prayer and Meditation*, 2nd part, c. iii.

which are advanced in this way, and even already contemplatives.[1]   He continually reminds them,[2] that the *distinct and particular* knowledge acquired by the senses and the labour of the mind, and preserved in the memory, is incapable of quickly bringing us to divine union; the more the soul is filled with this kind of knowledge, the less room is left for God to pour into it His infused light. We ought, therefore, to make fewer considerations in our prayer, when the proper time to do so has come; to suppress them in the act of contemplation, and full of trust in God to suffer Him, if He so will, to reduce us to an impossibility of meditating.[3] Neither does the *distinct and particular* knowledge, which results from visions, revelations, or supernatural voices, lead to divine union. We ought never to desire, but rather to reject these favours. When they come from God they produce their effect passively, without needing even the soul's consent. When they have passed away, it is useless and even hurtful to trouble one's mind about them, to count upon them, " to make of them a treasure and a store of memories."[4] Yet, " this care, to strip oneself of knowledge and of the remembrance of all things, is never to extend to Jesus Christ and His Sacred Humanity,[5] . . . nor to anything that belongs purely to God and can lead us to a simple, universal,

---

[1] *Ascent*, b. ii. c. i. and vi.
[2] *Ibid.*, b. ii. c. iv. v. &c.
[3] *Ibid.*, b. ii. c. xii.-xv. xxxii. *First Night*, c. x.
[4] *Ibid.*, b. ii. c. xi. xxiii. xxiv. &c. St. Liguori, *Praxis*, 143.
[5] *Ibid.*, b. iii. c. i. and xiv.

and confused knowledge of Him." [1] Moreover, if
the memory of divine favours awakens in us His
holy *love,* we may think upon them to excite love,
attaching ourselves to love alone, and not to its
rind or to its sweetness.[2] Neither ought we ever to
neglect the thought of our *duties* or the remembrance of *necessary* knowledge; in order that these
may do no harm, it is enough that we be not attached
to them." [3] With these exceptions, let us empty
the mind and memory of knowledge, memories,
impressions, and distinct [4] images, in order to fix
them on God alone or the Sacred Humanity of Our
Lord.

The high road to reach divine union is faith,
which has no need either to see or understand in
order to believe; hope, which forgets earth in order
to remember only God; charity, which abandons
the creature to concentrate all its power of loving
upon God alone.[5]

This doctrine seems to us fully to harmonise with
the well-known text of Denis the Mystic,[6] whom
St. Bernard [7] and the other contemplatives of the
Middle Ages so faithfully followed.

3°. We must cultivate *purity of heart.* The sight
of God is promised to the pure of heart [8]; and " he
who loveth cleanness of heart . . . shall have

---

[1] *Ascent,* b. iii. c. ii.

[2] *Ibid.,* b. iii. c. xii. xiii. and xiv.

[3] *Ibid.,* b. iii. c. xii. xiii. xiv.

[4] *Ibid.,* b. ii. c. iv. &c. *passim.,* and *Living Flame* . . . 3rd
stanza, verse 3 *passim.*

[5] *Ibid.,* b. iii. c. vi. &c. *Night,* b. ii. c. xxi.

[6] Abbé Saudreau, *Vie d'union,* c. ii. § 10.

[7] St. Bernard, *Sermon* 52. 8 *puncta perfect. asseq.*

[8] Matthew, v. 8.

the King for his friend.'' [1]   If we would succeed in
a kind of prayer which proceeds principally from
love, our heart should be empty of every idol and
filled with God.   None are so loving as the saints;
they have treasures of delicate affection and of
generous self-sacrifice for all around them.   Their
heart is no egotist in search of enjoyments, no slave
tyrannised over by its own caprices; perfectly free
and detached, it uses everything as a means to raise
itself to God; what it seeks in all things and in every
one is God; it is fixed in God alone; hence, nothing
troubles it and its peace is perpetual.   Here we
have the secret of divine union.   How can we pretend to the favours and intimate familiarity of the
Spouse, if our heart abandons Him for the love of
anything else, if it lets itself be carried hither and
thither by its voluntary likes and dislikes, if it is
tossed about by sufferings and afflictions which it
accepts with a bad grace?   We must, therefore, get
rid of '' all foreign affections and loves, all trouble
of mind and movements of passion.   In order to
pray and meditate, it is not less necessary to have
the heart well regulated, than it is to tune a guitar
in order to play upon it.'' [2]

4°. Finally, we must perfect *the purity of the
will.*   '' Divine Wisdom goeth about seeking such
as are worthy of her.''   Who, then, would not receive her with open arms and with all his heart?
But we must be to some extent worthy of her.
'' The keeping of her laws is the firm foundation of

[1] Prov. xxii. 11.
[2] St. Peter of Alcant., *Prayer and Meditation*, 2nd part, c. ii.

incorruption; and incorruption bringeth near to
God." [1] " We must, therefore, labour to strip ourselves of our caprices, our fancies, our projects, our
manifold desires, our judgments, our attachments,
our repugnances, in a word, of everything which is
not the will of God; and the soul shall be perfectly
pure, when she shall have reached such a state of
liberty and self-control as to obey without difficulty
the law of God, her rule and her superiors, to
abandon herself with filial confidence into the hands
of Providence, and no longer to will or not will anything but the self-same thing with God. In proportion as our souls draw near to this happy state,
God can elevate us in prayer, for there will be no
obstacle on our part.

Is there any need to point out how wisely our
rules combine to thoroughly purify us, how much
we ought to esteem and love our fasts, our watchings, our manual works and other austerities which
subdue the body, our silence, which tames the
tongue, our humiliations, as well those which are
part of our daily life as those which crop up unexpectedly, for they all keep down our pride; the
thousand details of our observances, which break
down the will, the great and small trials, which
stamp our whole life with the seal of the cross?
Far from lessening the austerity of our life by con-
venient compromises and lax interpretations, we
should set a high value on whatever is most mortifying in our rules, as a most powerful means of bringing to its perfection, that fourfold purity so dear to

[1] *Wisd.*, vi. 17, 19, 20.

God. But, amongst our observances, none should excite our zeal more than the VIIth Chapter of our Holy Rule: *On Humility;* for the observance of it alone, as St. Benedict says, would lead our soul on to perfect love by purging it from its sins and vices.

Such, in our opinion, is the negative preparation which our own activity, aided by grace, can make for attaining to mystical union : it removes the obstacles, by purging the conscience, by banishing from the mind all thoughts that have not God for their object or their rule, by expelling from the heart every love other than that of our only Spouse, by detaching the will entirely from self; our soul thus becomes a sanctuary into which nothing defiled or profane enters. What remains is to fill it with God, and this is the work of the positive preparation.

§ II.—POSITIVE PREPARATION.

1. We must adorn the temple in a manner becoming so lofty a majesty. We should therefore continually increase in grace in order to render our soul more beautiful with the beauty itself of God. All the virtues should be its adornment; our works and our merits should be its treasure; the innocence of Our Lord, His humility, His obedience, His detachment and His other perfections, reproduced in our soul by a faithful imitation, must render this temple agreeable in God's eyes. How can God the Father not be delighted if He beholds in us the living image of His Son? Can the divine Spouse refuse His

love to a soul in which His own virtues are reflected
as in a mirror? Yet there are two virtues that have
a greater attraction for the Holy Ghost, and that will
better prepare us for that look of love which constitutes contemplation; namely, a *lifely faith,* which
looks almost as though it beheld, and an *ardent
love,* which unites us with God in a mutual embrace.
St. John of the Cross incessantly repeats: If you
aspire to perfect union, " ask not of your eyes, your
ears, or your heart to show you the means; close all
those doors, . . . and expect nothing but from
faith.[1] . . . God communicates Himself more
freely to the soul that is more advanced in His love,
to her whose will is in more entire conformity with
His own." [2] St. Teresa also says that " in order
to make progress in this path, . . . the essential thing is not to think much, but to love much;
. . . the soul which has the greater love is not
the soul that experiences the most attraction and
consolation, but she that is most firmly resolved
to satisfy God in everything, that has the most
ardent desire to please Him, that makes the greatest
efforts to avoid offending Him." [3] . . .

2°. The temple is now adorned; God will take
pleasure in it, if He find there religious silence and
the incense of prayer.

Above all, let us love solitude and recollection.
We have no right, indeed, to fly from common life
and the occupations which obedience enjoins; but,
whilst showing ourselves obliging towards our

[1] *Ascent,* b. ii. c. iv.　　　[2] *Ibid.,* b. ii. c. v.
[3] *Castle,* 4th mans. c. i.

brethren and conscientious in performing our work and the duties of our charge, let us avoid pouring ourselves forth too much on outward things and being absorbed by them; without giving way to injurious intensity of thought, let us collect within us all the powers of our soul in order to keep them attentive to God. Our model ought to be our glorious Father St. Benedict, who, on returning to his well-beloved solitude, *dwelt with himself* [1] alone under the eye of the heavenly Watcher. There, shutting the doors and avenues of our soul by silence, modesty and recollection, let us make to ourselves an inner sanctuary entirely filled with God, and let us learn to entertain the infinitely great and infinitely loving Guest who dwells within us.

Let us converse with God who honours us with His presence. Let us abandon ourselves ever more frequently and in a better manner, to vocal prayer, to pious reading, and, above all, to mental prayer and the habitual thought of God.[2] Let us seek Him assiduously in aridities as well as in consolations; if He hide Himself, let us do Him violence by pursuing Him with a like ardour; let us check our pursuit of Him only at the boundary line of over-strain of the mind and indiscreet fatigue. We shall thus make acquaintance with God; we shall learn to hold frequent converse with Him, to enjoy His intimate friendship and to attract Him to us by our zeal in seeking Him. A prolonged course of mental prayer may, perhaps, one day obtain for

---

[1] St. Gregory, *Vitâ S. Benedicti, II. Dial.,* c. iii.
[2] *Life of Fr. Balth. Alvarez,* c. xiv. § 2 and 3, and c. xlii.

Q

us the favour of being raised to a higher form of
prayer. When our mind and heart shall have
learned to turn, as it were by instinct, to God, we
shall be very near to mystical contemplation, should
it please God to raise us to it.

Such, it seems to us, is the thought of St.
Bernard.[1] He depicts a soul who, in the purgative
way, kissing the feet of Our Lord, has obtained the
pardon of her sins; who, in the illuminative way,
kissing the hands of Our Saviour, has acquired
" many and not small virtues "; who, carried away
by a love stronger than her respect, now dares to
ask from God the gift of contemplation, the gift
" of a kiss from His divine mouth." Here are the
reasons she alleges to justify her boldness : " I beg
Him, I conjure Him, nay, I almost demand Him *to
give me a kiss of His mouth. Lo! I have spent
already many years,* striving by His grace to lead
a pure and mortified life, applying myself to pious
reading, resisting my passions, giving myself frequently to prayer, guarding against temptations,
recalling my years, in the bitterness of my soul, and
living, I believe, as far as in me lay, in peace with
my brethren; submissive to authority, and regulat-
ing my steps according to the will of my superiors.
I never covet the goods of others, but rather give
away my own goods and even myself to serve
them, eating my bread in the sweat of my
brow," &c., &c.

Such, also, is the thought of St. Teresa. In her
" Interior Castle " she teaches that " all our desires,

---

[1] St. Bernard, *IX. Serm. in Cant.*

all our meditations, all our tears, all the efforts we
can make (in order to raise ourselves to supernatural
quietude), are useless; God alone gives this
heavenly water to whom He pleases; often He
gives it just when we least think of it." However,
she requires as an indispensable disposition
" humility, humility, since it is by this virtue that
Our Lord allows Himself to be overcome, and is
induced to grant all our desires. . . . Let a
soul be humble and detached from everything, in
very truth, however, and not merely in imagination which often deceives, and the Divine Master,
I have no doubt, will grant her not only this grace,
but even many others surpassing all her desires." [1]
The same doctrine is found in the saint's " Life "
and in her " Way of Perfection." No one by his
own efforts can raise himself to mystical contemplation; yet " God invites us all to it." [2] He will
give it to those souls who prepare themselves for
it by an entire detachment, a perfect humility and
the practice of the other virtues,[3] and who, instead
of stopping on the road, march onwards with an
ever-renewed ardour towards the happy goal of
their desires.[4] To attain to contemplation, it is
not necessary to be already perfect,[5] but we ought
to have more virtue than is required for ordinary
mental prayer; [6] the saint " confidently asserts that,
as long as a religious fails in obedience, he shall
never arrive at being a contemplative." [7]

[1] *Castle*, 4th mans. c. ii. [4] *Way*, c. xxvi.
[2] *Way*, c. xx. éd. Bouix. [5] *Life*, c. xxiii.
[3] *Ibid.*, c. xviii. [6] *Way*, xvii.
[7] *Way*, c. xix.

All these things prepare the soul for making its first steps in mystical ways; they will dispose it, moreover, for making higher ascents, should it so please God. Though she should have reached heights far from common, she ought never to cease exercising herself in penance, humility, self-renunciation, obedience and the other virtues, and, above all, in faith and divine charity; for, the possibility of being lost always remains; progress in purity and love brings about progress in prayer; God requires more from a soul to whom He has given more; and we ought to correspond to those graces of predilection by a more perfect fidelity in the discharge of all our duties.

In all that has been hitherto said there is nothing which may not come from our own efforts aided by ordinary grace; this is the active preparation. The gift of contemplation is not, however, promised to it, but should we not obtain it, there will remain at least, as the reward of our efforts, an increase of grace and of glory.

St. John of the Cross depicts [1] in anything but flattering colours those souls who are already standing upon the threshold of contemplation: either they do not perceive all those defects which remain in them, or, if they do, they must embrace unsparingly humiliations and sufferings; but nature cries out and we treat ourselves too softly. God then puts His strong but paternal hand to the work; He humbles, washes, brushes, and polishes energetically in order to complete the cleansing of

---

[1] *First Night*, i.-vii.

the soul. Again, this latter must become simplified in its operations, weaned from sensible
devotion, disengaged from its dependence on the
senses; the mere subjection of the body to the spirit
and of the spirit to God is not sufficient. The soul
that God would elevate to a mystical state must
be fortified against the intoxication of pride. Such
are the reasons which explain the necessity of
passive purifications.

They are so called because they are not of our
own choice; we endure them, but it is God who
operates, and the soul has little else to do but to
submit to them with a good grace.

CHAPTER III

PASSIVE PURIFICATIONS

THESE are the passive purification of the senses, and that of the spirit : the former is rather common, seeing that it is the ordinary introduction to mystical contemplation ; the latter " is very rare." [1]

ART. I.—PASSIVE PURIFICATION OF THE SENSES.[2]

§ I.—NOTION OF THIS STATE.

The passive purification of the senses is not *any* kind of suffering, such as aridities, temptations, humiliations, scruples, cares, sickness, and the thousand other trials which abound in the spiritual life. It is an *habitual* and very *special* dryness, by its very nature related to mystical prayer, of which it is the preparation, the germ and the bud; or rather it is itself contemplation, but as yet too feeble, dry, full of desolation and purgative. It is passive; God it is who is operating, and the soul yields herself up to His operations. It purges the senses by subjecting them to the spirit, and by

[1] St. John of the Cross, *First Night,* c. viii. ix. xiii.
[2] Fr. Poulain, *Grâces d'or.,* c. xv.

fettering the sensible faculties in their natural functions. Thus these faculties enter as it were into an obscure night; for which reason St. John of the Cross calls this state the *Night of the senses;* this is the first night; another night still more painful succeeds this—namely, *that of the spirit.*

The concurrence of the following three signs characterises the former night.

1°. The first is *a total dryness of the sensible faculties,* "when a man finds no comfort nor pleasure in the things of God, and neither also in created things. It is God who produces this *universal loathing* in the soul in order to annihilate and purge away its sensitive desires."[1] He had carried the soul in His arms, had nourished her with the milk of sensible consolations, encouraged her by His caresses; now, that she has grown in grace, He weans her and places her upon the ground that she may learn to walk. Hence comes that aridity in prayer; God no longer smiles, the heart is devoid of all enthusiasm, the imagination no longer helps at all, but impedes her by its distractions. All is gloomy desert and desolation. Weariness weighs her down in the practice of virtue : the soul is plunged in bitterness, sacrifice terrifies, a mere nothing makes her suffer, temptation is more than ever burthensome. She feels a distaste for all created things; she experiences no liking for anything, "she cannot find sweetness or comfort anywhere.[2] On the other hand, she

---

[1] St. John of the Cross, *First Night,* ix,
[2] *Ibid,*

would not cherish any attraction for anything that
is not God. For although the sensible faculties
" are cast down, dulled and weakened, the spirit
remains lively and strong." [1]

It is true that it *appears* to be without strength,
being no longer sustained by the sensible faculties;
and has also its only too real weakness, as the life
of St. Teresa, during her eighteen years of trial,
superabundantly demonstrates.[2]   Still, in spite of
all this, the soul desires only God, seeks Him with
anxiety, and suffers bitterly on account of being
weaned from Him.[3]   This aridity is an infliction
which lasts for months and sometimes even for
years.

2°. The second sign is more characteristic.   It is
the *powerlessness* and vacuity of the mind, which
is, as it were, bound down hand and foot, *when engaged in prayer*.   In all other functions, to study,
for instance, or to reflect on its ordinary business,
the soul can freely use its mental powers; but in
prayer, notwithstanding all her efforts, the imagination remains inert, the memory without any distinct recollections, the understanding empty of
ideas.   The soul is no longer able to consider the
numerous details of a mystery, to study a truth and
draw conclusions and excite affections by it;
briefly, considerations become as it were impossible, or at least perseverance in making them is
an impossibility, though this powerlessness is less

---

[1] St. John of the Cross, *First Night*, ix.
[2] St. Teresa, *Life*, vii. and *ff. passim.*
[3] St. Liguori, *Praxis*, 128,

marked when meditation is made while writing down
one's thoughts. Sometimes the mind is so empty
that even a book is of no service; it is read but not
understood. Vocal prayers are difficult and tend
to become a torment. A man in this state cannot
meditate, but he can think on God, keep the eye of
his soul fixed on Him after a simple, general, and
confused fashion, by an affectionate look without
any scaffolding of considerations or too complicated
details.

It is only by slow degrees that the power to meditate disappears and a simple look becomes the only
prayer possible. This powerlessness augments
progressively, and tends to become more and more
profound. It may be subject to intermissions, especially in the beginning; there is then a kind of intermediate state, during which, at one time, the soul
has nothing to do but to receive infused contemplation, at another "she must correspond, by a
tranquil, moderate exercise of the understanding,
with the grace which wants to lead her into it." [1]

Is there any need to add, that the will, by this
emptiness of the mind, is reduced to turn herself
towards God by a vague and indistinct love, or to
make only short acts, and that she enters into this
dryness, unless, indeed, it pleases God to console
her without, however, restoring to the intellect its
power of reasoning on spiritual things?

Such is the doctrine taught by St. John of the
Cross,[2] and confirmed by experience. St. Teresa

[1] *Ascent*, b. ii. c. xv. *Night*, b. i. c. ix.

[2] *Ibid.*, b. ii. c. xii. xiii. xiv. xv. *First Night*, c. viii. and ix.
Living Flame, 3rd stanza, 3rd verse §6.

ceases not to repeat [1] that she suffered much during
a number of years from this inability to meditate;
afterwards, "it was very seldom that she could
reason with her understanding, because her soul
used to enter immediately into recollection, quiet, or
rapture." [2] . . . She teaches [3] that, "*generally
speaking*," souls after being elevated to "perfect
contemplation" can no longer meditate as before.
This is, at bottom, the teaching of St. John of the
Cross, though not quite so strongly accentuated.
According to her also,[4] Our Lord sends the pains
of prayer, "to some from the very beginning, to
others at the end." She herself had not experienced them, when she first began to enjoy the
prayer of quiet and of union at about the age of
twenty years.[5]

It was necessary to call attention to these slight
differences.

3°. "In the third place, the most certain sign of
this state is, when the soul delights to be alone,
waiting lovingly on God, in interior peace, quiet,
and repose, without any particular considerations;
without acts and efforts of the intellect, memory
and will, at least in a discursive way, that is, without passing by consideration from one subject to
another." [6]

The soul is, therefore, set towards God; in the

[1] *Life*, iv. ix. xi. xii. xiii. *Way.* xviii. and xxvii. (Bouix.)
[2] *Ibid., I. Rel.*
[3] *Castle,* 4th mans. c. vii. *passim.*
[4] *Life,* xi.
[5] *Ibid.,* iv.
[6] St. John of the Cross, *Ascent,* b. ii. c. xiii.

midst of its desolation, it has no wish for creatures, it wants God; it does not rejoice in His presence, yet has no pleasure but there; in spite of its aridities and repugnances, it thirsts after solitude; the omission of prayer would produce remorse and create a frightful void; it wants everything when it has not God.

The mind is turned towards God by only a simple, vague, confused thought, by a general and unvarying remembrance of Him. " God is not represented to the soul under any form, no words can convey the idea which she forms of Him; He is not conceived precisely as great, nor as beautiful, nor as good, nor as powerful; her idea of Him is not this, and yet it is all this; or, better still, it is something above all this. God, God, God, is the only word which the soul can utter to express her thoughts about Him." [1] Evidently the intellect is here not much engaged, a thousand distractions beset it; but the distractions once passed away, the occupations once ended, if we want to think of God, it is always the same simple and general thought that recurs to the mind, and we can find no other.

The will is fixed upon God by " a vague love and a secret instinct," [2] as indefinite as the thought just mentioned, by a *dolorous and persistent need* of a more intimate union with Him. It is as it were a longing, like home-sickness, after God absent, an unassuaged thirst, which cannot do without Him; the soul would like to be inflamed with divine love,

---

[1] Abbé Saudreau, *Vie d'Union*, c. viii. §3 nº 336.
[2] *Ascent*, b. ii. c. xiv.

and, above all, to *possess* God; merely to love Him no longer satisfies her, she aspires to union with Him. If she has had no experience of the state of quiet, this is a confused attraction, a dull need, an undefinable discomfort. If she has already tasted mystical union, it is a definite desire to return to this union. In order to reach this happy goal, the soul ends by abandoning her former exercises; she feels that they would not suffice for her object, and that that road is now closed for her.[1]

§ II.—Explanation of this State.

The three elements just described are easily discovered when this dryness has already lasted a long time. They characterise the passive purification of the senses, and form its whole essence. This state is, at bottom, a state of contemplation as yet too feeble, a state of quietude in process of formation, a "*dry and purgative contemplation,*" [2] as may be easily proved by a process of reasoning.

This state is not tepidity. Tepidity, in fact, has no thirst for God, and willingly seeks its satisfaction outside of Him; this purifying aridity, on the contrary, wishes for Him only; all its fear is the fear of offending Him; all its desire, only to serve Him better; all its regret, that of not being sufficiently faithful to Him.[3]

Neither does it proceed from melancholy,[4] which paints everything in the darkest colours. Melan-

---

[1] Fr. Poulain, *Grâces d'or.*, c. xv.
[2] *Night*, b. i. c. ix.
[3] *Ascent*, b. ii. c. xiii. *Night*, b. i. c. ix.
[4] *Ibid.*, b. ii. c. xiii. *Ibid.*, b. i. c. ix.

choly takes away our zeal in seeking God, allows disgust to invade the will, which becomes limp and languishing. This purging aridity, on the contrary, affects the sensible feelings only; the will may have some weaknesses, and the soul, feeling nothing, is inclined to think that she is doing nothing; she acts, nevertheless, and remains generous; for, in spite of all it costs her, she never ceases seeking God by prayer and progress in virtue.

Neither does this state come from physical indisposition or intellectual fatigue; for if it did the dryness and powerlessness of the mind would make themselves felt elsewhere than in time of prayer; they would come and depart along with the malady, whereas this trial may last for years.

Melancholy, indisposition, fatigue and other natural causes may serve to purify the soul, but they are far from sufficing to explain this state; we must admit in it a more special action of God.

According to St. John of the Cross[1] and St. Teresa,[2] the soul ceases to meditate, because discursive prayer has given her all it had to give; henceforth, there will be for her no pleasure and little profit in it; finding God by a more simple means, she no longer feels the need of reasoning; "she would like to be always occupied only in loving, without giving a thought to anything else." These reasons would appear a sufficient explanation in the case when the soul feels herself inundated with light and love in a contemplation full of relish; but, when

---

[1] *Ascent*, b. ii. c. xii. and xiv. *Night*, b. i. c. viii. and ix.

[2] *Castle*, 6th mans. c. vii.

this purging aridity makes her cruelly suffer, she
would experience a great relief, and think she was
making great progress, if she could arrive at making
use of meditation in order to inflame her desolate
heart; it is not, however, the desire to do so that is
wanting, but the power. We prefer the explanation
which St. John of the Cross gives elsewhere [1] : Our
Lord no longer communicates Himself to the soul
by helping her to meditate, " the state of contemplation has commenced, the divine communications
follow the way of the pure spirit, a way inaccessible
to the senses." He withdraws His former aid and
gives a new one.

1°. He withdraws the former consolations, in
order to humble the soul by the sense of her powerlessness, to detach her from sweetnesses, to purge
her thoroughly, to remove thus the obstacles to the
graces He destines for her.

Above all, " divine grace no longer favours meditation, because God's intentions are that the soul
should enter upon another way." [2] Deprived of
the divine concurrence, the imagination and
memory cease to furnish images and recollections,
and the mind has no materials to work upon; hence
the source of meditation is dried up. God wishes to
accustom the soul, through necessity, to receive her
light from Himself, instead of her procuring it by
the force of reasoning, and to abandon the toil and
turmoil of considerations for the simple look of contemplation.

---

[1] *Night*, b. i. c. ix.
[2] Abbé Saudreau, *Vie d'Union*, c. viii. § 3 n° 339.

This afflicting withdrawal of help is altogether an act of mercy. God takes away an inferior good, only in order to confer upon the soul a higher grace.

2°. He begins to pour into the soul " that loving knowledge " which is the groundwork of contemplation. St. John of the Cross repeats, in a hundred different forms,[1] that " this is a beginning of contemplation, dry and obscure to the senses, concealed and hidden, generally speaking, even from the soul herself." [2]

The mind, depending too much upon sense, has not as yet learned to appreciate this altogether spiritual manna. This grace, as yet powerless to make a vivid impression on the soul and to throw her into transports of inebriating joy, is nevertheless real and of great price; it alone it is which detaches the soul from everything created, and keeps her turned towards God by a constant remembrance and a sore need of Him. It is not as yet strong enough to crown all her desires; but it nourishes, strengthens, and is not without its charm.

Passive purgation of the senses is, therefore, not a mere disposition for infused contemplation; it is the entrance into it and the commencement of it. Purgative contemplation and consoling contemplation are only one and the same divine fire; weak at first, but destined to increase, it finds the soul like to the green wood full of sap, and it has to prepare it by

[1] *Ascent*, b. ii. c. xii. xiii. xiv. xv. *Night*, b. i. c. viii. ix. x. *Living Flame*, 3rd stanza, 3rd verse *passim*.
[2] *Night*, b. i. c. ix.

drying it up, that it may afterwards burst forth into a bright and burning flame.

This is no longer the prayer of simplicity. If formerly I confined myself to forming affections, and made them short and with little variety, that was by my own free choice; at most, I only experienced a certain difficulty in doing otherwise, and could conquer it. Now, however, a certain passiveness has commenced: passive is this inability to meditate, which is only just appearing, but will become more and more marked; passive, this obscure and confused remembrance, this afflicting need of God; passive, this desolating dryness in spite of fervour of spirit; passive, this state of prayer, in which I have now no longer the same liberty to choose my subject and my method. Nevertheless, I can still produce a crowd of acts like those of the prayer of simplicity, and I feel at times a need of doing so in order not to remain altogether idle. Here, then, we have a mixture of activity and passiveness; we have one foot in affective prayer, while the other is already planted in the dry region of the prayer of quietude.

§ III.—Sufferings of this State.

We must not exaggerate them.

Authors have mainly depicted what took place in the souls of certain saints; God, who wished to raise them up to lofty heights, made them strong and did not spare them; He lavished upon them, as upon His dearest friends, a superabundance of

His crosses. We are weak; God will proportion the burden to our weakness, or will increase our strength to bear it. Many persons, in every condition of life, endure sufferings as great as these first passive purgations, yet no one thinks of compassionating them. These pains, besides, lose their bitterness, once the soul has come to value them and to submit herself to them with a resolute will.

Nevertheless, they are real. St. Teresa, who had experienced them during a number of years, declares that they are very great, and that, in her opinion, more courage is required to support them than to endure many worldly afflictions; but, as she clearly saw, God recompenses them, even in this life, with a magnificent reward.[1]

The soul suffers on account of the good things she has lost. It was not thus she used to pray formerly; pious thoughts abounded, affections welled up as from a fountain; she used to feel what she was saying to God; God used to show Himself all loving, and was prodigal of His caresses; she could have spent nights and days in prayer; penances had a charm for her; nothing would have cost her anything in the service of so good a Master. Can it be that He is now angry with her? He has veiled the sun of His divine favours, closed the sluice-gates of the spiritual waters, and deposited the soul upon the ground; He has weaned her, and would seem about to let her die of hunger. What bitter regrets! Her former practices are powerless to reanimate her fervour;

[1] *Life*, xi.

R

the more recourse she has to them, the more her
trouble and aridity augment.

She suffers from this persistent dryness : on the
side of God, who says nothing to her, and her
prayer is full of weariness and ennui :— on the side
of creatures, for God makes them for her objects of
disgust by imparting to them a special bitterness,
or else in order to resist their seductions, she has to
do herself a violence which her dryness renders all
the more painful, and that, too, without any com-
pensation. She suffers from all her surroundings;
a mere nothing is to her a burden. She suffers from
herself; she feels herself to be powerless, stupid,
cold, entirely useless, with a tendency to evil, with
no impulse towards good, a veritable load even for
herself.

She suffers from her inability to meditate.
Whence comes it that the imagination and the
memory are devoid of pious memories, holy
images, and abound in distractions? And may
not this emptiness of mind be nothing but idleness,
loss of time, culpable inaction, a punishment only
too well deserved? And, even after the soul has
come to understand better the divine meaning of
this trial, her interior powers, deprived of their
natural occupations, " grow weary of having to
practice renunciation "[1] without end, at least so
long as they are only partially occupied by God.

The soul suffers from the light that God is
giving her. She has not yet understood that this
obscure, confused, and altogether spiritual know-

[1] *Night*, b. i. c. ix.

ledge is a most precious gift, which later on God need only increase to throw her into transports of spiritual joy. The more simple this light is, the greater the risk of its passing away unperceived; " it is at times so subtle and delicate—particularly when it is most pure, simple, perfect, spiritual and interior—that a soul may very easily be possessed of it, and yet neither perceive nor feel that she has it." [1] Moreover, this general and unvarying remembrance is monotonous in the extreme.

The soul suffers also from that confused sense of need, from that indistinct love, which inclines her towards God, but at first causes her an undefinable uneasiness. The spiritual palate has not as yet learned to relish this new, delicate and spiritual aliment; the heavenly manna has not made her forget the onions of Egypt; all the more because God gives it sparingly in the commencement. The soul hungers after God with a hunger that cannot be satisfied; when she thinks she has laid hold on Him, He escapes from her; feast days are for her like ordinary days, long days without light and without food. If she has already tasted God in the state of quiet, her desire becomes more lively, at times even anxious and very painful; but she lives upon memory and hope; God has come before, God will come again. The very ardour of this desire is a wound and a balm : a wound, because this desire is unsatisfied; a balm, because it proves that she loves and is beloved. On the contrary, when the soul has not yet tasted

' *Ascent*, b. ii. c. xiv.

God, if this desire is less lively, it is also more afflicting; for the soul, feeling herself empty and cold, believes she is travelling towards perdition rather than towards mystical union.

All these sufferings, which the night of the senses causes in spiritual persons, "are very little when compared with the fears they awaken. It seems to them, in fact, that spiritual goods are lost to them for ever, and that God has abandoned them." [1]

Profoundly wearisome, even when of short duration, this state may be prolonged for years; the soul sees nothing before her but an endless desert, which is monotonous, bleak, desolate and dreadful; she would be very soon discouraged, did she not know whither it leads.

These various pains belong to the very substance itself of the passive purgation; they are as it were the *natural* consequences of this dry kind of contemplation. But mingled with these pains there are often violent temptations, maladies and other trials, which, without being a necessary and characteristic feature of it, complete the passive purgation of the soul.

Trials of temptations.—These are fierce assaults against faith; the soul tells herself that she no longer has any belief, because she feels none.— Against hope; she fears that God has abandoned her, because He no longer consoles her.—Against the holy virtue; her disordered senses and imagination subject her to a torment worse than death

[1] *Night*, b. i. c. x.

itself.—Against patience; in the midst of so many
worries, " the demon arouses in us so much anger
and ill-humour, that every one becomes insupportable to us, and that, in spite of ourselves." [1] We
are inclined to murmur against our trials, to be
sullen towards God, even to doubt His justice and
His providence. Against Christian fortitude;
shall we persevere ? There are so many sacrifices to
be made ! Then weariness and disgust enervate
the soul and dispose it to abandon the ways of
prayer.—Temptations to diabolical wickedness;
execrable blasphemies seize upon the imagination,
and they are so strong and vivid that we almost
believe we have uttered them.—Temptations to
scruples; so many doubts confound the mind, that
the soul can neither solve them herself, nor remedy
them by blind obedience. " The horrible torments (of this spirit of unrest) form as it were
the transitional phase between the night of the
senses and the night of the spirit." [2]

These temptations, and others like them, may
be in every respect similar to those of the common
ways of prayer; but, in this state, they press more
heavily upon the soul, because they are superadded
to the pains of aridity, and, at times, "to that
great dryness, in which even the remembrance of
God is in some sort lost." [3] *When the soul has
made more progress,* these temptations may present themselves with such violence, suddenness,
persistence, &c., that it will be impossible not to

---

[1] St. Teresa, *Life*, xxx.   [2] *Night*, b. i. c. xiv.
[3] *Castle*, 6th mans. c. i.

recognise therein a special permission of God and a kind of obsession. Who does not know of the fierce assaults made upon St. Antony, St. Catherine of Sienna, and the Blessed Angela of Foligno? After enduring this sort of persecution for five years, St. Magdalen of Pazzi, unable to suffer them any longer, was upon the point of yielding to despair and committing suicide. St. Teresa during eight days, a fortnight, and even at times for three weeks, had her mind filled with a thousand foolish thoughts without being able to think of anything good; it seemed to her that the demons were playing with her, as with a ball, without her being able to escape from their blows.[1]

Trials on the part of men.—God permits that those whom He has charged with our direction do not understand us, or that they should be unable to console us; they have doubts about everything, apprehend all kinds of evils, or imagine that the souls to whom God grants the graces of prayer ought to be angels.[2] St. Teresa's confessors plunged her, for a length of time, into intolerable anxiety.[3] Father Balthazar Alvarez, her director, had himself to endure a kind of persecution on account of his manner of prayer.[4] But if we are to credit St. Teresa and St. Peter of Alcantara, "one of the greatest sufferings in this state of exile is the opposition our spiritual progress meets with from really good people."[5]

---

[1] *Life*, xxx.
[2] *Castle*, 6th mans. c. i.
[3] *Life, passim.*
[4] *Life of Fr. Balth. Alvarez*, c. xl.-xli.
[5] *Life*, xxx.

Trials of sickness and infirmities.—God has subjected the greater number of contemplative saints to these trials. Let us mention only St. Clare, St. Lidwina, and St. Teresa. It is not necessary that these trials should have a clearly supernatural character. When St. Teresa had to endure her great spiritual pains, and, at the same time, the miseries of sickness, "she underwent a real martyrdom." [1]—Add to all this, fatiguing duties, the cares of a position fertile in preoccupations, failures, which inexplicably overwhelm us from all sides, and which, by God's will, occur just at the most trying moments, loss of property and of honours, and a thousand other crosses which Providence may send. Sometimes these troubles have nothing extraordinary about them, sometimes they are manifestly due to the special intervention of God; but in all cases these trials, whilst remaining only accessory means with regard to passive purgation, are none the less very efficacious in perfecting it, by detaching the soul from all things, and almost compelling her in sheer desperation to throw herself into the arms of God. We must not, however, think that every soul called to divine union must of necessity pass through all these accessory trials. God distributes more of them to some, less to others, according as the soul has more or less need of purification, and is destined to ascend to a more or less elevated state.

[1] *Life*, xxx.

§ IV.—ADVANTAGES OF THIS STATE.

Let these poor suffering ones beware of believing that they are abandoned and upon the very brink of the abyss. The way in which they are walking is really a very excellent way: it purifies them; it endows them with the most solid virtues; it is the desert which leads to the Promised Land.[1]

1°. With good reason is this state called a purgation. For it purifies our souls from pride. Inebriated with divine consolations, they used to deem themselves good; plunged in a universal disgust, powerless to meditate, reduced to the production of a few meagre affections without variety or unction, assailed often by most humiliating temptations, they feel their misery, are convinced by force of evidence that they are worth very little, and that without God they can do nothing; they are, in consequence, disposed to make themselves very small in the presence of so much greatness and sanctity, to have a greater respect for His majesty, and to pray to Him with more humility. As they find themselves plunged in darkness, they more willingly have recourse to the wisdom of their superiors, and become simple and docile; they are also too much occupied and penetrated with the sense of their own miseries to observe those of others with a malignant curiosity; and thus indulgence towards the faults of others, mutual forbearance, esteem and charity increase along with humility.

[1] St. Liguori, *Praxis*, 128.

This state also purifies souls from spiritual gluttony and all inordinate love of spiritual joys. The soul was greedy of consolations, she wished to find her pleasure in the service of God; now, this inordinate love of spiritual pleasures dies for want of food; as time goes on she learns to do without emotions, to give herself to God without any selfish interest, to serve Him at her own expense and no matter what it costs; the animal part is weakened by being deprived of sensible sweetness, the passions lose their force, and are reduced to order; little by little she dies to herself, and the divine life meets with fewer hindrances.

The soul gradually learns to work after a more spiritual fashion and *to depend less upon the senses;* she abandons the coarser efforts of the imagination, the encumbrance and fatigue of reasoning, and begins to contemplate God by her superior part in an almost angelic way, just as she perceives evident truths by a most simple act.

By the very fact that she is more free from sensuality and sensible feeling, the soul gives less hold to the demon, who acts chiefly on the imagination and the senses, and her prayer is *more sheltered from illusions.*

2°. This purgation endows the soul with the most solid virtues.

Besides humility and self-denial, which, by purifying her, remove the obstacles to progress, all the other virtues gain, in this state, a more pure merit and an immense increase. This is the case with regard to faith, for instance; for she believes in the

midst of darkness without seeing or relishing anything, upon the sole word of God.—So, too, hope
is strengthened; she trusts in the Lord, even whilst
He leaves her and gives no longer and sign of
His goodness. Charity, obedience, and religion
develop; she sacrifices herself, prays, obeys through
pure love, and not for the sake of any pleasure she
finds therein. These trials are pre-eminently the
soil most proper for the growth of patience, abnegation, and especially of a trustful, filial and
loving abandonment into the hands of God.

Little by little the soul, humbled, detached from
everything, but submissive, generous and confiding, learns to become meek towards all; towards
herself, so as no longer to be angry with herself
on account of her faults; towards her neighbour,
for the sight of her own miseries makes her compassionate the ills of others; towards God, for,
having come to understand that He treats her
better than she deserves, she becomes less importunate in seeking divine favours and less sullen
when God chastises her.

In proportion as she is purified and is enriched
by virtues, she becomes *peaceful,* and enters into a
state of great repose. The divine consolations and
caresses hide from her her misery and the infinite
distance which separates her from God; she finds,
in the midst of the darkness, a purifying light,
which imparts to her a correct knowledge of God
and of herself, a light already great, but which will
grow greater still in the state of spiritual purgation. Finally, the soul learns to keep God con-

tinually in remembrance, and to have a great fear
of backsliding in the spiritual way.

All the soul's virtues develop and ripen in time,
provided that she is generous enough to avoid
tepidity and discouragement. To the soul herself
her virtues appear a mere nothing, so dry and
meagre they seem to be; but they are, on that
account, all the better safe-guarded and are extremely pleasing to God, who knows what disinterested and persevering efforts they have cost.

3°. This aridity is the desert which leads to the
Promised Land.

God weans the soul, removes the swaddling
clothes of infancy, and sets her down that she may
walk by herself. He deprives her of infant's food
in order to give her the bread of the strong, a
bread suitable to nourish the spirit, when, amidst
dryness and darkness, it is devoid of sensible
devotion; a bread, in fine, which is nothing else
but infused contemplation. Such is the chief advantage which the soul gains, and which is the
source of all the rest. "The joy that, by occasion
of all this, is felt in heaven now breaks forth in all
its splendour." [1]

§ V.—Conduct to be Observed.

Two things are to be done: to accept trustfully
the state in which God has placed us; and, in order
to draw profit from it, to act with courage, both
during prayer and in the practice of virtue.

[1] *Night*, b. i. c. xii.

1°. *To accept of this state trustfully.*—God withdraws His consolations and plunges us into a state of dryness and desolation. Let us first see whether we have provoked this trial by our faults, our attachments, our dissipation. If we have, the penalty is only just, and let us make it also salutary by accepting it and correcting ourselves. If our conscience does not reproach us with any fault, let us adore lovingly the will of God, who is a good Father and a wise director; " let us, *without afflicting ourselves,* put our confidence in Him, who never forsakes those who seek Him with a simple and upright heart." [1] He is too wise a guide ever to lead us to our ruin. Without ever abandoning prayer, let us accept, even to the last sigh, this dryness and desolation, and let us not leave Jesus Christ to carry alone the burthen of His cross. . . . We are near our Master, and He is certainly nigh unto us. Sure of pleasing Him, let us ambition no other satisfaction. . . . Let Him lead us by whatever path He pleases; we belong no longer to ourselves, but to Him. True love does not consist in tears and sweetness; it is proved by serving Our Lord with courage and humility. Trouble takes away liberty of spirit and the courage to undertake great things for God; . . . and if, at other times, we were to feel ourselves powerless to do anything in the shape of meditation during one hour, this state of trouble would make us feel so four times as much. [2]

This state furnishes an excellent occasion for

---

[1] *Night*, b. i. c. x.   [2] St. Teresa, *Life*, ix. *passim.*

exercising the spirit of faith, the hope of eternal goods, disinterested love, Christian fortitude and all the other virtues. No virtue, perhaps, is more useful than a filial and loving abandonment of ourselves into God's hands; let us be thoroughly convinced that dryness and desolation, the most dreadful temptations, the inability to meditate and this feeble germ of dry contemplation, all obey God and serve His merciful designs. One thing only is to be feared; our own want of confidence and docility. Our resistance is the only hindrance that can mar His bountiful designs.

2°. *We must persevere courageously in prayer,* but without opposing the action of God. Let us not leave off meditation and affective prayer till God invites us to do so; that is, let us keep to them as long as they are possible for us, and do us more good; and this especially with regard to the Life and Passion of Our Lord.[1]—If a book, a statue or pious picture would help us to excite affections and to fix our thoughts, let us make use of it,[2] unless God is drawing us towards interior repose. At the times when passive purgation is interrupted, ordinary prayer becomes again possible and we should return to it.[3] Should God render us incapable of meditating, in order to pour into our soul that loving knowledge which forms the groundwork of contemplation, let us embrace this state with all confidence; for this most simple

---

[1] *Castle*, 6th mans. c. vii.   *Ascent*, b. ii. c. xiii. xiv. xv. xxxii. *Night*, b. i. c. x.
[2] See 2nd Part, c. ix. § vi. p. 212.   [3] *Ascent*, b. ii. c. xv.

attention to Him, this interior look fixed on God, these motions of love, of humility, and other like movements which carry the soul towards God, are not idle occupations. Our occupation, indeed, is not manifested by outward expressions and sentences, but it is nevertheless real; and God, who beholds the depths of the heart, understands this silent homage.[1] Let us avoid at such a time everything that might obstruct the action of God. At such a moment let the soul cease from meditating; besides, "though she should wish to continue meditating, she would not be able to do so." Let her abstain also from seeking with attachment after sensible relish and fervour, and from making acts too multiplied or too complex. "This would be to create an obstacle to the action of God, the principal agent, who is secretly and calmly pouring into the soul a loving knowledge and wisdom. . . . Let her then assume an *almost passive* attitude,—keeping herself in a state of pure, simple and loving attention, as one would do who opens the eyes merely to look with love upon another. . . . If God requires her for a time to make some special acts . . . let her be satisfied with making those to which God inclines her," *without doing violence to herself* in order to multiply them or to produce others.[2] For the chief action here is that of God, ours should be to second this, or even to cease from action altogether.

[1] *Ascent,* b. ii. c. xii. xiii. xiv. xv. *Night,* b. i. c. x.
[2] *Living Flame,* 3rd stanza, 3rd verse, § 6 and *passim. Ascent,* b. ii. c. xii. xiii. xv. xxxii. *Night,* b. i. c. ix. and x.

However, as the soul is far from being lost in God, she must still fight against distractions, courageously keep her look and her heart lovingly turned towards God, carefully avoid idleness—*i.e.*, that state of slothful inaction, in which the soul is no longer employed in looking and loving either by distinct acts or by loving attention. In spite of our dryness and disgust, let us have the patience and the courage to converse with God in the church and elsewhere, just the same as if He were giving us consolations. If the duration of these conversations with God should make them monotonous and distasteful, we can make them shorter and more frequent, but, in any case, let us not show any sullenness towards God.

3°. *For the purification of the soul and its advancement in virtues,* this state is a golden mine which must be courageously utilized. There is a treasure to be gotten from it; let us not stand with folded arms through fear of the cost. Let us apply ourselves with ardour and perseverance to enrich ourselves with the humility, abnegation, abandonment to God and the other virtues which this state brings with it.

If we meet with painful temptations, let us combat energetically; our faculties are in bonds, only when we are in prayer, and, even then, only with regard to too complex considerations and acts; we can always watch over ourselves, have recourse to God and fight the good fight. St. Teresa[1] "had more fear of a single venial sin

[1] *Life,* xxv.

than of all Hell together "; with a crucifix in her
hand she would defy all the demons, " she found
them to be so full of cowardice that the very sight of
her seemed to strike them with terror; the moment
they are despised they lose all courage." What
gives them power is our wavering and the feebleness of our resistance. The saint " could not understand those fears which make people say: The
devil, the devil! when they could say : God, God!
and thus make the infernal enemy tremble." God,
for whom we combat, will sustain us; temptation
cannot cross the limit set to it by the divine good
pleasure; it always has a providential purpose; it
attacks us on our weak side, and obliges us to
fortify that; it instructs us, spurs us on, crushes
pride, excites to prayer, calls for austerities and
elicits great resolutions; thus the demon becomes,
in his own despite, one of the most active agents of
our union with God.

Amidst failures, contradictions and other crosses
sent by Providence, nothing hinders us from having
recourse to God : how often all our trials vanish,
as if by enchantment, at the moment appointed by
the divine decrees! How often, also, the soul,
strengthened anew by grace, hardly feels her sufferings and offers herself to undergo fresh sacrifices! [1]
The most generous way to act is to conduct ourselves, " like a sick person under medical treatment," [2] and to accept of the remedy, although
bitter, and to conform ourselves exactly to the
divine prescriptions.

[1] *Life*, xxx.   [2] *Night*, b. i. c. ix.

Should sickness and infirmities aggravate our other sufferings, there is nothing to prevent us from having recourse to God and to our superiors, and obedience is a duty. We must not, however, give way to a burning anxiety to escape this trial, nor abuse it, in order to unduly diminish the burthen of regular observance; a generous soul will receive the cross from God's hand with patience, humility, and abandonment, she will even take occasion from it to renew in herself the spirit of austerity. Father De Padranos said one day to St. Teresa "that perhaps God was sending her so many sicknesses, only in order to exact from her a penance which she had failed to perform."[1] The saint candidly admits that "since she began to treat herself with less care and delicacy, she enjoyed much better health."[2] Let us renew in ourselves, if necessary, the esteem and love of suffering, and let us valiantly practice those austerities which are compatible with the state of our health.

In this state of dryness, desolation and overwhelming temptations, we stand more than ever in need of a spiritual guide, from whom nothing—neither the bad nor the good that is in us—should be hidden, in order that we may be securely directed, encouraged and sustained. Woe to the presumptuous soul who dares to be her own sole guide! God grant that the director also may know the road by his own experience; at least, that he may be learned; "the most enlightened

---

[1] *Life*, xxiv.   [2] *Ibid.*, xiii.

S

will be the best," as St. Teresa says. Our Lord always required from the saint obedience to her confessor.[1]

§ VI.—Duration of these Trials.

"The purgation of the senses with its accompanying pains and temptations lasts a longer or a shorter time, . . . but how long the soul will continue in this state no one can with certainty tell. . . . This varies according to the Divine Will, and is proportioned to the imperfections, many or few, which are to be purged away, and also to the degree of union in love to which God intends to elevate a particular soul, to the nature itself of the sufferings she must undergo," and finally to the fidelity of her correspondence with God's action. "Those who are endowed with a capacity for suffering, and who have strength sufficient to endure, God purifies in more intense trials and in less time; but those who are weak are purified more slowly and with consideration for their weakness." In the case of certain souls, the inability to meditate and the dryness are continual; with others, the mind at times resumes its liberty, and God grants them some consolations, lest they should lose courage and fall away; "these latter seem to have only one foot in this night, . . . and also they come late to the pureness of their perfection in this life, and some of them never reach it here below.'[2]

[1] *Life*, xiii. xxix. xxxiii. *Castle*, 6th mans. c. ix.
[2] *Night*, b. i. c. ix. and xiv.

As to " souls still weaker, God tries them by showing Himself to them and again hiding Himself from them," in order to make them seek after Him. He does not use the same precautions in regard to strong souls, whom He wants to raise to the union of love; still, however quickly God may lead them, experience shows that they are wont to remain a long time in this state of sensitive purgation [1]; generally speaking, it lasts a certain number of years.[2]

The first night is the germ and bud of passive prayer; however, certain persons have to endure this trial later on, as St. Teresa [3] says. With time, the state of quiet becomes more marked, and the inability of the mind to meditate " goes on ever increasing." [4] But, " at the moment the soul least thinks of it, God makes her feel a most spiritual sweetness, and communicates to her a most pure love and a most delicate spiritual knowledge." [5] She passes then through an alternating succession of ardent prayer, whereby love is wonderfully developed, and of progressive aridity, whereby the soul is ever more and more purified, whilst the longing for God, having become more intense, singularly dilates her capacity of loving and receiving Him. This purgation pursues its course in this way throughout the primary stages of contemplation. If it is God's good pleasure, and the soul is generous, this state, after a period of repose, is commonly quitted only to enter into the night of

---

[1] *Night*, b. i. c. xiv.
[2] Scaramelli, *Dir. Myst.*, 5th treatise c. xiii. 4th counsel.
[3] *Life*, xi.   [4] *Night*, b. i. c. ix.   [5] *Ibid.*, b. i. c. xiii.

the spirit, which is more difficult and grievous, and by means of it, to advance towards the perfect union of love; but it is only "a very small number" who arrive there.[1]

Is it a duty to pray for the end of these trials, on the pretext that they are a sort of ailment, and that, being called to contemplation, we should hasten to enter into it? We do not think so.

1°. This arid contemplation is a remedy and not an evil. The wounds to be healed are pride, spiritual gluttony, and the too great dependence of the superior faculties upon the senses. Seeing that the soul continues on her way to be purified in the fire of mystical union, it is necessary that she should enter upon this passive purgation and stay a long time in the bitterness of this first night. We know whither it is leading us. Are we not all the more free, when we abandon ourselves courageously into God's hands and leave everything to the heavenly physician, who knows better than we do the remedy, the dose and the time it requires?

2°. We ought to make haste to enter into the state of contemplation. No doubt; but this is already done, since it is the self-same contemplation which is now purging the soul before setting it on fire. It will be developed in the same proportion as this purgation shall have better prepared the soul for union; the more God ploughs and harrows the soul, the better chance the precious seed has of living and of producing flowers and fruit.

[1] *Night*, b. i. c. xiv. and b. ii. c. i.

As, however, God's ulterior designs are concealed from us, it is quite permissible to pray for an end of these trials, provided it be with submission and purity of intention; but, in our opinion, it would be much better to leave God to act according to His pleasure and to ask Him only for generosity and patience. This seems to us the wisest and most valiant way to show our good will and to seek for progress.

ART. II.—PASSIVE PURGATION OF THE SPIRIT.

§ I.—WHEN IT TAKES PLACE AND WHAT IT IS.

St. John of the Cross teaches that, between the night of the senses and that of the spirit, God grants "long years" of repose, during which a much relished contemplation is developed in the exercises of the progressive way. The spiritual part, thanks to its first purgation, walks onward untrammelled; it is no longer attached to consolations; its powers are no longer entangled in the chains of reasoning; " the spirit soon reposes with ease in a serene and loving contemplation accompanied with spiritual relish." As the purification of the soul, after the night of the senses only, is yet far from being complete, this state of transition " does not exclude aridities, darkness and anguish; at times these are even more intense than during the purification of the senses; but they are less prolonged. After some days of these storms, serenity returns to the soul with its wonted joys." The senses, now

purified, begin to share in the joys of the spirit, but
are as yet too weak to support the intensity of the
divine communications. Hence it comes that, in
this intermediate time, ecstasies, raptures, and even
strange physical phenomena may happen ; all which
will no longer take place after the night of the spirit ;
for then the senses and the spirit, being freer,
stronger and purer, will be able to sustain the
action of God without giving way.[1]

This passive purgation of the spirit never pre-
cedes that of the senses, rarely accompanies it,
but, generally speaking, follows it, after an intermediate period of repose. Yet God remains always
master of His own action and time ; He is not bound
to follow any invariable course.[2]

In spite of the purgation of the senses, there still
remain in the spirit some habitual imperfections.
These are defective affections and dispositions,
which that first night has been unable to uproot,
because they have their *roots in the spirit* ; there is,
moreover, a sort of spiritual stupidity, which
renders the spirit subject to distractions and effu-
siveness. There remain also actual imperfections :
pride, for instance, which insinuates itself into
everything that wears an appearance of holiness,
such as ecstasies, visions and revelations ; a certain boldness and want of respect in God's regard,
a too great greed of spiritual sweetness, &c. " The
manner and operations of the soul are still on a
low level, . . . she thinks of the things of God

[1] *Night*, b. ii. c. i.

[2] Scaramelli, *Dir. Myst.*, 5th treatise c. xv, St. Liguori,
Praxis, 129 and 137.

like a child, she speaks of God like a child, her acts and sentiments are the acts and sentiments of a child."[1] On account of the intimate union of the sensitive with the intellectual part of the soul, "neither of them can be perfectly purified without the other"; the purgation of the senses prepares the soul to endure that of the spirit, which, in its turn, *completes* that of the senses.[2] The night of the senses is "rather a reformation than a purgation properly so called"; the night of the spirit proceeds even to the plucking up of the root of the evil; the former is painful, the latter terrible. Both are a purifying aridity which, remotely or proximately, leads on to the perfect union of love; the one is wrought out in the sensible part of the soul, the other, in the intelligence and the will; each is brought about by a special operation of God, which is none other than *obscure contemplation* itself in certain conditions. It is easy to conceive that this divine influence first penetrates the exterior and interior senses before entering into the superior and more inward faculties; in the beginning, contemplation was *too feeble,* and the soul was suffering from not enjoying God; now, it will be *too strong,* and it is its very strength which afflicts the soul in divers ways.

In short, the night of the spirit is a mysterious influence which God exerts, by means of a vigorous but obscure contemplation, upon the superior faculties, in order to *purify* them, and thus to prepare them for the perfect union of love.

[1] *Night,* b. ii. c. iii.   [2] *Ibid.,* b. ii. c. iii.

§ II.—Sufferings of this State.

1°. " God withdraws from the soul the relish and
feeling of spiritual things which it used to experience." [1]   The first state of aridity had dried up sensible devotion and the sweetness of meditation; this
takes away accidental spiritual devotion and the
sweets of contemplation.   The soul retains a
prompt and generous will to serve God in every
way, but she is plunged in darkness and dryness.

2°. God communicates to the soul such vivid
lights, that, unable to bear their strength and impetuosity, she is dazzled and pained by them. The
senses and the spirit suffer, as though they were
oppressed by an immense weight, and are plunged
in a cruel agony. Just so the pure and vivid
brightness of the sun dazzles and afflicts eyes that
are sore.   The light of contemplation, much
stronger now than formerly, trammels still more
our natural operations; the memory is more devoid
of every remembrance that has not reference to
God, the intellect experiences a more profound in-
capability, the will and the senses are plunged in a
more complete aridity.

3°. A horrible suffering, which St. John of the
Cross [2] and St. Teresa [3] have described in a thrill-
ing fashion, comes from the fact that this contemplation brings into a most vivid light God's infinite
greatness and our own nothingness, His holiness
and our sinfulness; it is, in fact, an only too evi-

Night, b. ii. c. iii.   [2] *Ibid.*, b. ii. c. v. and *ff*.
          [3] *Castle*, 6th mans. c. i. *Life*. xxx.

dently infused knowledge of God and of ourselves.[1] The poor soul is seized with trembling in the presence of so lofty a majesty; she is terrified at her own hideous deformity and numberless offences. Whatever good she has done is hidden from her; the divine graces given her stand out in strong contrast with her sins; a terrible anguish crushes her in the presence of God's holiness and justice; she believes herself to be all mud and filth, devoid of every virtue; it seems to her impossible that God could love so horrible an object or endure such infection; besides, was she ever worth anything? Has she not lived under a perpetual delusion? Is she not then justly abandoned, hopelessly lost? She wishes only for God, but God seems taken away from her for ever, she is drowned in an ocean of bitterness, horribly tempted against hope.—This, however, is but the vivid thrill of adoration, it is regret, shame, desire and love, not a falling away, not a back-sliding down the slope of negligence; for this soul fears the least fault more than death; she so loves God that she would sacrifice a thousand lives for His sake; in this dreadful storm faith has not foundered; the despair is only apparent, and has its seat only in the sensitive nature; it is the love of God and the fear of losing Him which subjects the soul to such a torture, and this alone should be sufficient to reassure her.

But God permits that no one is able to give her any lasting consolation. She is herself reduced to

---

[1] St. Liguori, *Praxis*, 129.

a state of utter helplessness; mental prayer is, as it were, impossible to her, vocal prayer and spiritual reading have no meaning for her; she finds everywhere a thousand subjects of affliction; nowhere anything to reassure her.

For souls in this state there remains no other resource [1] than to hope against all hope, to throw themselves with entire abandonment into the arms of God. St. Teresa advises that in such a time the soul should create a diversion by employing herself in pious occupations. The heat of these pains is felt only from time to time and not continuously, otherwise it would cause death. The assaults which St. Teresa herself endured lasted eight days, fifteen days, or even three weeks.[2] During this time the sufferer believes they will never end; but God dispels them, and "then it seems as if there never had been a cloud in the soul."[3] "When the union is to be serious and real, this night, however generous the soul may be, lasts for several years,"[4] with the above-mentioned alternatives of storm and calm. The suffering is sometimes so violent that the soul seems to see the abyss open at her feet and ready to engulph its victim. This state is a *hell* in its pain, a *purgatory* in its purifying power. St. John of the Cross affirms that those souls shall not pass through the fire of the next world, or at least shall not remain long therein; unknown to themselves, they are now being purified even to their inmost depths, and the spiritual

[1] St. Liguori, *Praxis*, 130.   [3] *Castle*, 6th mans. c. i.
[2] *Life*, xxx.   [4] *Night*, b. ii. c. vii.

marriage is the goal at which these terrible trials terminate.

4°. St. John of the Cross [1] and, in a more special way, St. Teresa,[2] describe another passive purgation, which is worked out in *the tortures of love.* There is no question here of those alternating states familiar to contemplatives, wherein God casts the soul into transports by manifesting Himself, and again plunges it into anxious desires by hiding Himself; for the trials here spoken of are very special, crucifying and sublime.

Previous to the period of her great raptures, St. Teresa had during some years very frequently received the *wound* of love. The soul feels that God is near her, and that He is calling her; fired, transported, desperate with love, she almost dies through her desire of seeing Him; and, not being able to possess Him at her ease here below, she is dying on account of not being able to die. She conceives a horror for the world and her own wretched body; she " is rudely tormented between the excess of her transports and that of her powerlessness." [3] It is as though a sharp-pointed arrow inflicted a deep wound upon the soul, and made it suffer a real martyrdom; and at times the body is almost deprived of feeling. This torture is so intense that the sufferer cannot help uttering groans, and at the same time so delightful that the soul

---

[1] *Night*, b. ii. c. xi. and *ff.*

[2] *Life*, xx. xxix. *Castle*, 6th mans. c. ii. and xi. *Rel. II. to Fr. Rodr. Alvarez.*

[3] St. Francis of Sales, *Love of God*, vi. 13.

would never wish it to cease. It lasts rather long
sometimes, now diminishing, now increasing; at
other times, rather a short while, either because this
flame becomes extinct, or because it all ends in a
rapture.

God completed the purgation of St. Teresa's soul
by a species of suffering still more painful and more
spiritual than the preceding. In the wound of
love, the body shared in the suffering and also in
the sweetness; here, it is admitted to a share of the
suffering, but not of the enjoyment, " the soul alone
tastes the delight of this new kind of martyrdom." In the former case, God made Himself
felt to be quite near, the soul understood that
He was calling her; in the latter, He shows
Himself at a great distance; there, the soul
transported with love, seized with a violent desire
of beholding God, was almost dying because she
could not die; here, she experiences the same impatient and torturing hunger, but with this peculiar
character, that, seeking after God and finding Him
nowhere, *she feels herself to be in a boundless
desert,* crucified between heaven, which she does
not yet possess, and earth, which is no longer anything to her. God communicates to the soul a most
vivid knowledge of His amiable qualities; and this
light sharpens her desires and her torment. The
pain is so great that the body is tortured by it;
but of this the soul has no perception at the
moment, so much more poignant is this wound of
the spirit. " It is a martyrdom of pains and of
joys "; a martyrdom which terrifies nature, but out

of which the soul would never wish to issue, because
she knows its charm and its value. It is of com-
paratively short duration, not lasting more than a
few hours. In it, life itself runs a real risk, both
on account of the extreme pains which accompany
it and the violent rapture by which it terminates.
Happy the victims whom this divine affliction torments! Alas! dare we say that we have ever loved
God?

This holy violence tears the soul away from
everything created; the great fear, which she experiences at the sight of her miseries, extirpates the
last roots of pride; the crucible of divine love completes the destruction of everything human that
remained in her; her faculties, reduced to a more
thorough emptiness, have become supple and docile
to receive the action of God; henceforth the soul is
purified, disciplined, illuminated, inflamed; she is
ready for perfect union with God.

To sum up, it is contemplation itself, which at
one time, darkens, dries up, tortures, and purifies
souls, at another, sheds over them a pure light and
inundates them with a love full of sweetness. It
produces different effects according to the various
dispositions of the soul : the same fire produces at
once a clear and burning flame, if the wood is dry;
but it begins by blackening, drying, and preparing
the green wood, before enveloping it in a pure and
delightful blaze.[1] This depends also upon the will
of God, who, ever wise and merciful, communicates to contemplation an activity, sometimes pur-

[1] *Night*, b. ii. c. x.

gative, sometimes enlightening and inflaming. He knows how to make Thabor succeed to Calvary, to humble and annihilate the soul by crucifying it, to fortify and prepare it for fresh trials by manifesting Himself. In the sweetness of these meetings with God, past agonies are dispelled like a dream and forgotten; yet the soul feels, as it were instinctively, that Calvary still awaits her, because she has not completely died to herself; for these trials will entirely cease, only when the fire of contemplation finds nothing more to purify and the faculties are well disciplined. If the divine action is strong and the soul docile, the trial will be less prolonged; let the soul submit to it with courage and not complain; for the rigour and duration of these mysterious pains are the announcement of and preparation for the more sublime ascents in prayer and perfection.

Is there any need to observe that the passive purgation of the senses marks the first steps in mystical ways, and that that of the spirit leads on to the summit? Both, however, belong to the same order of ideas and form a complete whole. This is the reason why we thought it best to explain both of them together, although, generally speaking, the passive purgation of the spirit does not take place for a long time after most of those states of prayer which it remans for us now to describe.

CHAPTER IV

OF MYSTICAL CONTEMPLATION

§ I.—SUPERNATURAL OR PASSIVE PRAYER.

MYSTICAL contemplation is a *passive contemplation;* or, if you prefer it, a manifestly supernatural, infused and passive contemplation, wherein God, who generally makes the soul feel His presence, becomes known in an ineffable manner, and is possessed by a loving union, which communicates to the soul repose and peace, and exerts an influence upon the senses.

It is a contemplation, a *prayer of simple look*[1] which proceeds from love and rests in love. So long as the soul has not reached this simple, amorous, and peaceful attention, she is still engaged in the noisy and complicated labour of meditation, or in the more simplified work of affective prayer. We have already[2] pointed out, with St. John of the Cross,[3] that there is an intermediate period during which the soul sometimes meditates, sometimes contemplates; when one and the same prayer may begin with meditation and end in con-

---

[1] See 2nd part, c. ix. § ii. p. 197.
[2] See 3rd part, c. iii. § i. p. 249.
[3] *Ascent*, b. ii. c. xv.

templation. Then comes a time when grace is given always for contemplation, never for meditation, so that whenever the soul prays, she does so by means of this simple and loving look. She has then acquired the perfect habit of contemplation, and enters upon it, as it were, *at her pleasure*.

This is a manifestly supernatural contemplation. In every kind of prayer there must be both God and man, grace and co-operation with grace. In acquired contemplation, the action of God remains hidden, we know it by faith and prove it by reason; in mystical prayer it is manifest, we feel it, it is a fact of our experience.—St. Teresa never loses an opportunity [1] of reminding us that mystical contemplation is supernatural, entirely supernatural, manifestly supernatural; she asserts that this is so even from the prayer of quiet.

Now, "she calls supernatural, whatever we cannot acquire of ourselves, no matter what care and diligence we employ. In this respect, all we can do is to dispose ourselves for it, and a great point, too, is this disposing of ourselves for it." [2] Speaking elsewhere of the prayer of quiet, the saint says: "Just as we cannot make the day dawn nor prevent the night from succeeding to it, so we cannot either procure for ourselves so great a good, nor retain it a single instant beyond the time fixed by the will of Our Lord. It is a favour entirely supernatural, we ourselves have no part in it, our

---

[1] *Way*, xxvi. xxxii. &c. *Life*, xii. xiv. xv. xvii. xx. xxi. xxii. xxiii. xxix. &c. *Castle*, 4th mans. c. i. ii. iii.; 5th mans. c. i. &c.
[2] *II. Rel. to Fr. Rodr. Alvarez. Ascent*, b. iii. c. i.

own efforts cannot attain to it." [1]   Alas! we can
only too easily banish God by our infidelities, or
oppose His action by doing things incompatible
with prayer.   " The impurity and the imperfections
of the soul are the only obstacles to this grace, just
as the spots of dirt upon a window-pane are
obstacles to the light." [2]   We can, on the other
hand, remove the obstacles and positively dispose
ourselves for this grace, as we have just shown. [3]
Notwithstanding all this, God remains master of
His gifts : " He distributes His favours, when He
pleases, in what manner He pleases, and to whom
He pleases." [4]   Here is the reason why all authors,
with St. Teresa, [5] so strongly recommend us not to
seek to thrust ourselves into supernatural contemplation.   This would be to deprive ourselves of
meditation without reaching contemplation ; a culpable presumption, a foolish attempt, a labour
absolutely thrown away.   By disposing herself, indeed, the soul reaches the door, but God alone can
open it.

Since mystical prayer is supernatural, it is consequently *infused on God's part, passive on the
part of the soul.* [6]   These expressions recur unceasingly in the writings of St. John of the Cross.
Now, God shows Himself to the soul whenever it

[1] *Way,* xxxii.
[2] *Ascent,* b. ii. c. xvi.
[3] See 3rd part c. ii. p. 228 and *ff.*
[4] *Castle,* 4th mans., c. i.
[5] *Life,* xii.
[6] The expressions "supernatural" and "infused" are here
synonymous, we use them both only because they serve to
mutually explain each other.

T

seems good to Himself : at prayer, at spiritual reading, at manual work, during conversation, or sometimes in the midst of the most ordinary thoughts and occupations. Sometimes the soul expects a visit, but God does not come ; at other times He shows Himself " at the moment when He is least expected and when the soul is very far from aspiring to any such favour." [1] " In the beginning, it is true," says St. Teresa, when speaking of ecstasy, " that this occurs almost always after a prolonged mental prayer. God at first is pleased to make the soul ascend towards Him step by step; afterwards He takes up this little dove and places it in the nest that it may rest itself there." [2] Likewise, God gives Himself to the soul in whatever manner He Himself wills : the contemplation will be consoling or dry, according as He judges it well to inflame the soul or to purify it. However well prepared a soul may be, the divine favours remain favours, and never become a right or the salary of our efforts. God gives such form and such intensity to her prayer as He wills; sometimes He inebriates her with light and love; at others, He only half satisfies her hunger, or hardly throws her some few crumbs; and it is not in our power to render this infusion more copious, nor to leave the state of quiet for complete union or ecstasy. Finally, He withdraws Himself when He wills, and none can keep Him when He wills it not.

This explains the constant fluctuations to which contemplation is subject. At times it is feeble, it is

---

[1] *Ascent*, b. ii. c. xxvi. and xxxii.   [2] *Life*, xviii.

at other times strong, but only to decrease again and grow strong again. " If sometimes it lasts a somewhat long while, it is always increasing or diminishing; in fact, it never perseveres in the same state, . . . but varies according as Our Lord is pleased to communicate Himself; . . . because this operation is altogether divine.'" [1] These fluctuations are to be met with even in one and the same prayer; for a stronger reason, amongst a succession of prayers, one will be ardent, another feeble, or medium, or very intense; the soul will be now in full union, the next moment in quite a low degree of quietude. Alas! this is an abundant source of bitter deceptions. The soul hopes to take hold of God, but He escapes from her. It is sometimes a paternal chastisement, when the soul has been in fault; often, it is a loving artifice to excite desire and pursuit. However, if the soul is faithful, and if such is the good pleasure of God, the level of the prayers, taken all together, should ascend to a higher point, and the virtues should ever be on the increase.

Thus, " The Divine Majesty communicates Himself to the soul *which remains passive,* as light is communicated to the mind of him who has his eyes open." [2] It is necessary, therefore, " for the soul to assume an *almost passive* attitude without any thought of acting by herself; but keeping herself in a simple, pure and loving attention, as a person would do who voluntarily opens the eyes to look with love upon another." " God is the agent

Castle, 6th mans. c. ii. *Life*, xviii.   [2] *Ascent*, b. ii. c. xv.

who infuses and touches, whilst the soul is the recipient." *During the whole time that God is pouring into her His light and His love,* the soul should be attentive to gather in what God deigns to give her. If she tries to meditate as formerly, to multiply distinct acts, "other than those which God inclines her to," to seek spiritual relish and fervour by the old methods, in a word, to act by herself instead of lovingly yielding herself up to receive, she thereby hinders God's action. "God wants to speak to her, . . . but she makes a disturbance in the midst of silence." He is pouring into her a supremely desirable light and love; "but she will receive this benefit only in small measure and imperfectly, and not in all that plenitude with which it is offered her." Or, rather, she throws obstacles in its way, and will lose this benefit altogether.[1] "This is," in the words of St. Teresa, "to throw water on the fire, to blow so strongly upon the torch as to extinguish it."[2] It is at the same time to increase dryness, trouble, fatigue, disgust. On the contrary, "the more the soul accustoms herself to this repose, the more it increases, the more, also, increases that general and loving knowledge of God, in which she finds a peace, a repose, a relish and an enjoyment exempt from all effort and more agreeable than all else."[3]

For the very reason that contemplation is in-

---

[1] *Living Flame*, 3rd stanza, 3rd verse § v. vi. vii. viii. *Ascent*, b. ii. c. xi. xii. xiii. xv. *Night*, b. i. c. ix. and x. &c.
[2] *Life*, xv. *Way*, xxxii.   [3] *Ascent*, b. ii. c. xiii.

fused on God's part, and passive on the part of the soul, *it demands less labour,* in proportion as it is more elevated; in complete union, the labour is reduced to almost nothing; in ecstasy, there is no longer any. This, however, is far from being the case in the state of quiet.[1]

In short, "it is very seldom"[2] that contemplation is completely passive. The co-operation of the will is necessary, in order that the mind may remain fixed in this simple look, and the heart continue in this movement, or these acts of love; this is a pleasure, and, as it were, a necessity rather than a labour, when the soul is powerfully affected; but if God's action is weak, there is need of energy and of a wearisome labour, in order to repel distractions, to overcome weariness and disgust. The soul is then in a state of painful dryness, wherein she feels the need of making acts that are dry and without relish, in order to supplement the insufficient occupation which she is receiving from God. Infused light and love, nevertheless, still remain the constituent elements of the contemplation. There is then a double operation : God's and our own, infused and acquired, passive and active. But obviously the principal action is that of God, our own action should be subordinate to this, and should second it, or altogether vanish.

Here, then, is the first characteristic of mystical prayer. It is impossible for the soul to raise herself to it by any efforts of her own; God gives it, she

---

[1] *Life,* xi. xiv. xvi. xviii. *Way,* xxxii. *Ascent,* b. ii. xv.
[2] *Life,* xxvii.

receives it. It is by experience that the soul
acquires the certainty of this. In the common ways
of prayer, we feel that we ourselves are acting; we
can tell precisely the thought that has moved us,
and, by using the same means again, we can reproduce more or less the same effects. Here, on
the contrary, we are conscious that we are passive;
when light and love inundate the soul she feels
that it is another that is pouring them into her,
that all her own efforts are powerless either to give
rise to them, to keep them, or to bring them back
again. When all has disappeared, she perceives
that she is again alone and abandoned to herself;
He who was operating in her has withdrawn.
When God's action is so slight as to leave the soul
in a state of desolation, she sees too well that her
understanding is fettered, and that she is powerless
to enlighten and inflame herself. A great lesson
this in humility, dependence and filial fear towards
God!

§ II.—How in this state God is known in a way that is ineffable.

Let us enter more deeply into the interior
nature of passive contemplation and consider its
constituent elements.

These are at once both light and love mysteriously produced in us.—According to St. John
of the Cross, contemplation is "the science of
love, the infused and loving knowledge of God, it
enlightens and inflames the soul so as to raise it

by degrees towards God its Creator; for love is the sole means to unite the soul to God." [1]   God communicates, then, "a light which warms." "The knowledge thus received is general and obscure; as the intellect does not understand distinctly what it conceives, so the will also loves generally and indistinctly; [2] it is a vague love, a secret instinct, which carries the soul towards the object beloved.   For, as God is light and love, in this delicate communication He informs equally the intellect and the will, though at times His presence is felt in the one more than in the other; one, for instance, finds himself more filled with knowledge than with love, in another, love is deeper than intelligence." [3]—"The mystical influence is exercised directly upon the intellect, and the will participates in it; . . . sometimes it strikes simultaneously both intellect and will, and then love redoubles in strength, tenderness and perfection. . . . As long as the intellect's purgation is not completed, it is the will that most frequently takes fire under the divine touch, before the intellect receives any perfect communications." [4]

This loving knowledge has for its object God or Our Lord.   "It is God Himself that is tasted and felt in this state, not, indeed, with that luminous evidence that we shall have in heaven, but by a view so elevated, so consoling and so penetrating

[1] *Night*, b. ii. c. xviii.

[2] *Living Flame*, 3rd stanza, 3rd verse, § x.

[3] *Ascent*, b. ii. c. xiv. *Living Flame*, 3rd stanza, 3rd verse, § x. *Spir. Canticle*, stanza xxvi., 2nd verse. St. Francis of Sales, *Love of God*, b. vi. c. iv.   [4] *Night*, ii. c. xiii.

that the soul is impregnated by it even to the inner-
most depths of its being," [1] when this mystical
influence is strong.

This light does not come from the work of our
mind, from the force of our reasonings; on the
contrary, the more vivid the light is, the more
our understanding is fettered and reduced to
impotence. God it is, who pours this light into
the soul, sometimes, in the midst of some pious
occupation, sometimes, unexpectedly, and even
amidst the most common kinds of work. He
measures it out at times with a sparing hand, and the
soul suffers from this low diet; at other times,
" without arguments or reasoning, in the space of
a single *Credo,* He illuminates the soul with more
light than she could with all her efforts acquire in
several years." [2] When this mystical light is
more sensible and less pure, it is then more accessible to our view, and we very wrongly judge it to
be clearer and of greater value. But when it is
very pure and excites a quite spiritual love, " the
soul may very well be occupied with it without
her perceiving that it is so. . . . This light
escapes our notice then, only on account of its very
purity, perfection and simplicity." [3]

It is, above all, an *experimental* knowledge,
which teaches us more than any amount of reasoning and books. No one knows God like those
who have experienced the union of love. Before,
they had only heard of Him; now they know

[1] *Ascent,* ii. c. xxvi.   [2] St. Teresa, *Life,* xii.
[3] *Ascent,* ii. c. xiv.

Him by experience because they have felt, tasted, and, as it were, touched with their finger His goodness, His tenderness, His infinite condescension, His character. This knowledge is both light and savour ; it has the taste of God, the aroma of eternity.[1] The soul, beneath these divine touches, resembles a child, whom its mother presses lovingly to her heart; this silent embrace expresses more than any words; the child has heard nothing, seen nothing, neither has he reasoned, he has merely felt that loving embrace, and now he knows the heart of his mother.

This mystical light ends by giving us a most exalted knowledge of God and of ourselves, of His infinite greatness, of our own littleness, and of the nothingness of all created things. Notwithstanding its vividness, it remains *obscure* and *confused,* vague and general. For it shows us God in one simple and collected view, without fixing our attention upon His divers perfections, His wisdom, His power, His immensity, &c. It makes us take, as it were, a general view of Our Lord without bringing into relief each of His different mysteries, or the details of what He has done to save us ; or, if it does fix our attention upon some attribute of God, on His beauty, His goodness, His love, His mercy, or upon some mystery of Our Lord, it does so in a general sort of a way, which, not stopping at details, remains of necessity vague and confused.[2] Besides, God so secretly and mys-

---

[1] *Living Flame,* 2nd stanza, 4th verse.
[2] St. Francis of Sales, *Love of God,* b. vi. c. vi.

teriously pours this light into the soul that " she herself does not perceive how it is done." At times, also, " the contemplation is so simple that it can hardly at all be perceived. The soul only knows that she is satisfied, tranquil, content, she tastes God, and feels that all is well; but it is only in very vague and general terms that she can tell what it is she possesses."[1]

Truly those authors are very right who say that obscure contemplation is " an experimental perception of God," [2] " God ineffably perceived," [3] in a confused and mysterious light.

Besides this obscure and general contemplation, there is another which is distinct and particular. This sees, hears, grasps clearly particular objects, or concrete truths, which are supernaturally presented to the soul. It operates especially by visions, revelations, interior words, &c. It is not our intention to speak of this. St. Teresa,[4] St. John of the Cross,[5] and a number of excellent authors,[6] have superabundantly treated of this subject. We shall merely call attention to the fact that obscure contemplation is always without danger: it is a loving look upon God, a simple view of faith, into which no error can glide. We cannot say the same of particularised and distinct contemplation: for, it is easy to mistake for a divine illumination, the work of our own mind,

---

[1] *Night*, ii. c. xvii.   [2] Gerson, Tr. 7 c. ii.
[3] Ven. John of St. Samson, *Maxims*, c. xxi.
[4] *Life* and *Castle, passim*.   [5] *Ascent, passim*.
[6] Fr. Poulain, *Graces of Prayer*, xx. and *ff*.

our reveries, the illusions of the demon, and also
to misinterpret the sense and bearing of the divine
communications themselves. A certain nun, who
had ecstasies, perhaps too, quite genuine ones, has
had two of her works put upon the Index, namely,
" Views upon the Priesthood " and her " Life."

§ III.—How God in this state is ineffably LOVED.

St. John of the Cross, following St. Thomas,
never ceases repeating that, in the mystical kinds
of prayer, light and love are inseparable, or,
rather, that love is the principle of contemplation;
" it is love which teaches this secret science of God,
it is love which renders it so sweet." [1]   " It is by
means of love that it is communicated to, and
spread throughout the world." [2]   St. Francis of
Sales, in like manner, teaches that " meditation is
the mother of love, but contemplation its daughter.
.   .   . The desire of obtaining divine love makes
us meditate, love, being obtained, makes us contemplate; for love makes us find so agreeable a
sweetness in the object beloved, that we can never
satiate our mind with seeing and considering it." [3]
Nor could it otherwise be explained how a mother
has the patience to remain for hours near the cradle

[1] *Spirit Canticle*, stanza xxvii.
[2] *Night*, ii. c. xii. and xvii. *Living Flame*, 3rd stanza, 3rd
verse, § 10.
[3] *Love of God*, b. vi. c. iii. b. vii. c. v.

of her child and to take pleasure in doing so; so, likewise, in arid contemplation, there must be a secret, but very real and living love which keeps the soul enchained near God, despite the pain and weariness of her condition.

In its turn, contemplation " gives rise to a greater and more fervent love, which, at last, is crowned with perfection, when it comes to enjoy what it loves. By this perpetual movement from love to sight, . . . and from sight to love, . . . love urges the eyes to look ever more attentively upon the beauty of the Well-Beloved, and this view compels the heart to love ever more ardently." [1]

It is God who inflames the will when and how He pleases. " The soul finds itself at times agitated by outbursts of the most pure love, without being able to understand from what cause this proceeds, . . . without even knowing (by a distinct knowledge at first) what it is loving."[2] Nevertheless, that it is God, that it is Our Lord she loves, there can be no doubt. This love may be almost imperceptible, whether it be that God pours in only a few drops of it, or that it is too pure and spiritual to be grasped by the senses; it is to be judged by its fruits. This love will be at times neither very strong nor very weak, in fact, one might have as much and even more of it during ordinary prayer. At other times, it will be like an overflowing of tenderest affection which transports

---

[1] *Love of God*, b. vi. c. iii. b. vii. c. v.
[2] *Ascent*, ii. c. xiv. and xxiv. *Way*, xxvi.

the soul out of herself. At such times she remains fixed and, as it were, motionless, lost in admiration, in trembling delight, respect and joy; she says nothing, or almost nothing, she speaks not of her love; but she shows it by loving. Her attitude, her tremulous joy, her silence, the movements of her heart which incline unceasingly towards God—all this is a splendid hymn of praise and a delight to Him who holds her captive. Or again, there may take place those violent and burning outbursts, those transports of spiritual inebriation, which spring from a too full heart in noisy and oft-repeated effusions, like the waves of a tumultuous torrent. One may be seized " with such strength and in so sensible a fashion, that not only the soul, but even the body itself trembles. At other times, it happens that without even the least shock, but with a most elevated sentiment of relief and enjoyment, the soul is taken by surprise in the midst of repose. . . . There is found in this an inexpressible something of divine being and of eternal life, which the demon has not the power to imitate. He, who is the ape of God, can indeed make the soul experience a very sensible elevation and satiety, which he will pass off for the inward action of God; but such modifications do not sink very deeply, and do not renovate the whole interior of the soul by filling her with noble sentiments and love, as this infused knowledge of God is wont to do." [1]

Besides the fact that this love is passive, general

[1] *Ascent*, b. ii. c. xxvi.

and obscure, its proper character is to be unitive.
The soul, now pure and rich in virtues, is no longer
a slave who fears, a mercenary who gives his services for pay, a timid friend who loves from afar
off; she is a spouse who wishes to possess the God
of her heart, to unite herself to Him by love, and
to make but one with Him. In the night of the
senses she experiences a dolorous need of this
union, and calls for it with all her prayers; in the
sweet state of quiet she begins to find it; she aspires
only to make progress in mystical ways, in order
to tighten these bonds so much desired, and to
arrive at the perfection of this union.[1]

§ IV.—How in this state the presence of God is felt.

In the ordinary kinds of prayer we *think* of God,
we *remember* God, we know Him by faith. In
passive contemplation, the soul generally feels a
mysterious impression. God, who dwells in the
soul of the just, manifests His presence there in a
manner which must be experienced to be understood. The soul has an experimental perception
that she possesses God and is united to Him, that
she is, so to speak, plunged in God and all penetrated by Him; and, when this impression becomes
strong, it is like a loving clasp of the hand, a
spiritual embrace. Then the soul is as sure of the

---

[1] *Ascent*, b. ii. c. xxvi. and xxxii. Abbé Saudreau, *Degrés*, b. v.
c. iii. St. Francis of Sales (*Love of God*, b. vii. c. i. and *ff*.)
explains very well this mystical union.

presence of God as if she saw Him with her eyes and touched Him with her hands, because she *feels* Him in herself.   This is a fact established by the experience of all mystics, and no author denies it. Father Poulain brings forward in support of this statement authorities both various and decisive.[1] St. Teresa, amongst others, learned in this way that God resides in our soul; she could never believe that a person had been favoured with the prayer of union, unless there remained when the prayer was ended a most firm certainty that the soul had been with God.   She affirms in ten places that this sentiment of God's presence is to be found from the time of the state of quiet.   It remains obscure and veiled, when the mystical influx is feeble; but when this influence grows strong this sense of God's presence manifests itself more clearly.   Here, however, authors begin to differ.

One set of writers, relying upon the authority of Scaramelli and many other authors, think that this mysterious impression may be explained by saying that everything takes place as if there were a contact of God with the soul, a contact which would exite in the soul a spiritual perception realised by an interior touch.   Others,[3] while admitting that, perhaps, in exceptional cases, certain divine touches, of which St. John of the Cross speaks, must be understood of a contact of sub-

[1] Fr. Poulain, *Graces of Prayer*, c. v. and vi.

[2] *Ibid*, especially No. 11.

[3] Abbé Saudreau, *Etat Mystique*, c. x.

stance with substance between God and the soul,
yet say that, generally speaking, the presence of
God is made evident by a manifest action which
He exercises over the intellect and the will. In
support of their opinion they quote St. Teresa,
saying that, " in the state of quiet and of union,
certain divine impressions are rendered sensible;
yet the presence of God is there indicated only by
the effects of grace, which are an ardent love, a
lively faith, firm resolutions and a great spiritual
tenderness; " [1]—St. Francis of Sales, according
to whom God manifests His presence by the
suavity, the heavenly consolations, the attractions
and certain sweetnesses which He pours into the
soul [2];—St. Bernard, teaching that " sighs and
tears indicate the arrival of the Spouse, the soul
recognises His presence when she feels His
grace," [3] &c.

Those who hold the first opinion go so far as to
maintain that this presence of God, so peculiarly
felt, and this interior possession of God, are the
two fundamental characters of all mystical states.
The others absolutely deny this; for, if this impression of God present and possessed was essential
to mystical states, it would be necessary to exclude
from them the night of the senses and that of the
spirit, which nevertheless form a considerable portion of them; far from tasting God's presence in
these states, the soul therein suffers cruelly from
His absence. It would also be necessary to exclude

---

[1] *Life*, xxvii.   [2] *Love of God*, b. vi. c. vii. and xi.
[3] St. Bernard, *Serm. in Cant.*, lxxiv. *Scala Claus.*, vi.

certain contemplations so spiritual and so pure, that they are hardly, so to speak, perceived by the soul on account of their very simplicity.

We leave to more enlightened judges the task of deciding these difficult controversies; besides, we want to write a practical not a scientific treatise. Perhaps, however, it might be concluded, that this very peculiar sentiment of God's presence, when clearly realised in a prayer of simple look, gives to that prayer a distinctly supernatural character, but that the absence of this sentiment does not suffice to prove that such a prayer is not mystical.

§ V.—INFLUENCE OF THIS STATE UPON THE SOUL
AND THE BODY.

This loving union, wherein the soul sometimes feels so vividly that she possesses God, produces an impression "of interior peace, repose, and quiet," [1] which penetrates even to the depths of her being. St. John of the Cross and St. Teresa never fail to point out this character of mystical prayer. Our faculties receive light and love, and are not any longer obliged to seek these by the painful labour of meditation; "they are, therefore, in a state of repose, and their whole operation consists in a simple, sweet and loving attention to God." It is especially the appeasing of a hunger which is being satisfied, of a consuming thirst which is being quenched by living waters. The soul was

---

' *Ascent*, b. ii. c. xiii.

hungering after God, she was seeking for Him everywhere, and could not do without Him; she finds Him and possesses Him; He is the light which satisfies the mind, the love which gives rest to the heart. Now that she feels Him to be within her she no longer desires anything but to possess Him still more perfectly and that for ever. This sense of being appeased becomes more marked, in proportion as the prayer is more full of sweetness and the presence of God more strongly felt.

This union produces, moreover, a joy which may even cause transports and a kind of spiritual inebriation; but mystical states have also attached to them cruel sufferings. In the midst of this delicious repose, " in this profound peace, the will is inebriated with love,"[1] forgets its past pains, is strengthened for fresh trials, makes great progress in virtue, advances with giant steps towards that complete "transformation of the soul in God by love,"[2] which is perfection itself; whilst the mystical trials facilitate this advance by the detachment they produce.

Speaking in general, mystical union exerts an influence upon the body, weaker and barely outlined in the state of quiet, very marked in full union, and altogether overwhelming in ecstasy.--- The interior powers undergo an analogous influence, slight in the state of quiet, but which goes on increasing even to rapture. It is called a *binding* of the faculties, when it is weak; a *suspension* of

' *Way*, c. xxxii.   ² *Ascent*, b. ii. c. v.

them, when it is very strong.[1]   In the commencement, it is only a more or less pronounced difficulty in meditating, in reciting vocal prayers, in
multiplying distinct and particular interior acts,
except when God's action impels the soul towards
effusions of love and other like acts; but, alas! our
faculties do not experience the same difficulty in
creating distractions.   Later on, the making of considerations becomes impossible; and, in full union
and in ecstasy, the mystical action seizing upon
our faculties with a sovereign intensity, suspends
their activity with regard to their natural operations, and applies that whole activity to the receiving of infused light and love.   The senses and
interior faculties regain more liberty in the spiritual marriage.[2]

Hence we see how deservedly these forms of
prayer are called mystical.   They are, in fact,
mysterious even for the initiated.   Mysterious is
this void of the mind, this incapacity to meditate,
and that, only when engaged in prayer; mysterious
also, these strange passive purifications in an
anguish bordering almost upon despair, or in the
tortures of love; mysterious, that divine infusion,
so secret that it is at times imperceptible to the
very recipient; mysterious, that general and
obscure light, which defines nothing precisely, yet
imparts such a high esteem of God and creates a
disgust for everything else; mysterious, that vague
and confused love, that sense, at times so intense,

---

[1] Fr. Poulain, *Graces of Prayer*, 2nd part, c. xiv.
[2] See 3rd part, c. iii. art. 2 § 1 c. viii. and ix. pp. 278, 352, 361.

of God's presence, that sweet and tranquil union, those impetuous transports, that profound peace, that binding of the soul's powers, that influence, which seizes upon the body itself, that mighty transformation of the soul in God caused by love. The soul thus finds herself introduced into a new world, as it were, where the supernatural may be almost touched by the hand.

CHAPTER V

DIFFERENT KINDS OF MYSTICAL PRAYER

WE purposely omit all mystical phenomena; visions, revelations, interior locutions, &c., which are not, properly speaking, union. We are treating only of the graces of union with God. Their classification is a most difficult task, and there is among authors a difference of opinion not easy to reconcile. Several distinguish far too great a number of kinds. One of the best known authors, Scaramelli, enumerates twelve; manifestly, circumstances, which are mere varieties or modes of the same state, are counted as different degrees of prayer. Such, for instance, are the transports of love or spiritual inebriation, the sleep of the faculties, the pain and thirst of love, the divine touches described at such length by Scaramelli. All these features belong to the state of quiet, to complete union, or to ecstasy, just as mystical espousals are to be referred to the spiritual marriage.—St. John of the Cross is less intent upon classifying, describing, and analysing mystical forms of prayer than upon pointing out clearly the active and passive ways which lead on to the summit of Carmel, that is, to the spiritual marriage or perfect union. Let it, however, be noted that he describes minutely the night of the senses and that of the spirit,[1] before he sings the praises of the transforming union.[2]—St. Teresa, on the contrary, gives us a clear and precise, sober and rational classification, which we shall adopt in preference to any other. The saint states it already in her " Life ";[3] she reverts to it in her " Interior Castle," [4] but warns us, on three different occasions in this latter work, that she has now more experience and a better knowledge of her subject.[5]

This classification has for its principal basis the faculties affected by the mystical action. It comprises four degrees : the state of quiet, full union, ecstasy, and spiritual marriage.

1°. The state of quiet. The powers of the soul are not all seized upon, and distractions remain possible.

2°. Full union. All the interior powers are seized upon, the soul is fully occupied by God; the body itself is more under the mystical influence than it was in the state of quiet, but it can still act.

3°. Ecstasy or ecstatic union. All the powers of the soul are strongly grasped by the mystical influence; and the senses are so much absorbed that communication with the exterior world is entirely, or almost entirely, suspended.

4°. The spiritual marriage, or transforming union, differs entirely from the preceding states. Ecstasies are still met with, but they are of rarer

---

[1] *Obscure Night.*   [3] *Life*, ix. and *ff*.
[2] *Spiritual Canticle* and *Living Flame.*   [4] *Castle, passim.*
[5] *Castle*, 1st mans. c. ii. ; 4th mans. c. i. and ii.

occurrence; the senses being purified and strengthened are less liable to give way under the divine
action.[1]

After all we have said, it is plain that the ways
of prayer exhibit an admirable progression. Vocal
prayer consists altogether in formulas and words,
recited, however, with attention and devotion, and
so it makes much noise as it were :—meditation is
more interior, but still it requires quite a din of
reasoning ;—affective prayer simplifies the work of
the mind ;—the prayer of simplicity simplifies even
that of the will ; and prayer ends by becoming, at
least occasionally, hardly anything more than a
loving attention to God, and the soul has become
a most silent sanctuary :—God, who fills this sanctuary, makes His presence mysteriously felt, He
Himself pouring into it light and love amidst the
peacefulness of a sweet and holy union. His
action at first affects only a portion of the soul's
faculties, afterwards it affects all of them ;—later
on, the body in its turn is fully grasped by the
divine influence; and the soul at last arrives,
should it so please God, after so much preparation,
at the spiritual marriage, which is itself a preparation for the beatific vision.

Such is the logical development and the ordinary
order of ascent in the ways of prayer; but the fact,
that many saints have been ecstatics from their
earliest childhood, shows that God has reserved to
Himself the liberty of making the soul overleap
these various stages when He pleases to do so.

[1] Fr. Poulain, *Graces of Prayer*, c. iii.

We by no means maintain that these various steps in the ladder of prayer manifest exteriorly the exact degree of light, love and perfection which reigns within ; this is God's own secret.[1] We have described merely the ever onward path, which prayer and perfection generally travel. The author of grace may, when He so pleases, communicate to a soul more light and love in meditation than in contemplation, and perhaps even in a well-marked state of quiet, than He does in a weak state of union involving all the soul's powers.

All authors call the degrees of mystical prayer stages, periods, spiritual ages, to indicate that a rather prolonged stay must generally be made in each before passing on to the following degree; "and this transition is difficult. Hence many souls stop short upon the road. But St. Teresa often repeats a reflection calculated to humble those who remain stationary : it is, that God probably called them to mount higher; and, if they never reach that higher point, she thinks that by their own fault they have placed some obstacle in the way of the divine plans in their regard. Thus, instead of conceiving a certain pride in having reached the state of quiet, they should ask themselves with fear why they have not passed beyond it.[2]

[1] Abbé Saudreau, *État Myst.*, n° 109
[2] Fr. Poulain, *Graces of Prayer*, 2nd part, c. iii.

CHAPTER VI

OF THE STATE OF QUIET

§ I.—Description of this state.

The prayer of quiet is the first step in mystical ways. In it the will is united to God; the superior part of the soul also is affected by the divine action; but the understanding, the memory and the imagination remain free and may help or impede prayer by their own natural activity; in a word, the powers of the soul are not all grasped by the divine influence; distractions remain possible and are not uncommon.

This term *repose or quietude* is of very frequent occurrence in the writings of St. Teresa and St. John of the Cross. It means: 1°. that the mind which heretofore had wearied itself, seeking after convictions and affections in the long and painful labour of reasonings, now ceases from these discursive acts, rests itself and has nothing to do but to look upon the truth discovered.—2°. The will reposes in a tranquil and loving union with God, whom it feels present and whom it possesses.—It is well to remember, when reading the authors who treat of this subject, that this word quietude is taken in various senses: it sometimes is used to express

that feeling of repose, which the soul experiences
in all the degrees of mystical union; in the writings of St. Francis of Sales [1] and others, it ex-
tends to every union inferior to ecstasy, whether
all the powers of the soul be affected or only some;
we, with St. Teresa, restrict it to the first degree of
supernatural prayer, in which "the will alone is
captive," [2] whilst the other faculties remain free.

St. Teresa calls it also: the *second heavenly
water,* [3] to indicate that, in the stage of quiet, the
soul is already passive, and that, with less labour,
it now finds itself better watered with the dews of
heavenly grace;—the *fourth mansion,* [4] to indicate
the degree of spiritual progress corresponding to
this prayer;—the *taste of God,* the *prayer of divine
sweetness,* [5] because it is the first in which God
makes Himself experimentally known to the soul,
and wherein His presence is realised as by a spiritual sweetness and savour.   Other authors call it
the *prayer of silence,* because it is the first prayer
wherein the soul leaves off reasoning and arguing,
and the noisy work of the intellect begins to disappear.

The prayer of quiet is "almost always preceded" [6] by a supernatural and passive recollection.—In active recollection, the soul labours by
her own industry to withdraw her faculties from
created things, to turn them towards God and so to
create a silence within herself.   Here, however, it

---

[1] *Love of God,* b. vi. c. xi.   [4] *Castle,* 4th mans. c. i. ii. and iii.
[2] *Way,* xxxii.   [5] *Ibid.*
[3] *Life,* xi. xiv. xv.   [6] *Ibid.,* 4th mans. c. iii,

is God Himself who suddenly establishes her in a state of recollection, without the need of any effort on her own part.[1] The soul then no longer resembles the tortoise of its own accord drawing into its shell its head and its feet; but, without even giving it a thought, she finds herself established in recollection by God, who calls her to Him as a shepherd, so to speak, calls his flock, and attracts her, as the magnet does the needle. This sudden recollection of the soul's faculties effected by God without her aid, is the forerunner of the state of quiet, in the words of St. Teresa it is " the principle and vestibule "[2] of this state. At first, of rare occurrence, it becomes afterwards more frequent. It belongs, indeed, to the mystical state; but, in our opinion, it does not constitute a special degree of prayer. For, either the divine action is confined to producing a state of recollection, without establishing the soul in the state of quiet, and then it is only the entrance into prayer which is passive, while the prayer itself remains active; or, the divine operation goes further, and then we have the state of quiet, of union, or of ecstasy, and not a mere passive recollection.

§ II.—INFLUENCE OF THE STATE OF QUIET UPON THE FACULTIES.

The state of quietude being rather frequent, we shall try, at the risk of repeating ourselves, to outline a fairly complete description of it, and to

[1] St. Liguori, *Praxis*, 133.   [2] *Castle*, 4th mans. c. iii,

show how our different faculties behave in that state.

And first let us consider *the will.*

As we have said, when speaking of the passive purgation of the senses, contemplation begins by a state of quiet that is *very feeble,* and *hardly perceptible.* A remembrance of God, vague, obscure, persistent and monotonous, a love not less vague and indistinct, and a dolorous need of possessing God by a closer union form the groundwork of this state. The quietude is too feeble to allow the soul to taste the sweetness of the divine presence. The soul thirsts, and God gives her to drink not of " a stream " but of " a puny rill of water " as " to a child." [1] She is far from swimming in delights, but she is, in some small degree, relieved of her thirst, and held captive, for she feels the need of being alone with God, and, if she suffers in that state, she would be far worse off elsewhere.

Often in the sequel, and, so to speak, most of the time, this same state of quiet will be *slightly strengthened,* sometimes more, sometimes less; at certain moments the soul feels that she possesses God by a sweet union, but not as much as she would wish, and it is impossible to oblige God to be more liberal of Himself. Often this divine presence hides itself, and the attraction and facility gives place to a profound aridity. Generally, the intellect is but little held, the will itself only imperfectly occupied; there is in this state a mixture of joy and deception; the puny rill of water has

[1] *Way,* xxi.

become a tiny stream, in which the soul may more fully quench her thirst, without being able as yet to swim in delights.

Finally, the prayer becomes more elevated, and, although the soul does not reach to the full union of all her powers, the will is *strongly grasped* by the divine influence.   Divers cases occur; we shall mention several.

With some, or at certain moments in the same soul, it is light which predominates; but more generally it will be love.   "In quietude," says St. Liguori,[1] "love is communicated directly to the mind, to the centre itself of the soul, . . . it thence spreads to the exterior senses, but not always; whence it often happens that one may have the prayer of quiet without any sensible sweetness."   This dry state of quiet, therefore, proceeds either from the weakness of the mystical influence, or from its being purely spiritual; in this latter case, the light and love may be strong, but God communicates them to the mind only, without their redounding upon the senses.[2]

At times, in the language of Cassian,[3] "a person may feel himself transpierced with so lively a compunction and grief (or so penetrating a tenderness of love), that it must be in some fashion digested, find a vent and evaporate in a copious effusion of tears."

"Sometimes the whole soul concentrates herself within herself, and is buried in a profound silence;

[1] *Praxis*, 134.

[2] See upon arid quietude. Abbé Saudreau. *État Myst.*, xi. § 2 and *Degrés*, b. v. c. v. § 5 and 6.   [3] *Ninth Conf.*, c. xxvi.

the admiration she is in, at what she feels and what
she beholds, stifles her voice and prevents all
speech; the astonished spirit keeps the senses suspended, and can only by her sighs convey to God
the fervour of her desires.'' The mind then remains fixed upon God, whose presence it feels;
leaving reasoning aside, it keeps silence and looks
with admiration; it enfolds its Well-Beloved in
one long look, which, without any words, says a
great deal, because it expresses the astonishment,
the joy, the charm, and the love by which the soul
is fascinated. The will, plunged in God, inflamed
by its union with God, expanding itself in God by
a fusion full of sweetness, is not inclined to formulate a multitude of acts; it is enjoying God in a
union that is calm, tranquil, and full of unction, it
is reposing deliciously on the bosom of its Divine
Master in a silence full of love. The whole soul,
like to a mother who devours her infant with her
eyes, passes into this ardent look; the more she
contemplates, the more she is inflamed; the more
she is inflamed the more pleasure she takes in contemplating; she loves without saying so; but the
fire of her eyes, her tears, her sighs, her attitude,
the dispositions of her heart, the immobility of her
astonishment, the discreet outbursts of her tenderness, all speak with eloquence and ravish Him who
is charming her. The intellect and will remain
silently occupied with God, often during a somewhat long time; some simple and ardent acts, at
the most, are made by the heart, just what is needful to sustain this loving union. These two facul-

ties are, therefore, very active, noiselessly so, and it is then especially that quietude best deserves to be called *the prayer of silence*.

At times, on the other hand, the soul, all penetrated by divine love, pours herself forth in a *sweet colloquy*, in effusions full of tenderness, without violence, without transports, in a most delightful intimacy. Our Lord, on his side, is pleased by these outpourings of love, for it is He Himself who keeps alive this fire upon the altar of the heart, and bestows these pious effusions.

Sometimes, finally, adds Cassian,[1] the holy compunction of love " shows itself by an ineffable joy, by transports of an altogether divine gladness. Hence those exclamations of joy, from which the soul cannot refrain, . . . those impressions, . . . with which she is penetrated." God inflames the soul to such a degree that, out of herself, lost in love, inebriated with God, she cannot contain her love and her joy, but bursts forth into transports. She darts forward as though to seize God and would wish to lodge Him in her inmost heart; she feels vividly that He is there, that she possesses Him; she abandons herself to effusions of love, pretty much as a mother who catches up her child, clasps him lovingly to her bosom, bathes him with her tears, lavishes caresses upon him, calls him by the sweetest names and pours forth her feelings in a flow of burning and almost frantic words. The mind and the heart, in such moments, so superabound with life, that acts of love,

[1] Cassian, *Ninth Conf.*, c. xxvi.

confidence, admiration, and such like others, flow
inexhaustibly, and crowd upon each other like tor-
rents of burning lava.—Soon, however, astounded
at her own boldness, and recalling to mind the
majesty of God, her own nothingness and miseries,
the soul adores, humbles herself, makes herself as
little as she can ; then love seizes upon her again,
and, according to the expression of St. Teresa,[1]
" she utters a thousand holy follies, which delight
Him who has put her in that state." It must, indeed,
be believed that God takes a delightful pleasure in
all this, for He responds to the soul in His own
way, by continuing or increasing this spiritual
inebriation and these transports of love. He Himself seems to catch up the soul, to kiss her with
His divine lips, to caress her with an infinite love,
to press her to His heart more tenderly than the
most loving of fathers could do. The soul feels
that for the one drop of love she has given, she has
received an ocean. Happy moments, in which she
knows by experience that she loves and that she is
still more loved in return ! Moments, prepared by
long trials and forerunners of fresh purgations !
These meetings with her Divine Spouse make her
forget past pains and wonderfully strengthen her
for the trials to come.[2] These outbursts, however,
subside, prayer grows weaker, then stronger, only
to diminish anew ; and by means of these fluctuations it may last some time ; " one day, two days,
or even more," says St. John of the Cross.[3]

[1] *Life*, xvi.   [2] *Ascent*, b. ii. c. xxvi.
[3] *Spir. Cant.*, stanza 25.

We must not think, however, that these transports have always such intensity. The joyous inebriation of beginners resides rather in the senses; like to new wine, it has more of violence and effervescence, but its fruits are not so certain; it is coarser, less elevated, and the demon can easily produce its counterfeit; the soul is sometimes seeking herself in it, and that, too, not a litle, and her beautiful zeal is liable to subside altogether when this sweetness vanishes.—The spiritual inebriation of more advanced souls is less violent, because it is more spiritual; being founded upon well-established virtues, it is more solid, more profound, more sheltered from illusions; the old wine has less of effervescence, but it keeps well and does good.[1] The best, or rather the only good kind of inebriation, according to St. Francis of Sales, is that " which alienates us, not from the spiritual sense, like corporal inebriation, but from the bodily senses; which does not dull or stupify us, but angelifies and, so to speak, deifies us; which raises us out of ourselves . . . in order to elevate us above ourselves."[2]

Connected with this spiritual inebriation is a grace rather frequent, which St. John of the Cross calls *the spark of love*.[3]—Just as a spark falling upon the hand, quickly burns it and is immediately extinguished, so the soul is seized, either in prayer or during any other occupation, with a violent and sudden outburst of love which subsides rather

[1] *Spir. Cant.*, stanza 25.   [2] *Love of God*, b. vi. c. vi.
[3] *Spir. Cant.*, stanza 25. See Scaramelli, *Dir. Myst.*, 3rd treatise, c. vii.

quickly, but whose effects may last a much longer
time. This happens especially when the soul is
passing through a *state* of *fervour,* and these outbursts may surprise her a number of times in the
same day.

This spiritual sleep and these loving embraces
generally require that the soul should have already
made serious progress in the prayer of quiet and in
virtue; for they suppose an intensity of mystical
prayer that approaches to full union.   Nevertheless,
this state, so long as it does not go as far as the
union of *all* the powers of the soul, is as yet only
a marked state of quiet.

Here, then, is how the *will* is grasped in the state
of quiet : at times, feebly, and then prayer is dry
and wearisome; at other times, with more strength,
and then the soul experiences neither great consolation nor profound desolation; again, with great
energy, and then prayer is accompanied with a
gentle and penetrating sweetness, or with an
ardour that rises even to transports, unless, indeed,
the mystical action should be purely spiritual, for,
in that case, it would be, as it were, imperceptible,
on account of its very simplicity.[1]

The *other powers*—that is, intellect, memory
and imagination—even though they be recollected
and enter more or less into a gentle repose, still are
not lost, nor fixed upon God, nor suspended. They
retain their liberty.   The will alone is united with
Him by love, it alone is held captive, without its
well knowing how, and " without being as yet
entirely lost in God," as it will be later on.   The

[1] See above, part iii., c. iv. § iv. p. 304.

other faculties may separately share in the union of the will, but not all at the same time, or, if they do so, it is only in an imperfect way; otherwise, we would have the state of full union and no longer that of simple quietude.[1]

Of course the understanding must be more or less illuminated in its superior part; the will would not love, if the intellect did not show it the amiable qualities of God. The soul feels that the intellect receives this light from above, and that it does not evoke it by the force of reasoning. She contemplates, but does not reason; for quietude is an infused prayer of simple look. Still it is true that, *in the beginning*, "the understanding may have to co-operate, by a tranquil and moderate action, with the grace which is leading it into repose."[2]; it works some moments at turning the well-wheel in order to fill the channels"; and during the prayer, "it acts at intervals and in a most tranquil manner"; "thus the gardener obtains a greater supply of the celestial water, has less fatigue and enjoys some moments of repose."[3] A time will come when discursive acts will be impossible; all that the soul will then be able to do in order to nourish the divine fire will be to throw upon it "some little bits of straw"—that is, a few direct, simple and affective acts.

The mind is seized sometimes powerfully, sometimes feebly.[4] When this is the case, the intel-

---

[1] See St. Teresa. *Life*, c. xiv. and xv. at the beginning. *Way*, xxxii. at the beginning. *Castle*, 4th mans. c. ii.

[2] *Ascent*, b. ii. c. xv.

[3] *Life*, xiv. [4] Fr. Poulain, *Graces of Prayer*, ix.

lect, memory and imagination will come forward
sometimes in order to share in the joy of the
will, and will have the wisdom to remain as if
asleep, to be silent and to leave the soul in
peace.—At other times, however, they will want
to be meddling, and, upon the pretext of helping
in the prayer, will strive to depict its happiness to
the will, to discover fine reasons, to make elaborate
considerations, to represent to the soul in vivid
colours its own faults and the divine goodness,
. . . &c. Their activity, if wisely directed, will
sometimes succeed in sustaining the state of quiet,
and in supplying for its weakness, whence will
result a mixture of mystical repose and ordinary
prayer. Often, however, the action of the other
powers will only injure the will. Besides, this
peace and this co-operation hardly ever have any
duration in the state of quiet, especially when it is
a feeble quietude. The mind is then solicited by
a thousand distractions, the memory and imagination become a torment. "While the will is in this
profound and supernatural tranquillity," says St.
Teresa, "it is not uncommon for the intellect,
on the other hand, to be quite troubled and
astonished, and, not knowing where it is, to flit
from place to place without being able to settle
anywhere. It is importunate, foolish, silly,
following after the most extravagant thoughts."[1]
The intellect, however, lets itself sometimes be
attracted and captivated; but the imagination is
still more foolish: "it is a veritable clapper of a

[1] *Way*, xxxii. *Life*, xv.

mill that wearies by its inconvenient noise;[1] . . . but just as we cannot stop the movement of the stars, which travel with such a prodigious velocity, so it is not in our power to check the movement of the imagination."[2]—Happily, the wanderings of these three volatile faculties do not prevent the will from remaining united to God in a profound peace. Instead, therefore, of losing its time and risking its supernatural repose by going in pursuit of them, let the will strive to maintain itself in its loving union, which also is the best means to bring them back; besides, "if the bees were all to go chasing each other, how would the honey be made?"[3]

As for the *body*, it also is slightly affected, at least when the quietude is well-marked. Besides that "it shares in a very high degree in the delight and transports of the soul,"[4] this latter is already experiencing some difficulty in praying vocally and in meditating.[5] St. Teresa nevertheless advises us "not to abandon altogether mental prayer even in this state, nor even, from time to time, certain vocal prayers, if the soul has the desire *or the power* to recite them; for, when the quietude is great, she experiences an extreme difficulty in speaking,[6] . . . and she may require a whole hour to say a single *Pater*."[7] The mystical action, therefore, is beginning to embarrass the

---

[1] *Castle*, 4th mans. i.   [2] *Way*, xxxii.
[3] *Life* xiv. and xv. *passim.* *Way*, xxxii. *Castle*, 4th mans. iii. St. Francis of Sales, *Love of God*, b. vi. c. x.
[4] *Way*, xxxii.   [6] *Life*, xv.
[5] *Second Rel. to Fr. Rodr. Alvarez.*   [7] *Way*, xxxii.

movements of the body; these, in their turn, may thwart or altogether extinguish the former, if they be prolonged, violent, or absorbing. This is not, however, the case with regard to a mere passing movement, and St. Teresa pleasantly rallies the "excessive simplicity" of those who are afraid to move, and would wish not even to breathe, because it seems to them that, upon the least movement, they shall lose this sweet peace.[1]

§ III.—Various Forms of Quietude.

The variations we have pointed out in the state of quiet, depending on the manner in which the divine action seizes upon the will, may be reduced to three forms only.[2]

1°. *Silent quietude.*—The soul contemplates God in a silence full of love; the mind and heart, instead of pouring forth a flood of distinct and express acts, are completely or almost completely, silent. They are, indeed, occupied with God, sometimes even with supreme intensity, but their activity is concentrated in their attentive look and their movements of love.

2°. *Praying quietude.*—In this form, not only are we able to make simple acts, but we are impelled to do so. It is, as it were a need; the soul is full to overflowing and must relieve itself. These loving aspirations resemble a stream flowing from its source, or even a torrent rushing on wave after wave in rapid succession.

[1] *Way*, xxxii. St. Francis of Sales, *Love of God*, b. vi. c. x.
[2] Fr. Poulain, *Graces of Prayer*, ix. 24 and xiv. 13 and 47.

3°. *Acting* [1] *quietude*.—Generally speaking, exterior occupations prove rather an embarrassment to the state of quiet; but, sometimes, a special grace "keeps the will, as it were, enchained to the divine object which captivates it, for the space of one or even of two days, . . . whilst the other powers remain free to attend to business and to works required by the service of God." But it is clearly perceptible that the soul is not altogether absorbed in this exterior occupation; the will is in contemplation, while the mind and hands are engaged in action : " in this happy state, Martha and Mary go hand in hand." St. Teresa, much surprised at an experience of this sort, asked St. Francis Borgia whether it was not an illusion. He replied that the same happened to himself, and that it was a thing of frequent occurrence.—At first,[2] the saint considered this kind of mystical prayer as a case of full union; later on,[3] being better instructed, she considered it to be only a variety of elevated quietude, and rightly so, since the will alone is in the state of union, the other powers preserving their liberty.

§ IV.—Genesis, Progress and Cessation.

" We shall speak of only the ordinary conduct of God, leaving aside those extraordinary cases, in which He grants this grace (of quietude) solely because He so wills."[4]

---

[1] St. Teresa, *Life*, xvii. *Way*, xxxii. *Second Rel. to Fr. Rodr. Alvarez.*   [2] *Life*, xvii.

[3] *Way*, xxxii. *Second Rel. to Fr. Rodr. Alvarez.*

[4] *Castle*, 4th mans. ii.

In general, he does not wait to give it till the soul is already perfect, for to whom then could He grant it? Moreover, is not this favour one of the most powerful instruments to lead us on to perfection? But He usually waits till the soul is prepared to receive it. The soul, then, although not yet exempt from faults and defects, must have exercised herself, ordinarily speaking, for years in purifying herself by penance, humility, and abnegation, and have made some serious progress in virtue and in ordinary prayer. Generally, the state of quiet begins to appear, when the soul is already familiarised with the prayer of simplicity; [1] God thus makes the soul ascend progressively, step by step, and, during the state of quiet, she may often have to return to the exercise of the prayer of simplicity, rather than to meditation.

Infused contemplation may commence before the night of the senses; but, generally, the passive purgation of the senses is the sign which reveals to an experienced eye the germination of the state of quiet; it contains it in germ, and is already the mystical life in process of being *born* and of being *developed*. This night of the senses alternates with the state of consoling quiet and lasts until this latter has attained to its full development. Then comes an intermediate period, in which the soul enjoys the full union of all the powers and that of ecstasy, not without still meeting with some great trials. Finally, she enters into the dreadful passive purgations of the spirit which conduct her

[1] Fr. Poulain, *Graces of Prayer*, xvi.

to the spiritual marriage. It is a constant law that active and passive purgation do not cease so long as there remains anything to be purged away.

In the beginning, the state of quiet occurs only occasionally, and is usually of short duration.[1] St. Teresa[2] says that, before the age of twenty, she was sometimes raised to "quietude and full union," but she knows not if it lasted the space of a single *Ave Maria*. As time goes on, quietude becomes more frequent and more prolonged. Grounding their opinion on several passages in St. Teresa's works, authors think that the duration of this state, *in its full force*, hardly exceeds half-an-hour. But it does not always come on suddenly, nor does it suddenly depart; often enough, God seems to raise the soul to it by degrees, in order to arouse her attention and inflame her love. When the height of this grace has passed by, there usually follows a period during which the soul remains quite impregnated by the divine visit. In this way, quietude, with its dawn and its twilight, might last an hour, and even more. We have already said, with St. John of the Cross and St. Teresa, that acting quietude and spiritual inebriation may last for one, two, or even more days.

Quietude ends by becoming habitual. The soul then enters into it, as it were, at pleasure, the moment she begins to pray; often even the divine action seizes upon the soul unexpectedly, in the midst of the most common-place occupations. Sometimes strong, at other times weak, it rises pro-

---

[1] Fr. Poulain, *Graces of Prayer*, xvi.   [2] *Life*, iv.

gressively in a constant ebb and flow, and, generally, ceases only to give place to the state of union of all the powers, and of ecstasy. Nevertheless, when the soul has reached the period of full union or of ecstasy (for we must not forget that each degree of prayer is an age of the spiritual life), she very frequently returns to the state of simple quietude; even then, prayer rises and falls, and cannot abide constantly upon the loftiest summits.

Let us add, finally, that God is the master of His gifts; He may take them away, either to punish the soul for her infidelities, or to purify her and detach her from creatures by this trial, or for some other wise and merciful motive. The soul may always lose the state of quiet, and, what is more, may abandon the path of salvation. If the soul whom God has so favoured turns back her thoughts and affections to the things of earth, He goes elsewhere to seek for hearts that truly love Him. As St. Teresa [1] says, He does not altogether take away what He had given her, provided she keeps her conscience pure; but His favours become rare and of short duration; the soul profits only imperfectly of the state of quiet, and advances no further in the ways of prayer.

§ V.—Practical Direction.

As soon as the soul enters upon the passive purgations and mystical prayer, she has more than ever need of a learned and experienced guide, for whom she has no secrets, though from every other

[1] *Way*, xxxii.

she should conceal the favours of God. Simplicity, humility and docility are the best safeguards, and obedience has always its merit and can never be abandoned.

Both director and directed should have for these states the esteem they deserve. Nothing purifies the soul like the night of the senses, and, above all, that of the spirit, in which God Himself operates with as much power as wisdom. Nothing attaches the soul so entirely to God as those prayers, in which she feels that she possesses Him by a loving union. Nevertheless, all that is in itself only a means to perfection, not itself perfection, a gift of God rather than any merit of her own.

In the same way, prudence is necessary in order to avoid being deceived by counterfeits of the divine action. If the sweetness comes from nature, "it produces no good effect, disappears very quickly, and leaves the soul in dryness. If the author of this repose is the demon, . . . he leaves behind him trouble, little humility, and but little disposition " for virtue. St. Teresa never ceases recommending "to souls given to prayer to undertake it with humility, without curiosity, without attachment to even spiritual consolations, . . . with the one sole resolution of helping Jesus Christ to carry His cross." [1] But when once it is clearly understood that it is God who is operating in the soul, no one has any right to distrust Him and to oppose His action; for both director and directed should follow the guidance of the Holy Ghost.

[1] *Life* xv.

We have pointed out the characteristics of supernatural contemplation. If the penitent is of an observant turn and can account to himself for what he experiences, nothing is easier for him, given a little time, than to recognise the way in which he is walking. After all, though it may be more interesting to know exactly to what degree of prayer one has attained, this knowledge is not necessary. It is enough to know that the occupation of the soul with God is good in itself, and that we are meeting with success and profit.

During prayer, we ought to abandon the complicated acts of meditation, or the less varied and more simple acts of affective prayer, only " when God, raising the soul to a higher kind of prayer, keeps her united to Himself by love." [1] Until then, we must continue to employ ourselves in that kind of common prayer at which we best succeed, and from which we derive most profit. So, likewise, when the soul no longer experiences the mystical union, she ought to return to this active prayer, in order not to remain idle.

On the contrary, when the soul feels the divine action, she should suspend personal effort, as far as such suspension is necessary to enable her to yield herself up to the action of God. It is a duty of obedience to comply with what He wills in our regard. It would, indeed, be a strange kind of humility, that would wish to remain, in spite of the Holy Ghost, in the common ways of prayer, and would not fear to become His instructor, by im-

---

[1] *Castle*, 4th mans. c. iii.

plicitly saying to Him by our conduct: I know better than you what way is suitable for me.

If our soul is drawn to contemplate God in *a silence full of love,* let us be satisfied to look and to love, without saying anything; or, let us make only simple acts of love, adoration, humility and such like others, and that, only in so far as is needful to keep the soul engaged in this loving look. " The most one ought to do in this sort of prayer," says St. Teresa,[1] " is to utter from time to time some loving words which may reanimate the soul; let them be as the light breath which rekindles an expiring flame, and not like the strong blast which would extinguish a flame already lit." To persist obstinately in seeking for considerations and in multiplying affections, would be to trouble this loving repose in which God has placed us. " This would be to act like little children, whom their mother is carrying in her arms," says St. John of the Cross;[2] " they would not be able to walk a single step, and yet they cry and struggle to be put upon their feet, and so neither advance themselves, nor let their mother advance. An artist, when painting a portrait, makes his sitter take a suitable pose, and does not allow him to move."—But this, you will say, is mere idleness! No, it is work, noiseless, indeed, but productive of much fruit. The soul is in reality very active. The mind is entirely occupied with gazing upon God, and the will absorbed in loving Him. Should this prayer degenerate into a mere reverie, the soul would at once

---

[1] *Way,* xxxiii.   [2] *Living Flame,* 3rd stanza, 3rd verse, § 16.

be conscious that her faculties had got loose, and
that she is no longer lovingly looking upon God.
On the contrary, the soul is entirely absorbed in
this loving look; she is advancing and feels no
fatigue, because God is carrying her.

If, on the other hand, our soul is inclined to
make acts, be they tranquil or ardent, and if affections well up of themselves, let us freely follow this
attraction; such an occupation cannot be anything
but very profitable, since it is grace which calls us
to it. We may then, following the impulse from
above, adore God, admire His mercies, praise His
perfections, love Him, declare our trust in Him,
place ourselves entirely in His hands, humble ourselves exceedingly before Him, &c. . . .
" Seeing ourselves so close to Our Lord, we ought
to ask for grace, to pray for the Church, for those
recommended to our prayers, for the souls in purgatory, and this, without noise of words, but with
a lively desire of being heard." Our heart is too
full and it overflows under the pressure of the divine
action, all the time, however, "guarding itself
against the noise of the understanding, which is
ever fond of fine considerations," . . . and
always upon the look out for "choice and elegant
terms and all the artifices of rhetoric."[1]

Most frequently, the state of quiet will be feebly
marked, and not sufficient to keep us occupied;
then a need will be felt of supplementing by our
own efforts the action of God, in such a way,
however, as not to stifle this latter, but rather so

[1] *Life*, xv. —*Life of Fr. Balth. Alvares*, xli. 1st dif.

as to complete and second it. Here is how we should act :

Above all, we ought to accept the action of God such as it is, and not thwart it. We must never force ourselves to produce acts which would embarrass it, unless such acts be of obligation. We should make those acts for which we feel a facility, and never deliberately exclude them from our prayer.

Now, as regards reflections, the soul cannot, in this state of quiet, *meditate* on God, on Our Lord, and His mysteries by a sequence of considerations, developed reasonings, and a complicated work of the imagination; but nothing hinders her from *contemplating* these objects by a simple thought, by a general remembrance and a loving look. We should do so, therefore, according as we find this profitable, in order to give occupation to our mind, to nourish affections, and to enter into the intentions of the Church, whose will it is that Our Lord and His mysteries should play the chief *rôle* in the formation of our spiritual life.

As for affections, the soul generally experiences no difficulty in making acts of love, humility, confidence, abandonment and such like others, provided they be simple, short and but little varied. We may, therefore, multiply them in order to fill up the time of our prayer, except when God's action invites us to contemplate Him in silence, to love Him without saying anything, to raise ourselves towards Him rather by movements of love than by formal acts. On the other hand, to wish to give

too much variety and a complicated turn to these
acts would be to disturb this mystical repose. Still
more disturbing would it be, if the soul " were to
cling too much to saying a quantity of vocal
prayers which she had resolved to say daily, and
that, too, by saying them in a hurried way, as if
to finish her self-imposed task." [1] Those vocal
prayers, however, which are imposed by our rule,
or by general custom, should never be omitted.
Mental prayer, on account of its calm and silent
character, is particularly favourable to this mystical
quiet; but when the soul passes from it, all in union
with God, to the Divine Office, she will find in this
latter a wonderful aid to inflame her devotion, and
to enable her to keep herself raised to God during
long hours.

It is to be noted that we must never abridge our
prayer because it is dry, nor prolong it to the detri-
ment of our other duties because it is consoling;
the will of God and our own spiritual profit, not our
desire for consolations, should determine us in this
matter.—If God should visit us, let us endeavour
not to let this appear exteriorly; humility loves to
hide itself, close intimacy loves silence and mystery. Let us also avoid excessively fatiguing our
head, heart, or nerves by violent and indiscreet outbursts, whenever we are able to moderate this sort
of inebriation.

Finally, let us not imitate those " who are not
satisfied with being content, if they don't feel, see
and taste their contentment, . . . ever tor-

[1] *Way*, xxxii.

menting themselves to know if their tranquillity is really tranquil, and their quietude really quiet." [1]

After prayer, the directed and the director should never forget that, though prayer in itself is the best means of perfection, yet its end is to prepare our heart for upward progress, and to make us ascend from virtue to virtue; by our progress towards this end, its value is to be judged. Though our prayer should contribute greatly to develop faith and charity, still the chief fruits we should draw from it are that spirit of abnegation, which receives, without attachment, the divine favours, is resigned to be deprived of them should it so please God, and, with a holy indifference to all things, abandons itself to the divine good pleasure;—and that humility, which, far from attributing the gifts of God to our own efforts and our own merits, makes us abase ourselves all the more, the more elevated the degree of prayer to which He has deigned to raise us. "We ought to take care," says St. Peter of Alcantara, "to show the greatest humility and the greatest possible respect in our dealings with God; in such a way, that the soul should never receive spiritual joy, or divine favours, without falling back upon herself to consider her own baseness, in order to lower her wings, and humble herself in presence of so sublime a Majesty. . . . Nothing is more useful (in the ways of prayer) than a profound humility, the knowledge of oneself and an unbounded confidence in the divine mercy.—Humility obtains for us what

[1] St. Francis of Sales, *Love of God,* b. vi. c. x.

Y

we desire, humility preserves it, and it is increased by humility.'' [1]

Instead of complacently admiring himself, a religious should ask himself, why it is that, after so many years and such floods of graces, he has not arrived at a higher degree of prayer and of perfection. Besides, from him to whom more has been given, more also shall be required; and, if he does not generously correspond with grace by the practice of solid virtues, he will remain poor notwith- the treasures given to him, he may even lose them, and come himself to get a fall all the more crushing, because he falls from a greater height.

[1] St. Peter of Alcantara, *Prayer and Meditation*, 2nd part, v. counsels 4 and 8.

CHAPTER VII

UNION OF ALL THE POWERS
OF THE SOUL

" I HAVE treated at some length of this fourth mansion (the prayer of quiet), because, I believe, it is that into which the greatest number of souls enter. Moreover, in it, the natural being mingled with the supernatural, souls are more exposed to the artifices of the demon than in the succeeding mansions." [1]—We shall give only a rapid glance at the other degrees. St. Teresa, in fact, adds : " There are very many souls who arrive at this state (of quietude) ; but those who pass beyond it are few, and I know not where the fault lies. Most assuredly not with God. As for Him, after having granted so great a favour, He ceases not afterwards, in my opinon, to be prodigal of new ones, unless our infidelity checks the course of them." If souls then do not pass beyond this state it is because they look back ; no longer appreciating the Promised Land, they regret the flesh-pots of Egypt ; and their greatest misfortune is that they have ceased to esteem and love " the way which had led them to the possession of so great a good. . . . Great

[1] *Castle*, 4th mans. c. iii. at end.

is my grief, when, amongst so many souls, who to my knowledge have gone thus far and should go further, I am ashamed to say I see so few that do so." [1] These words should not be taken too literally, for the saint, a little further on, adds, that "the number of such persons is no doubt great" [2]; and, when beginning to explain to her daughters the treasures of the "fifth mansion," she declares, that "some amongst them habitually enjoy them," and that "the greater number" of the others "share in them more or less." The union of all the powers of the soul is called by St. Teresa "the fifth mansion," or the "prayer of union," in a restricted and special sense. Father Poulain calls this stage "full union," because in it the soul is fully united with God; Scaramelli calls it "simple union," because it is the lowest degree of those mystical kinds of prayer in which the soul is entirely united with God.

Between quietude and ecstasy there is an intermediate stage, in which the soul is more deeply immersed in God than in the former, and the unitive embrace less close than in the latter.

As its name implies, all the powers of the soul are simultaneously grasped by the divine action and fully occupied by God, without the senses being absorbed and ceasing to act at least partially; when at its height, this stage is semi-ecstatic.

We have said [3] that, in the state of quiet, the will is held captive, without being "entirely lost in

---

[1] *Life*, xv.   [2] *Ibid.*, xviii.
[3] Preceding chapter, § ii. p. 322.

God "; this supposes that a divine light has absorbed the superior part of the soul, while the other powers may be affected separately and in an imperfect manner, by the mystical action, but are not lost or suspended, and remain free.—In this state, on the contrary, they are all simultaneously seized upon and occupied by God. It seems, however, that there may be *a greater or less degree* of this. If this is the prayer described by St. Teresa, under the name of the " third water," in the beginning of the sixteenth chapter of her *Life*, " all the faculties of the soul are entirely occupied with God, without being capable of anything else . . . ; in order to distract them from this, *a great effort would be required;* " . . . they " are not, however, entirely lost in God," and the union is as yet imperfect, since the saint could, during this time, make verses to express her transports, and even write down what was taking place in her soul at the time. Assuredly she could not have done this, during the " union of all the powers " such as she describes it, in her letter to Father Rodriguez Alvarez, and in her " fifth mansion "; where she thus expresses herself :

" When God raises a soul to union, He suspends the natural action of all her powers, in order the better to infuse into her true wisdom. Thus she neither sees, nor hears, nor understands, while she remains united to God." At the same time, God " inebriates all her powers with a joy which keeps them all ravished at the same time, without their **either** knowing or being able to understand how that is brought about. . . . At such a time, the memory is as though it had no existence, the imagination likewise.   . . The understanding would like to try to comprehend something of what is taking place; but, finding itself incapable, and deprived of its natural action, it remains quite dumb and astounded at what it contemplates; the will loves more than the understanding has any idea of, yet without the soul comprehending or being able to tell (at the time), either whether she loves or what she is doing."[1]   She contemplates God, therefore, in a light so pure and penetrating, she possesses Him and clasps Him to her in so close and sweet a union, that she forgets all her surroundings, no longer makes any reflection upon herself, and passes with all her affection into her most amiable Well-Beloved.[2]

Hence flow three consequences[3]:

1°. Absence of distractions. Since all the powers of the soul are absorbed in God, the understanding, memory, and imagination, as well as the will, there is no longer any faculty which can give rise to distractions; and this characteristic can be easily recognised after the event. Importunate thoughts, like slender and agile little lizards, were wont still to glide into the state of quietude by the thousand openings of the imagination, of the memory, and of the understanding; but these

---

[1] *Castle*, 5th mans. c. i. *Second Letter to Fr. Rodr. Alvarez, passim. Way*, xxxii.

[2] St. Liguori, *Praxis*, 136.

[3] Fr. Poulain, *Graces of Prayer*, c. xvii. 2,

cannot penetrate into this fifth mansion, seeing that the natural activity of these powers is for the moment suspended, and the whole soul lost in God. " This latter is now very attentive and alert as regards God, but fully asleep as regards all earthly things, herself included. In fact, during the short time union lasts, the soul is, as it were, deprived of all sentiment, and, even though she would wish to do so, cannot think at all." So speaks St. Teresa.[1] But this complete union is rare and of short duration, and so the prayer comes down again to the state of simple quietude, and is subject once more to distractions.

2°. Personal effort is reduced to almost nothing.

No doubt the soul must make some efforts to prepare herself for this state of prayer and to draw profit from it. But, during actual union, it is God Himself who waters His garden, and " does almost everything.[2] . . . All He asks of the soul is merely to consent to receive the graces which He is heaping upon her, and to abandon herself absolutely to the good pleasure of the divine wisdom.[3] . . . She suddenly feels the heavenly manna within herself, without knowing how Our Lord put it there, being thus exempted even from that light labour, so full of sweetness, required in the prayer of quiet." [4]—Here, therefore, personal labour is reduced to almost nothing, and it is even accompanied with so much pleasure and glory, that the soul would wish to have it last for

[1] *Castle*, 5th mans. c. i. [3] *Life*, xvi.
[2] *Life*, xv. [4] *Way*, xxxii.

ever; it is not so much a labour as a foretaste of heavenly glory.[1]

3°. A much more vivid certitude of God's presence in the soul is found in this state; and in this consists, according to St. Teresa, the most certain mark of this kind of prayer. . . . " *When the soul returns to herself,* she cannot entertain the slightest doubt but that she has been in God and God in her; and this truth remains so strongly impressed upon her, that, though many years should pass without her being again elevated to this tate, she cannot forget the favour that she received, or doubt of its reality."[2] While this prayer is at its height, the soul, all absorbed in God, makes no reflection on what is taking place within her. "Our Lord unites her to Himself, but, at the same time, strikes her dumb and blind, like St. Paul at the moment of his conversion; He deprives her of perceptive power to such a degree, that she cannot understand either what the favour is that she is enjoying, nor how she enjoys it."[3] It is only afterwards that she can analyse her state; she then remains certain that she was in God and God in her "by a certitude which remains with her, and which God alone can impart"; and St. Teresa, "believes that the soul, which has not such certitude, has not been *wholly* united to God."[4]

The great Saint Antony must have experienced at least this degree of prayer, since he was wont to

---

[1] *Life,* xviii.
[2] *Castle,* 5th mans. c. i.
[3] *Castle,* 7th mans. c. i.
[4] *Ibid.,* 5th mans. c. i.

say: "Prayer is not *perfect,* if the solitary still perceives that He is praying." [1]

"*As for the senses,* they not only no longer possess their natural activity, but they seem, one would say, to be altogether lost.[2] . . . A person in this state does not know whether he even breathes.[3] . . . Rapture differs form union only in the following points: it lasts longer and manifests itself more exteriorly; little by little, it stops the breathing, and one can neither speak nor open the eyes. Union, it is true, does produce this effect; but rapture produces it in a much more energetic form; . . . all these ways of prayer admit of different degrees of intensity." [4]—And, in fact, St. Teresa says elsewhere, when treating of the "third water," that the soul " can help herself exteriorly to make known, at least by signs, what she is experiencing." [5]—In short, the senses are much more fettered than in the state of quiet, and less so than in ecstasy. Union has so close a relation with this latter, that it is almost the same thing: they differ from each other only by the energy of their effects, but this difference is very great.[6]

At first, this union, in the case of St. Teresa, was of short duration, about that of an *Ave Maria;* [7] it continued to recur, getting more pro-

---

[1] Cassian, 9th conf., 31.
[2] *Second Rel. to Fr. Rodr. Alvarez.*
[3] *Castle,* 5th mans. i.
[4] *Second Rel. to Fr. Rodr. Alvarez.*
[5] *Life,* xviii. at beginning.
[6] *Castle,* 5th mans. ii.   [7] *Life,* iv

longed, " but its duration is always short and
seems still shorter than it really is." [1]—The saint
does not think " that it ever lasts even half-an-
hour." [2]   Speaking elsewhere of ecstasy,[3] she
says, " hardly any time passes but some one of the
powers comes back to itself; it is the will which best
maintains itself in divine union; but the two other
powers soon begin again to trouble it.   As the will
is in a calm state, it recalls them and suspends
them anew."   The prayer, therefore, descends
from complete union to simple quietude, but it
may reascend afterwards to its highest point.
" With these alternations it may be prolonged, and
actually is prolonged during some hours." [4]   St.
John of the Cross, likewise, speaks of a prayer in
which " the divine light enfolds the soul with such
energy, . . . that she enters into a forgetfulness of everything, no longer knowing what she
has done, nor what is becoming of her, nor how
long she remains in this state. *After several hours*
of such a prayer, the soul returning to herself,
believes that only a short moment has elapsed." [5]

" *Let us earnestly beseech* Our Spouse," says
St. Teresa, " to aid us by His grace, and so to
strengthen our soul, that we may not grow weary
of working, *until we shall have at last found this
hidden treasure. . . .* In order that He may
enrich you with the good gifts of this mansion, He
wants you to make an *absolute gift* to Him of your-

[1] *Castle*, 5th mans. i. and iv.   [3] *Life*, xviii.
[2] *Ibid.*, 5th mans. ii.   [4] *Ibid.*, xviii.
                    [5] *Ascent*, b. ii. c. xiv.

selves, and of all that concerns you without the least reserve. According as this gift of yours is more or less perfect, you will receive more or less abundant graces. This total gift of oneself to God is the best of all signs by which to recognise whether we are arriving at this prayer of union."
. . . Let us make haste then to dispose ourselves for this grace, " by removing from our souls self-love, our own will, every attachment to earthly things, by works of mortification and penance, by praying much, by practising obedience and all the virtues, in a word, by discharging faithfully all the duties of our state. May this work be accomplished most speedily, and then, let us die, let us die (to ourselves and to all things). . . . This death will show us God, in the way in which He gives Himself to be known in this sort of union." [1]—Let us add, that before this state is reached one must, generally speaking, have passed through the night of the senses. We see from this how little reliance can be placed upon the pretended state of union of a soul less purified, less advanced in virtues, especially when she is of an impressionable and excitable temperament.

According to St. Teresa, " this union, when it is real, is the greatest grace, or, at all events, one of the greatest, which Our Lord grants in the spiritual way." [2] It is the " short-cut " [3] to perfection. The habit of this union transforms the soul to such

[1] *Castle*, 5th mans. c. i. and ii.
[2] *Second Rel. to Fr. Rodr. Alvarez.*
[3] *Castle*, 5th mans. iii.

an extent that she no longer knows herself. It
causes in her "a burning thirst to endure great
crosses for the sake of her Well-Beloved, . . .
an incredible love for retreat and solitude," . . .
a wonderful detachment from all things; in fact,
"whatever the soul sees upon earth is displeasing
to her," she "is here as in a strange country";
"she now regards as contemptible her former
labours, and whatever she does for God in this new
state seems to her nothing, in comparison with what
she would wish to do "; she begins also to experience such an ardent love for God, so great a sorrow
at seeing Him offended, that she "counts all other
evils as nothing."[1]—Above all, she will not forget
that, as this state of prayer supposes a real conformity of her will with God's, so much so, that it is
impossible to attain to this prayer unless the will is
already far advanced in this submission, the
divine favours ought to result in rendering more
perfect the union of her will with God, by producing in her an active obedience to all whatsoever
God, the Church, her Rule and her Superiors command, and a loving and filial conformity to the
dispositions of Divine Providence. Perfection,
indeed, consists in the transformation of the soul
by love, but love is proved by works and not by
mere sentiments. Despite the glowing praises
which St. Teresa gives to the union of love, she
prefers the union of the will, just as we prefer the
term to the journey, the fruit to the flower; this is
"that union of the will which she desired all

[1] *Castle*, 5th mans. ii.

her life, and which she constantly asked of Our
Lord." [1] "The prayer of union," is the "short-
cut," the most rapid and most powerful conveyance to bring us to perfection; but it is not the only
one. If we arrive there without the sweetnesses
and the holy and powerful aid of the mystical
union, more time, labour and fatigue, indeed,
will be required; but there will also be more
merit. [2]

The soul must remember that she is still capable
of falling and of being lost; this prayer even marks
out a period in the spiritual life difficult to be
traversed in safety. "If the soul," says St.
Teresa, "instead of giving herself entirely to her
Divine Spouse, happens to attach her affection to
anything else whatsoever, she will immediately
find that He has withdrawn Himself, and perceive
that she is bereft of these inestimable favours. . . .
She is not as yet strong enough to expose herself
to temptation without danger, . . . and I have
seen highly favoured souls, who, when they arrived
at this state, fell into the snares of the enemy. All
hell, you may be quite certain, will combine to
hinder such a soul from being faithful. . . .
The demon comes with his artifices, and, under the
pretext of some good object, engages the soul in
some dereliction of duty which appears to be very
slight; little by little, he darkens her understanding,
cools her good will and causes her self-love to
revive and grow strong, in such sort that she

[1] *Castle*, 5th mans. iii
[2] St. Liguori, *Praxis*, 136.

departs from God's will in order to carry out her own." [1]

The soul ought never to believe herself to be at the end of her journey and to fall asleep in a false security; her whole and only safety is to be placed in an humble distrust of self, in abnegation and obedience.[2]

[1] *Castle*, 5th mans. iv.   *Life*, xix.
[2] St. Liguori, *Praxis*, 136.

CHAPTER VIII

ECSTATIC UNION

ECSTATIC union, which St. Teresa places in that class of prayer which she calls the fourth heavenly water and the sixth mansion, seizes strongly upon all the soul's powers, and, at the same time, so absorbs the senses, that communication with the exterior world is suspended or nearly so.[1]

We are considering here only that ecstatic *union* which is a grace of prayer. Our definition designedly does not include those ecstasies which are rather mystical phenomena and favours, and which may not, perhaps, imply any powerful union of the soul with God. In this point of view, with which alone we are concerned, there is an abyss between the sublime kinds of prayer described by St. Teresa and the ecstasies of Bernadette at Lourdes, or those with which God has favoured some saints from their earliest years.[2]

Two well-defined elements compose the ecstatic union; they are the absorption of the whole soul in God, and the alienation of the senses. Does Our Lord exercise a direct action on the senses, in order to render them powerless to trouble His intimate

[1] St. Liguori, *Praxis*, 137.
[2] Abbé Saudreau, *État Mystique*, n° 111.

communications with the soul? Or, is it the excess
of light, of love and of joy, which, by absorbing the
soul within herself, impedes for the moment exterior and sensible functions? We do not know.[1]
But, whether the alienation of the senses proceeds
from the mystical union as from its cause, or is
produced by God with a view to this union, this
element is always the principal one in ecstasy considered as a grace of prayer. The alienation of the
senses supposes that these latter are not pure
enough nor strong enough to bear the divine action
without succumbing altogether. This is at bottom a
happy weakness, which tends to become more rare
and to disappear, in proportion as the operations of
grace become more purely spiritual, or the senses are
better prepared for their reception.[2] This explains
why ecstasies are of less frequent occurrence in the
state of spiritual marriage, and also why "the
blessed in heaven will have the perfectly free use of
their senses. The Blessed Virgin was raised to a
higher degree of contemplation than all the angels
and saints together, and nevertheless she had no
raptures. Our Lord enjoyed the beatific vision
without any ecstasy:"[3] In proportion as the soul
advances, her union with God becomes always
more spiritual and more perfect.

All the powers are absorbed in God, as in the
preceding degree. But here, the vividness of the

---

[1] Abbé Saudreau, *Etat Mystique*, n° 111. Fr. Poulain, *Graces of Prayer*, xxxi. § 5.

[2] St. John of the Cross, *Second Night*, c. i.

[3] Fr. Lallemant, *Seventh Principle*, c. iv. art. 7.

light, the fire of love, the inebriating joy, and the certitude of God's presence attain to a wonderful degree of intensity during prayer, and prepare the soul for an astonishing transformation in her conduct; and this is what gives so high a value to the ecstatic union. In the time of ecstasy, " God begins to unveil to the soul some marvels of the kingdom prepared for her. . . . He ordinarily discovers to her during the rapture some of His great attributes. . . . She has never more light to comprehend the things of God than at this time." St. Teresa " is persuaded that, if the soul does not hear these heavenly secrets, the raptures are not genuine; . . . when the ecstasy is genuine, Our Lord, treating the soul as His Spouse, shows her a small portion of the kingdom which He has acquired, and however little so great a God may reveal Himself to the soul, she always contemplates wonderful things. . . . To this effect He grants her visions, which take place in the imagination and which she can afterwards relate, and these remain so impressed upon the memory that she can never forget them. The Divine Master gave her also intellectual visions, some of which are so elevated that the soul cannot find words to express them." [1]

" In these raptures the soul appears no longer to animate the body. She perceives, in a very sensible manner, that the natural heat of the body is becoming diminished; so great a cold gradually prevails

[1] St. Teresa, *Life*, xx. *Second Rel. to Fr. Rodr. Alvarez, Castle*, 6th mans. c. iv. *passim.*

Z

in the hands and in the whole body, that it seems
to be separated from the soul.   The rapture checks
the breathing to such an extent, that it is sometimes
impossible to detect any breathing at all.   As long
as the rapture lasts, the body remains as though
dead, and often absolutely incapable of movement;
.   .   .   the hands remain icy cold, and sometimes
rigid as wood; the body remains erect or kneeling
according to the position in which it was when the
rapture occurred.   If at times the use of the other
senses is retained during some moments, not a
word, however, can be uttered.   Most frequently
perception is not lost; St. Teresa retained it in such
a way as to be able to see that she was raised above
the earth.   Although persons thus affected cannot
act exteriorly, yet they do not cease to hear; the
sound, indeed, appears to them confused, and
coming, as it were, from a distance; but, when the
rapture is at its height, they neither hear, see, nor
feel anything.—When St. Teresa wanted to resist,
she seemed to feel a prodigious power under her
feet which lifted her up.   Often her body became
so light that it had no longer any weight.—However short the duration of this state, all the bodily
members feel its effects for a long time; yet it
never injures the health.   It was so at least in St.
Teresa's case; she did not recollect having ever
received this favour from God, even in the height
of her sickness, that she did not experience a very
sensible improvement in her bodily condition." [1]

[1] St. Teresa, *Life*, xviii. and **xx.**   *Second Rel. to Fr. Rodr.*
Alvarez.   Castle, 4th mans. c. **iv.**

St. Thomas, St. Teresa, and the greater number of authors teach that ecstasy does not interfere with liberty and merit.

There are lesser and greater degrees in these divine communications and in the alienation of the senses. This is the reason why authors distinguish between simple ecstasy, rapture, and the flight of the spirit. They have borrowed this division from St. Teresa, who, however, does not always employ the same words in the same sense.[1]—Rapture seizes upon the soul with such promptitude and impetuosity, that she can hardly ever resist it; feeling herself carried away, as a straw in the hand of a giant, she experiences at first an exceedingly great fear, and she needs to have a great deal of courage to abandon herself to the action of God. Some authors affirm that the skin retains its natural flush, that the eyes have a special beauty, and that the features are lighted up, whereas in ecstasy, the body is thrown aside like an old suit of clothes or rather like a corpse.[2]—The flight of the spirit is a rapture so impetuous, that " it appears to really separate the spirit from the body. Does the soul remain united to the body, or is it separated from it ? St. Teresa does not know, and would not like to affirm either statement."

It is to be noted that St. Paul speaks in the same terms of his great rapture.[3] " It seems to the soul that it is in a region entirely different from that in

---

[1] *Second Rel. to Fr. Rodr. Alvarez. Life*, xviii. *Castle*, 4th mans. c. iv.

[2] Sauvé, *États Mystiques*, v. 3.   [3] *II. Cor.*, xii.

which we are; she beholds a light incomparably
more brilliant than all those of this earth; she finds
herself in an instant instructed about so many marvellous things, that, with all her efforts, she would
not be able to imagine the one-thousandth part of
them in many years." [1]

Ectatic union is shorter at first; it is always of
short duration. St. Teresa, agreeing in this with
St. Gregory,[2] thinks that it does not last beyond
half an hour in its full strength; but, whilst the will
remains absorbed in God, the other faculties become
more or less free, and "the body then appears to
resume some life, only in order to die again after
the same manner"; it is during these intervals
that visions, revelations, and divine locutions occur.
Then the ecstasy regains all its strength only to
subside and then to increase again; and, owing to
this ebb and flow, it may last many hours, and
even days. When it is ended, "often for the rest
of the day, and sometimes for many days, the will
remains, as it were, inebriated, and the understanding altogether occupied with what it has seen; the
soul, it appears, is incapable of applying itself to
anything else but the love of God." [3]

Certain saints have often enjoyed these favours;
the life of many of them has been only a succession
of ecstasies. When people wanted to find St.
Joseph of Cupertin in his monastery, they began
by looking for him in the air. On the other hand,

[1] *Castle*, 6th mans. v. *Second Rel. to Fr. Rodr. Alvarez.*
[2] St. Gregory, *Moralia*, l. xxx. c. xvi.
[3] *Castle*, 6th mans. iv. *Life*, xviii. and xx.

nothing, or almost nothing similar is to be found in the lives of certain other great servants of God. In the life of St. Vincent de Paul none of these divine favours are met with, and very few in that of St. Francis of Sales. Had these great saints no experience of them? or, did they more carefully keep them concealed? We know not.

Perfection does not consist in these mysterious favours, but in the perfection of charity, which is manifested by the perfection of obedience and of conformity to God's will. For this it is necessary to go out of oneself by humility and self-renunciation. Mystical prayer is indeed a powerfully efficacious means to lead us on to this, but it is not the only means.

Divine ecstasy must not be confounded with its *counterfeits*. Such are: 1°. *lethargy, fainting-fits, hypnosis,* and certain maladies like *hysteria*. All these morbid states may render the body motionless, suspend the senses, and resemble ecstasy externally. But, internally, some of them suppress, for the moment, intelligence and will, so that persons can remember nothing afterwards, because they had no thoughts at all. The purely nervous affections go further still; they benumb the intellect, the imagination becomes predominant, a mere nothing absorbs the attention, and the will exhibits an unhealthy feebleness. On the contrary, in divine ecstasy, the soul is flooded with light, the heart inflamed with love, the intellect is elevated and broadened in an extraordinary way, the will gains such strength that this prayer of ecstasy ends by producing a complete transformation of one's life. Genuine ecstatics are always distinguished by strength of mind, great courage, moral elevation and fruitfulness in good works.

2°. There are also *diabolical ecstasies*. The demon can ape God, by rendering the body motionless, by acting on the imagination, by producing deceitful pleasures in the soul. But " to live in the state of sin, to enter into ecstasy at will, to exhibit unbecoming contortions, to utter incoherent words, to have no recollection of them after the ecstasy, to select frequented localities in order to make a display of themselves, to remain a long time troubled and agitated on returning to themselves, finally to receive while in ecstasy communications of evil tendency, or of good tendency but for an evil end, are the distinctive characteristics of diabolical action." [1]

The only certain proof of the divine origin of ecstasy is its effects. If it produces a wonderful progress in virtue, it comes from God; but if it does not effect that energetic transformation, which St. Francis of Sales calls the ecstasy of life, that saint regards ecstasy as a deceit of the evil spirit.[2] Now, the principal signs of the divine ecstasy may be reduced to seven.[3]

The first of these is found in the condition of the body. The body requires some little time to regain its wonted suppleness and elasticity. Often,

---

[1] Fr. Meynard, *Mystique*, b. iii. c. iii., after Benedict xiv.

[2] *Love of God*, b. vii. c. vi. and vii.

[3] Fr. Maynard, *Mystique*, b. iii. c. iii., after Benedict xiv.

"though previously infirm and harassed by grievous pains, it issues from the ecstasy full of health, and wonderfully disposed for action." [1] St. Teresa speaks thus from her own experience. Nevertheless, many saints might be mentioned who were made ill by divine ecstasies.

The second sign is an ardent desire to serve God. " This is the hour for *heroic* promises and resolutions. . . . The soul makes astonishing progress. Those who have to do with her believe her to be at the summit of perfection, and yet, a little afterwards, they find her still higher, because God is continually pouring into her fresh graces. For all that, she herself believes she is doing nothing, and would wish to have a thousand lives to sacrifice them for God, and to change all creatures into so many tongues to praise Him."

The third sign is a wonderful detachment from everything and from self. " The things of earth appear to the soul mere mud, she endures this life only with pain, and it is for her a torment to return to it, to be a spectator of the pitiful comedy which is being played here below, and to have to spend precious time in repairing her bodily strength with food and sleep. It is not only a perfect spiritual detachment; but, in this state, God seems to will that *the body itself* should really attain to this complete disengagement."

The fourth sign is " a wonderful knowledge of God, of oneself, and of earthly things. God gives

[1] St. Teresa, *Life*, xix. xx. xxi. *Castle*, 6th mans. c. iv. and *ff*. *Second Rel. to Fr. Rodr. Alvarez, passim.*

to the soul a higher idea of His incomprehensible greatness; the soul experiences a lively grief and a profound humility, at the sight of her own incapacity, unworthiness, nothingness, and faults; earthly things seem to her worthy only of supreme contempt."

The fifth sign is an ardent thirst to behold the living God, and an eager desire of death.

The sixth is that torment of love, as dolorous as it is delightful, which we have described above when speaking of passive purgation. The seventh is an " excessive joyfulness, which God from time to time imparts to the soul, which sometimes lasts an entire day, and whose strange transports she cannot understand. At such times, the soul, in the excess of her joy, forgets everything else, herself included, and can neither trouble herself nor speak about anything but the praises of God."

Truly St. Teresa had good reason to say : " If wealth could purchase the happiness I enjoy, I would have an extremely great esteem for wealth; but I see, on the contrary, that to obtain this happiness, we must renounce everything." She adds elsewhere that " the soil which bears these fruits very seldom fails to have been deeply furrowed by sufferings, persecutions, calumnies, and sicknesses." Finally, she remarks that these effects of raptures are sometimes greater, sometimes less, and that the journey towards perfection is gradual, and requires a certain time.[1]

[1] *Life*, xix. xx. xxi.　*Castle*, 6th mans. *passim.*

CHAPTER IX

TRANSFORMING UNION

THE supreme goal of mystical unions is the spiritual marriage of the soul with God, or transforming union, consummated union, deification. St. Teresa calls this the seventh mansion.

God has made captive the will, in the prayer of quiet, all the powers, in the state of full union, and the very body, in ecstasy; but now He is about to take hold of the substance of the soul and of its life; her whole being will now be taken hold of in a *more perfect, permanent* and *definite* way. God will no longer have any need to *bind* the faculties, for they now move at His good pleasure. The other unions were only transitory states, this one is stable.[1]—The union of all the powers was " the preparation for, and, as it were, the road to " spiritual marriage, and, so to speak, the *preliminary interviews*, before the *espousals*.[2] These latter have been celebrated in a sublime rapture; numerous ecstasies have made known to the soul the riches, the infinite perfections, the boundless love of Him who wishes to become her Spouse; these divine favours elevate her mind, inflame her heart, adorn

---

[1] *Castle*, 7th mans. c. ii.   St. Liguori, *Praxis*, 138.

[2] *Ibid.*, 5th mans. c. iv.

her as with so many jewels; the torments of love have completed her purification, and all is now ready for the celebration of the spiritual wedding.

This ceremony takes place in the very centre of the soul,[1] where the Holy Trinity dwells in a special manner, having there erected Its throne. Into this God introduces His betrothed, showing Himself to her, not indeed in the full light of the intuitive vision, but in a very clear and distinct intellectual vision. The sacred Humanity of Our Lord also manifests Himself to the soul, at first in a vision of the imagination, afterwards in an intellectual vision. Then it is that this most happy contract is signed by mutual consent. The form of the ceremony and of the secondary details may vary; the essential point is, that this contract establishes henceforth a permanent and indissoluble union of the soul with God.

The two spouses will dwell together in the inmost centre of the soul. Already God dwelt there by His sanctifying grace without the soul's being conscious of it. Here, however, the soul constantly enjoys an intellectual view of the Holy Trinity who is her companion. This view was very clear at first, and will become so again whenever God so pleases; but, generally, it is more obscure, otherwise " the soul could not attend to anything else, nor even live amongst human beings." This view is almost uninterrupted, even in the midst of exterior occupations; even when engaged in the works of Martha, the soul enjoys the

---

[1] *Castle*, 5th mans. c. i. and ii.

repose of Mary. Every time she thinks upon Him, she enjoys the company of her Divine Spouse; if she should cease to be attentive to Him, He Himself arouses her.[1]

There is in this state something infinitely more precious than even this continual perception of the Divine presence. " This is the total transformation of the soul into her Well-Beloved, a transformation in which . . . God raises the soul above herself, makes her divine, and renders her, so to speak, a participator in the Divine nature, as far at least as such a thing is possible in this world." [2]—Sanctifying grace had already made her sharer in the Divine nature and the life of God in a way as real, but not accompanied by a consciousness of it. Here it is impossible for the soul to doubt that the Holy Trinity is within her, communicating to her divine life, and aiding her to perform divine acts. " She sees clearly, by certain secret but very vivid affections of love, that it is her God who is giving her life, that He is within her like a living fountain, watering her with graces, that it is He who shoots the arrows by which she is wounded, that He is the life of her life, and the sun that sheds its light from her inmost centre upon all her powers."[3]

This perception of transformation in God is something very strange; its effects are not less so. The soul forgets, so to speak, her own interests,

---

[1] *Castle*, 7th mans. c. ii. and iii.
[2] St. John of the Cross, *Spir. Cant.*, stanza 22.
[3] *Castle*, 7th mans, c. ii,

and thinks only of those of God. She has an insatiable desire of suffering, but it is a tranquil
desire, for in all things she wishes only the good
pleasure of God. The impatient longing she previously had to die in order to be with her Well-
Beloved, has given place to such a desire to serve
Our Lord and procure His glory, that she would
willingly consent to live for long years to come;
yet she regards death rather as a " sweet rapture " ;
meanwhile she would wish to be ever occupied
with Our Lord or for Our Lord, and to do nothing
else but praise Him and win souls for Him.[1]

St. Teresa affirms that " the soul arrived at this
state hardly ever again experiences those impetuous
raptures of which she had spoken; ecstasies and
even flights of the spirit become very rare, and
hardly ever happen to her in public. . . . The
distinguishing feature of this mansion is that there
hardly ever occur in it any aridities," or interior
troubles; a profound peace reigns therein, " God
alone and the soul enjoy one another in a very
great silence."—Yet this is the case, " not invari-
ably, but as a general rule, . . . for some
times Our Lord leaves these souls in their natural
state "; then concupiscence awakens, and attacks
them fiercely, but this trial occurs only at rare intervals, and lasts hardly more than one day.
God wishes thus to show these souls how much
they stand in need of Him, to incline them to live
in an humble watchfulness, in a continual fear of
losing His favours. These souls, therefore, have

---

[1] *Castle*, 7th mans. c. iii.

their own trials, but they have also greater strength, and God protects them with jealous care.[1]

St. John of the Cross [2] and Scaramelli [3] maintain that in this state the soul is confirmed in grace. According to St. Teresa, she can commit only imperfections and "indeliberate" venial sins; "from mortal sins committed with advertence, she is exempt"; . . . for all that, "the soul is not assured of her salvation, nor of never again falling away," . . . except perhaps, "during the time Our Lord is leading her, as it were, by the hand."[4]

---

[1] *Castle*, 7th mans. c. iii. and iv.
[2] St. John of the Cross, *Spir. Cant.*, stanza 22.
[3] Scaramelli, *Dir. Myst.*, tr. 2 n° 258 and tr. 3 n° 225.
[4] *Castle*, 7th mans. c. ii. and iv.

CHAPTER X

SPIRITUAL ADVANTAGES OF
MYSTICAL PRAYER

WE have already shown the powerful effects of the
passive purgations, when God Himself, wishing
to purify and simplify a soul, operates with an un-
erring wisdom which knows the evil and its
remedy, with a strong hand which has none of our
over-tenderness and weakness. As we went along
we pointed out certain results which belong only to
the most elevated forms of prayer. It now remains
to set forth the general advantages which are to be
found in every species of mystical contemplation.

It is quite certain that mystical contemplation is
neither perfection, nor a necessary means to arrive
at it; for God gives it only to whom He wills,
whilst all are invited to be perfect. At all times
there have been great souls who were not contemplatives, and contemplatives who were far from
being perfect. "Many saints are in heaven,"
says St. Francis of Sales, "who never enjoyed an
ecstasy or a rapture of contemplation; for how
many martyrs and great saints, both men and
women, does history tell us of, who have never had
in prayer any other privilege than that of devotion

and fervour."?[1] St. Teresa, who extols so highly the advantages of contemplation, teaches that we can be saved without it, and none the less be very perfect, and even surpass in merit those who were favoured with it; for all our goodness and the most sublime perfection consist in the perfect conformity of our will with the will of God, and this conformity is the full development of divine love.[2] Mystical union, indeed, is " the short-cut "[3] to reach it, but it is not the only way. It always remains a favour which cannot be claimed as a right, no matter how advanced one may be in virtue. It, ordinarily speaking, requires dispositions already well-marked, but the precise moment, when the soul may safely leave off ordinary prayer and enter into mystical ways, cannot be determined. God always remains master of His gifts.

It is none the less true that supernatural prayer, especially of the more elevated kind, is a wonderful instrument of sanctification. " When God gives a soul such precious pledges of His love, it is a sign that He destines her for great things; and, if she be only faithful, she will make wonderful progress in perfection." So speaks St. Teresa, who had herself gone through this experience.[4]

What, then, are the advantages of mystical prayer?

1°. *On the part of the intellect.*—They are an incomparable knowledge of God, of ourselves, and of creatures.

---

[1] *Love of God,* b. vii. c. vii.
[2] *Way,* xviii. *Castle,* 2nd mans. i.
[3] *Way,* xxxii.
[4] *Ibid.,* xxxii.

A.—Before she has tasted God, the soul has only
a hearsay and feeble knowledge of Him. From
the time of the prayer of quiet, she has an experimental perception of God, she feels Him, tastes
Him, and is intimately united with Him; it almost
seems that she is going to see Him and take hold
of Him. This is not as yet the clear vision of God,
nor is it quite the obscurity of faith, but an intermediate state, wherein she treats with God, the invisible God, almost as if she beheld Him.[1]—Besides
this, she beholds Him under a new aspect. It is
His beauty, His goodness, His love which excite
in her admiration and astonishment. The Deity
hides from her His majesty; the Father, the
Brother, the Friend, the Spouse lavishes upon her
so much tenderness, so deep a love, such affectionate caresses, that it seems to her, transported
as she is out of herself, that she had never hitherto
really known God.—Later on, when she has pro-
gressed in the mystical way, she will, perhaps,
come to contemplate in a blinding light, in "the
great darkness," the incommunicable attributes of
God, His immensity, His eternity, &c.; but, from
the very first, she feels that God is incomprehensible; and, the more she advances the more she is
thrilled by a sense of this. No meditation, however
lightful you may suppose it to be, could ever give
her such an idea of Him. The same happens with
regard to things divine. "To meditate upon
Hell," says Father Lallemant, "is to see a painted

---

[1] *Invisibilem tanquam videns sustinuit*, Heb. xi. 27.

lion; to contemplate Hell, is to look upon a living lion."[1]

B.—Oh, how well the soul understands the dignity she receives from faith and grace, now, when the Sovereign Master deigns to manifest to her His presence, and to caress her with all the tenderness of a loving Father!—How she now feels overwhelmed with shame, penetrated with sorrow, animated with a holy hatred of herself, when this powerful light unveils to her, in all their hideous ugliness, her misery and her sins; or, when God persists for weeks or months in repelling her, although she never ceases seeking Him! Behold here the reason why the saints believed themselves to be the greatest of sinners.—In the same way, when the soul perceives by a kind of evidence her own nothingness and God's greatness, when she feels herself powerfully affected by the action of God upon her, the same grace, which raises her to contemplation, plunges her in an abyss of humility; the more she is struck by the majesty and power of God, the more need she feels of making herself quite small, of sinking down and annihilating herself in adoration and obedience. She cannot pardon herself for having so often offended so good and so great a Master; the only fear she now feels is that of offending or losing Him.

C.—In proportion as she grows in the knowledge and love of God, the things of earth cease to fascinate her. What the world calls honour appears to her "a huge lie; she despises, as so much worth-

---

[1] *Spiritual Doctrine*, 7th principle, c. iv. 5.

less mud, those riches, for which men often descend
to Hell and purchase an inextinguishable fire, an
endless torture "; she holds in horror " those
pleasures, by which people gain, even in this life,
only pains and bitter troubles." The bustling
activity, which worldings display, seems to her
" mere children's play. . . . For whatever
comes to an end and is not what pleases God, is
nothing, and even less than nothing. . . .
How much she is ashamed of her former attachments! How she is amazed at her own blindness!
What compassion she feels for those who are in-
volved in that same darkness! She would wish to
raise a warning voice to let them know how far they
are going astray." [1] Everything appears so insipid to a soul that has tasted God and experienced
a foretaste of Heaven! To enable her to make the
comparison she has now something better than any
amount of arguments, she tastes God, she has an
experimental knowledge of Him, in fact, a kind of
evidence. Whatever does not lead to God has no
charm for her; whatever rises up as a barrier
between her and her Well-Beloved excites her
horror.

2°. *On the part of the heart.*—Nothing is so well
calculated to nourish the fire of divine love as
mystical contemplation. When the soul feels that
she loves and is beloved, when God evinces towards
her an incomparable tenderness, there are moments
when, quite bewildered and transported out of herself, she is inebriated, and beside herself with love;

---

[1] St. Teresa, *Life*, xx. *passim.*

one might say, without fear of exaggeration, that she loves God a hundred times more ardently than in her natural state. She rushes towards Him, she possesses Him and unites herself to Him with such impetuosity, that she would wish to be dissolved in Him and to make only one thing with Him. It is a fire, a flame, a furnace, one great conflagration of love. St. Teresa complains of the hardness of her heart, and yet " it used to drop like an alembic." [1]   If this occurs in the state of quiet, when somewhat pronounced, what shall it be in the state of full union and the still higher degrees?

This glorious delirium of love is not of everyday occurrence. For the most part, the soul is, as it were, abandoned; she is seeking God but cannot find Him; the more He hides Himself, the more ardently she pursues after Him. But is it not love which thus runs after Him? This desire dilates the heart, increases its capacity to receive Him, intensifies the closeness of the unitive embrace, perhaps quite as much as did the ardours which preceded. For a long time severed from her Well-Beloved, her only one, the soul comes to seek Him with an impetuous though transient desire, which constitutes *the anguish of love*; if this restless desire should remain fixed in the depths of the heart, it is called *the thirst of love*.[2] We have described elsewhere *the wound of love*, when " God closely pursues the soul, and, from time to time, discharges at her countless arrows of His love,

---

[1] *Castle*, 6th mans. c. vi.   [2] Scaramelli, 3rd tr. xi.

showing her by new means how much more
lovable He is than loved.[1] " These secret ardours,
these amorous touches, like so many burning
arrows, wound and transpierce the soul, and leave
her all tortured by this violent fire." A dolorous
torture : " He alone who caused this wound can
cure it. . . . . But the soul cruelly feels His
absence and the grief of not being able to possess
Him here below as she desires." A sweet torture :
for the soul feels that she loves and already possesses
her Well-Beloved. " She would be willing to suffer
death a thousand times by means of these arrows,
which make her leave herself and all things, only
in order to unite her "[2] more perfectly to Him,
whom she invokes with all her desires.

Oh, how those souls who hunger and thirst after
God alone, how those souls, wounded with love,
honour and delight God, whether it be that they
are seeking Him with so much ardour, or, that they
have already found Him, with so much contentment to themselves ! No doubt, souls that have
reached this degree of love are rare ; but religious,
engaged in contemplative ways, are often met with
who already love God to an astonishing degree.

3°. *On the part of the will.*—God enlightens the
mind and inflames the heart, only in order the
better to secure the will. Mystical action, by
rendering faith more lively and love more ardent,
develops the energies of these holy virtues. It
multiplies, elevates, and strengthens the affections

[1] St. Francis of Sales, *Love of God,* b. vi. c. xiii.
[2] St. John of the Cross, *Spir. Cant.*, stanza i. 15, 16, 17.

in prayer, and imparts to them at times a marvellous intensity. It communicates to the soul a well-marked impulse towards all virtues, and leaves her better armed, than she could be by ordinary meditation, for the combat and for spiritual progress. Under its influence the mists of faith clear up, love grows stronger, the mind adheres more closely to God, the heart conceives a holy passion for Him; hence, the soul becomes more easily detached, and obstacles diminish. At the same time, urged by her love, she strives to avoid whatever is displeasing to her Well-Beloved, and to omit nothing that may please Him. She becomes more delicate and generous in her obedience to all the prescriptions of His law, and in her loving conformity to all the dispositions of His divine Providence. She conceives a supreme horror of the least sin, and can never pardon herself for having so much offended the " God of her heart." She peacefully accepts, lovingly seeks opportunities of sacrifice, she even becomes insatiable for them, in order to make some small return to Him who has so exceedingly loved her. Her happiness would be to be always, like Mary, at the feet of her Divine Master, contemplating Him, loving Him, and singing His praises. She devotes herself to the occupations of Martha, as far as duty requires; but, as soon as she is permitted, she makes haste to return to Him, who is the repose of her mind and the joy of her heart. Solitude attracts and captivates her; she feels the imperative need of being alone with God alone, that nothing may trouble the serenity of her mind and the pious effusions of her heart. A time even will come, when it will no longer suffice for her to feel the presence of her Well-Beloved; with impatient desire she will long for death which she deems too slow in coming, in such haste shall she be to see at last Him, whom she loves, and to possess Him quite at her ease; unless, indeed, divine love, growing still stronger, should urge her to wish to live for ever, in order to labour unceasingly to communicate to others the fire which consumes herself. For she would wish to show to the whole world the treasure that excites her admiration and her raptures; and, not being able to praise or love Him as she would desire, she would be happy to see all the earth on its knees before Him.

This soul is possessed by an ever-increasing divine love; God, on his side, operates with so much the more energy because He meets with fewer obstacles in a heart so well disposed. So St. Teresa is not afraid to say : " Weak and bowed down to earth as we are, we should have much trouble in arriving at perfect detachment, at that sovereign disgust of things here below, did not our soul already possess some pledge of the goods above.[1] . . . As for me, miserable that I am, I have need of all these helps. . . . Previously to my receiving these helps, it was my own life I led; this life, which began with these states of prayer, is, I may say, the life of God in me; for, otherwise, I acknowledge, it would have been impossible for me to have been delivered, in so short a time, from the habits

	[1] *Life*, x.

of a life formerly so imperfect."[1]—The same saint says elsewhere, that "the state of quiet is incomparably more efficacious than meditation to make us grow in virtue. . . . It is a spark which God casts into the soul, a real conflagration, which sets the soul on fire with a most ardent love of God."[2] In proportion as prayer rises to the higher degrees, this saint extols it more eloquently; for these degrees have not all the same relative value, and differ also in intensity and frequency. Their efficacy is all the greater as the soul becomes more purified, reaches the higher degrees, and utilises with greater zeal the influence they have to make her grow in holiness. Taking them altogether, they are a marvellous instrument of perfection, and Father Lallemant[3] had good reason to say : "With the aid of contemplation, a man will do more for himself and others in one month than he could do in ten years without it."—According to Father Surin, in meditation, souls travel on foot, are greatly fatigued, and advance little; in affective prayer they travel on horse-back with less labour and increased rapidity; in contemplation, they travel in a carriage, to-day we would say by rail; they advance still more rapidly and with much less fatigue.[4]—Louis of Blois had said before him : "Those who are united to God and leave Him full liberty to work in them at every moment what He pleases, do more for the Church in one hour than others, whoever they may be, do in several years."

---

[1] *Life*, xxiii.   [3] *Spiritual Doctrine*, 7th principle, iv. 4.
[2] *Ibid.*, xiv. and xv.   [4] *Spiritual Catechism*, vol. i. part i. c. iii.

St. Teresa never ceases repeating [1] that those, to whom God gives such graces, are destined to win a great number of other souls to God, and to render great services to the Church.

According to St. John of the Cross, " certain lights and divine touches so enrich a soul, that a single one of them is able to deliver her at once from the imperfections she had not been able to get rid of during her whole previous life, and to endow her besides with virtues and divine gifts." [2]　St. Teresa is not less formal upon this point : Oftentimes God in the space of a year or six months raises certain souls to a higher degree of contemplation than others in the course of ten or twenty years. He obtained a progress from certain generous persons in three months, and from one of them in three days, that He had not obtained from herself after many years of prayer.[3]　She mentions, in many places,[4] cases in which the soul was changed rapidly, and, as it were, in an instant, and certain faults, until then intractable, were corrected, how she knew not.— But these rapid ascents, these sudden illuminations, these unexpected transformations, are rare exceptions.　Very rash, mad even, would he be who would count upon such favours and lie down in idleness !　Generally speaking, the soul becomes detached and advances in prayer only little by little, as also occurs in the habit of meditation,

---

[1] *Life*, xi. xv. xviii.　*Castle*, 4th mans. c. iii. &c.
[2] *Ascent*, b. ii. c. xxvi.
[3] *Life*, xxxiv. and xxxix. *passim.*　*Cant. of Cant.* c. vi.
[4] *Ibid.*, xvii. xxi. xxiv. xxv. xxvii. xxxi.

although with less energy. " The soul's whole
good, therefore, depends on her perseverance," [1]
and the generous efforts she makes to prepare herself and to correspond. It would be very unjust to
require that she should be perfect even from the
state of quiet, time is necessary as well as grace.—
Alas! she may, even after such favours, backslide
and become tepid, as it happened to St. Teresa.
The saint beseeches these souls not to abandon
prayer, " they will find in it light, sorrow for their
faults, and strength to rise again." [2]

[1] *Castle*, 4th mans. c. iii.   [2] *Life*, xv.

CHAPTER XI

JOYS AND SUFFERINGS

ST. JOHN OF THE CROSS describes the rough ascent
which leads to Carmel, the pains which purge the
soul and prepare it for the divine union.[1] St.
Teresa sets more in relief the joys of contemplation. They do not contradict, but rather supplement each other, and in order to have the whole
truth, we must take them conjointly. Besides, St.
John of the Cross does not conceal the consolations,[2]
and St. Teresa clearly sets forth the crucifying
trials of the contemplative way.[3]

I.—There are joys of the mind, which, having no
longer to labour so hard and possessing the truth,
enjoys a sense of repose; the lights the intellect receives are at times so vivid that it remains dumb
with admiration.—There are the joys of the will:
" the soul experiences in her inmost depths a pure
calm, a profound peace, a very great contentment
of her will, an interior and exterior satisfaction, a
very sweet unction of which she can give no precise
description. She does not know whence nor how

[1] The whole of the *Ascent* and of the *Obscure Night*.
[2] *Spir. Cant.* and *Living Flame*, &c.
[3] *Life, passim*, and especially c. xi. xxx. xxxi. *Way*, xix.
Castle, 6th mans. c. i. and *ff.*

378

this has come to her, but she finds herself so happy that it seems to her she wants for nothing." This is what St. Teresa in many places affirms to be the case, even in the state of quiet.[1] She shows its clearly supernatural and infused character, and points out the differences which distinguish the sweets of contemplation from the consolations which spring from meditation. The soul has found Him whom she was seeking, and, finding herself in possession of God, she feels that she loves and is deeply loved in return. What a happiness to be clasped to the heart of God in a loving and spiritual embrace, though it were for a few instants only! But when this delight is prolonged it produces a sort of spiritual inebriation, which sometimes resembles the state of a person half asleep, and at other times is full of ardour. And these joys go on increasing in proportion as the prayer ascends to the higher degrees; the union of all the powers is more full of consolation than a simple state of quiet, and ecstasy still more than either. At certain moments the soul believes herself to be at the very gates of Paradise; half-an-hour, or even fifteen minutes, of these delightful interviews with her Well-Beloved makes her forget all past sufferings, and strengthens her wonderfully for trials to come.[2] For such is the rôle of these sweetnesses: they detach the soul from earth, and attach her to God; they are the harbingers of new sufferings, and predispose contem-

[1] *Life, passim,* and especially c. xiv. and xv. *Way,* xxi. xxxii. *Castle,* 4th mans. c. i. and *ff.*
[2] *Ascent,* b. ii. c. xxvi.

platives to embrace them generously. " I know," says St. Teresa, " that the tribulations, through which God makes them pass, are *intolerable*; they are of such a nature that if God did not strengthen these souls by this delightful interior nourishment, they would never have the strength to support them. . . . Thus it is necessary that Our Lord should give them, not the water which refreshes, but *the wine which inebriates,* in order that, under the influence of a holy inebriation, they in some sort no longer feel their sufferings. . . . Persons who are engaged in the active way, when they witness some favour granted to souls raised to the contemplative prayer, imagine doubtless that there is nothing but sweetness and delight in this state; but I can tell them that perhaps they could not bear even for one single day the sufferings which contemplatives have commonly to endure." [1]

Contemplation, then, is not the way of delicate and soft souls, but rather that of brave and generous hearts, who love their crucified Saviour, and have no fear of the cross; tribulation and anguish are their daily bread; though, from time to time, God sends some sweetness to comfort them, and to show the boundless extent of His enduring love for them.

We may remark with Father Poulain, that " the pleasure experienced in the prayer of quiet is affected by the dispositions in which the soul is at the time. If she is passing through a period of peace and joy, it is more marked. It is so, likewise, when these graces have a certain novelty. If,

[1] *Way*, xix. *Castle*, 7th mans. c. iv.

on the contrary, she is passing through a state of sorrow and of trial, the pleasure imparted by the prayer of quiet may be in some degree troubled or veiled."[1]

II.—*As for sufferings,* contemplatives have still to endure many of those which they formerly suffered. Besides physical pains, separation from their dearest friends, loss of temporal goods and other common trials, they have still temptations to overcome, inclinations to subdue, passions to govern, virtues to perfect. They suffer on the part of God who seems to have abandoned them, on the part of their superiors who reprehend them, of their brethren who have neither the same views nor the same tastes, of the world which misunderstands them, of the demon who tempts them, of the elements which afflict them : all this is the lot of poor humanity, even in the cloister.—It may even happen, through a special design of God, who wishes to render these souls more pure, more humble and more detached, that many of these ordinary trials afflict them with an uncommon persistency and severity.[2]

Just as contemplation has its own joys, so also it has its own peculiar sufferings.

We have already sufficiently described the trials, so various and so prolonged, of the passive purgation of the senses, and the rarer, but much more acute, pains of the passive purgation of the spirit. We need not further revert to them here.

Mystical contemplation, taken in general, intro-

---

[1] *Graces of Prayer*, 2nd part c. xi. 8.
[2] See 3rd part, c. iii. art. i. § iii. p. 263.

duces the soul, in an evident manner, into the midst
of the supenatural; it has something mysterious
about it which strikes the mind, especially at first,
and causes trouble in a soul as yet inexperienced in
this way. We become still more anxious, should
we meet with no one able to give us an explanation
as to what it all means. What, then, will happen
if you clip this poor soul's wings, if you hinder her
from flying whither God is calling her, under the
pretext of preserving her simplicity and avoiding
singularity? At bottom, it is the Holy Ghost
whom you are lecturing and forbidding to lead that
soul by any other way than such as is in accordance
with your own narrow views.

When the state of quietude is weak, the soul
suffers. St. Teresa declares that " while her will
was united to God, her memory and imagination
waged so fierce a war against her that she conceived
a horror of them, and was altogether worn out by
their assaults." [1] We shall, therefore, have to
struggle against distractions, weariness and disgust, and to strive to supplement the divine action,
which it is not in our power to increase, by the
efforts of our own activity; now, at such a time we
shall be able to make nothing but little, dry,
short, monotonous acts devoid of all relish. God's
company becomes a downright fatigue, His conversation has no charm for us; yet, if we fly from Him,
our state becomes still worse, for, in spite of all, the
soul has need of God and cannot do without Him.

The soul hoped to ascend, ever to ascend higher,

[1] *Life*, xvii.

and now she must remain months, perhaps even years, in the same degree; hence, she is inclined to become discouraged and to look back.

Even when the soul has attained to a high degree of prayer, and when she is passing through one of those periods in which a mere nothing sets her all on fire, she still has to suffer; for, however closely she may be united to God, she will always long for a closer union. The visits of her Well-Beloved appear to her so short and so few; . . . she thinks she holds Him fast, and, behold, He escapes from her grasp; it seems to her that she is flying upwards to a higher union, and lo! she falls back again; . . . her desire is impetuous, her need imperious, but never satisfied. The soul comes at last to experience a real hungering after God, a painful thirst for Him, without being able ever fully to satisfy it; sometimes it is a wound of love, which the entire possession of God alone can heal; and yet He hides Himself from her, and, by His absence, enlarges the wound and renders it more painful. Should He give Himself to her to the full extent of her desires, she is too weak to bear so excessive a joy. She ends by conceiving such a taste for God "that she would wish to be at once freed from all necessities; eating is death to her, sleeping is a torment; she beholds the precious time of life consumed in providing for countless necessities, and yet she can find no satisfaction but in God alone."[1]

The contemplative soul suffers also from the ever-varying fluctuations of this state which constantly

[1] St. Teresa, *Life*, xvi.

toss her about, being sometimes raised to the heights of mystical union, at another time brought down to an almost imperceptible union, or even plunged once more into all the horrors of the passive purifications. How full, then, of desolation is this soul so loving, this soul that hungers so after God, desires only Him, and yet nowhere finds Him! Above all, when these trials are prolonged, and when He, who is the sole object of her love, persists in abandoning her and seems to despise her! At times this is a merciful chastisement, at others, it is an artifice of her Divine Spouse, who wishes to make her seek more earnestly after Him, in order that the increasing ardour of her desire may inflame the fervour of her love.

St. Bernard was well acquainted with these painful trials, and bewails them in the bitterness of his soul. "When we seek Christ our Spouse in watchings and in prayer, at the cost of many efforts, and amidst a torrent of tears, He comes to us; but suddenly, whilst we think to keep Him, he escapes from us. Yielding again to the tears and pursuit of our soul, He allows Himself to be laid hold of, but by no means to be retained; for suddenly He escapes a second time from our hands. If the devout soul perseveres in prayers and tears, He will return again and not disappoint the desires of her heart; but soon again He will disappear and she shall see Him no more, unless she recalls Him again by the whole strength of her desires. Thus, then, even while the soul is in this body, she may taste frequent, but not full, delight in the presence of her

Spouse, for, though His visits give her joy, those vicissitudes make her suffer." [1]

Finding it impossible to keep her Well-beloved with her, and impossible also to rekindle the fire of her love, she bewails her negligence and bitterly accuses herself in the language of St. Bernard : " I was running well, but lo! I struck against a stumbling-block in the way, and I have fallen. Pride has been found in me, and the Lord has turned away in anger from His servant. Hence, this barrenness and this dearth of devotion which I now experience. How has my heart become so dry, like curdled milk, like to a land without water ? . . . I can find no tears of compunction, so great is the hardness of my heart. The psalms have lost their savour, reading pleases me not, prayer has no charm, I can no longer make my customary meditations. What, then, has become of that inebriation of the soul ? Where, then, is that serenity of mind, that peace and joy in the Holy Ghost ? This is the reason why I am so lazy at manual work, so drowsy at watching, so prompt to anger, so slow to forgive, so weak in my preaching. Alas! the Lord visits all the mountains round about, but never draws near to me . . . ! "

The soul suffers also, when God shows her in contemplation His terrifying justice, the multitude of her personal sins, her own long life so empty of virtues, the countless offences which outrage His sanctity, the rage of those who hate Him, the loss of so many souls, the evils of the Church, the suffer-

[1] *Sermons on Cant. of Cant.*, xxxii. 2.

2 B

ings of His Passion, the little return we make for the love of our Divine Master, and many other such like subjects for sorrow. " Six years had passed away since St. Teresa had had her vision of hell, and yet such was the terror that seized her, when writing about it, that the very blood froze in her veins."[1] When the same saint considered what she was, the favours of her God used to throw her into inexpressible confusion ; the memory of her good works seemed to be blotted out, her imperfections alone presented themselves to her mind, and she needed more strength to receive such graces than to carry the heaviest crosses.[2]—She used to suffer almost continual pain and look upon herself as the greatest sinner in the world, when she thought how little gratitude she had shown towards Him who had heaped upon her so many favours.[3]—She was overwhelmed with shame, that she was able to make only so poor a return to that God who had given her so much, and this inability was for her the greatest of penances.[4]—She suffered from being exposed to the complaints, criticisms, and suspicions of some persons, and to the praise and admiration of others, when the favours she had received from God became public.[5]—Add to this the fear of losing God and of being a prey to those illusions, which have made so many victims. St. Teresa suffered all this during long years; her humility and the delicacy of her conscience rendered her fears only the more alarming.[6] In the midst of

[1] *Life*, xxxii.
[2] *Ibid.*, xxxix.
[3] *Castle*, 6th mans. c. vii.
[4] *Castle*, 7th mans. c. ii.
[5] *Ibid.*, 6th mans. c. vii.
[6] *Life*, c. xxiii. and *ff.*

so many afflictions, she sought for a long time in vain for some guide who would understand and console her. If she met with any such who re-assured her for the time, her fears quickly revived to assail her once more., It often happens in the designs of Providence that no one can assuage our pains.

To resume, then, " at all times, in the beginning, in the middle, at the end of our career, we all have our crosses, though of different kinds; " [1] for this is the royal way traced out for all by our Crucified Saviour; in this way alone, we shall find Him and become united to Him; there would be no security in a way always exempt from trials and strewn with roses. Suffering, by purifying the soul, assures advancement in the path of prayer; moreover, it is amply compensated for, and is by no means an un-mitigated evil. From the hour that St. Teresa gave herself entirely to God, she never had to endure a pain that did not bring with it its own consolation. If God sent her something to suffer, He afterwards lavished upon her His favours. " It seems to me," she adds, " that to suffer is the only thing worth living for, . . . and I sometimes say to God from the bottom of my heart: O Lord, let me suffer or die." [2]

[1] *Life*, xi.   [2] *Ibid.*, xl.

CHAPTER XII

DANGERS AND ILLUSIONS

§ I.—DANGERS.

THERE are some dangers when the graces of prayer abound, others when these graces are withdrawn.

I.—In the midst of the joys of divine consolations we have to fear vain complacency and spiritual gluttony.

These faults may be met with in simple meditation; but when the soul feels herself sought after by God, tenderly loved by her Divine Master and treated with marked predilection, she has a more specious pretext to look upon herself with complacency, and to believe herself to be something. In another way, spiritual consolations are so sweet, that one is led to seize upon them with a greediness which turns into poison the generous wine of contemplation. Mystical action, however, strongly urges the soul towards humility and detachment. Far from being the cause of those miseries, it is only their innocent occasion, the whole fault comes from ourselves. It would, therefore, be unjust to regard that action with suspicion and to avoid it, on the pretext that it exposes us to the malice of the demon and of nature; it would, in fact, be just as reasonable to omit the practice of virtue through fear of pride, which finds therein its most delicate nourishment.

But the more God elevates us, the more ought we to humble ourselves. These things are graces and not our merits; they are powerful instruments of perfection, not perfection itself; in spite of them, a man may be much inferior to his brethren, may grow tepid, and be lost. God will require more from him to whom He has given more.—In the same way, we must renounce our greediness for consolations, and combat it with unremitting energy. It is better to accustom ourselves to will only God's good pleasure, to remain in a holy indifference with regard to sweetness or bitterness, consolations or trials. Provided that we belong entirely to God and God to us, what signify the ways and the means, consolations or aridities, sweet contemplations or passive purgations? The one thing essential is to arrive at our end by the shortest and best way. After all, it is God we want rather than His gifts. His will and not our pleasure is the rule of what is good, the sole road of progress, and we should study to serve Him with disinterestedness and at our own expense.

Can the inebriation, produced by the strength and sweetness of divine love, occasion any disorder in the senses? St. Teresa never experienced anything of the kind "in the supernatural phenomena" which she has described, and this kind of thing seemed to her not even possible.[1]   Quite

[1] *First Rel. to Fr. Rodr. Alvarez.*

different is the opinion of St. John of the Cross, when there is question of souls imperfectly purified; [1] and that of St. Gregory the Great is not less formal on this point. " It often happens," says this latter, " that the soul is elevated by the Divine Spirit even to the heights of prayer, and, nevertheless, the flesh makes painful assaults upon her. At the very moment when she is led to the contemplation of heavenly things, imaginations of illicit actions present themselves to her, and the sting of the flesh makes itself painfully felt in him, who had been raised above the flesh by contemplation. It seems as if heaven and hell were here mingled together, since the same soul finds herself at once illumined by the lights of contemplation and clouded over by importunate temptations." [2]

In such a case, let the soul strive to avoid all danger of consenting to such temptations; let her moderate, if she can, the excess of sensible devotion; let her humble herself on account of her misery, and not be discouraged. This purely material disorder is not willed by her, either as an end or as a means, and is superabundantly compensated for by the fruits of contemplation. This painful condition, therefore, ought not to lead us to abandon so desirable a form of prayer.

For a stronger reason, contemplatives are not exempt from this kind of humiliations outside the times of mystical union. " Contemplation lifts them above themselves," says St. Gregory [3] elsewhere, " and, behold, immediately temptation

[1] *First Night*, iv.　　[2] Saudreau, *Vie d'Union*, n° 129.　　[3] *Ibid.*

comes upon them from their growing vain of these gifts. Compunction, in fact, or contemplation raises them up towards God, but the weight of temptation makes them fall back again upon themselves. Temptation depresses them in order that contemplation may not puff them up; and contemplation elevates them lest temptation should utterly cast them down."

An humble and detached soul has nothing to fear in mystical ways. "God forbid," says St. Teresa, "that any one could say that there is danger in the ways of prayer. It is the demon, never doubt it, who has invented all these fears. . . . The danger really to be feared is that of failing in humility and the other virtues."[1] The soul, therefore, should practise humility, detachment, and strive to become better; otherwise God will be obliged to withdraw His favours which we abuse, and to crush our pride under the severest humiliations, and, perhaps, by even allowing us to fall heavily into sin.

II.—*When the graces of prayer are withdrawn,* especially if for any length of time, the resulting aridity exposes the soul to discouragement. One may weary in the pursuit of God, when one constantly fails to get hold of Him. The blessings of contemplation, however precious they may be, lose their relish for a soul that is wanting in generosity, and appear to her to be too dearly purchased at the cost of so many trials. Oh, let us never give way to discouragement; it is the worst of all scourges. Great graces and sublime virtues are not imparted to cowardly

[1] *Way,* xxii.

souls. Our Lord loves the brave hearts who have
no fear of His cross. We are the brothers of the
Crucified God, we must be willing to be crucified
with Him, if we would resemble and please Him.
Besides, if we profit much during the outbursts of
divine love, perhaps we may derive as many advantages from trials and abandonments well borne.
Let us allow God to lead us by the ways which seem
to Him to suit us best; let us place our perfection in
following Him with love and docility, especially
when He leads us by paths wherein self-love
perishes and falls exhausted for want of food.

§ II.—Illusions.

One of the first illusions is to believe ourselves
more advanced than we really are. We possess a
theoretical knowledge of mystical ways, and then
we let ourselves believe that we are already in these
ways, merely because we have received some more
vivid light in prayer, or some more marked devotion. The holy mountain of contemplation is still
really very far away, and yet we think we have
already reached it; we have hardly begun to ascend
this mountain when we imagine we are upon its
summit. This illusion is the daughter of pride.—
St. Bernard tells us[1] that " if there are amongst
monks contemplatives who imitate Mary, they are
not to be looked for amongst novices,[2] who,
having only just died to sin, are labouring, in

[1] *Sermons on the Cant. of Cant.*, lvii. n° 11.
[2] He means such as are novices in virtue.—*Trans.*

groanings and the fear of judgment, to heal their still fresh and bleeding wounds. No, but they are found to be those who, after a long co-operation with grace, have arrived at a better state, wherein they are less occupied in turning over and over the sad picture of their sins than in making it their joy to meditate day and night on the law of the Lord, without ever being able to have enough of it." Generally speaking, therefore, a person must have practised meditation and affective prayer for a long time, and must have made great progress in virtue, before contemplation is reached. The slow and painful passive purgation of the senses is the gate of contemplation; its every degree is a long stage, which usually requires years for its accomplishment; and very few are the souls that get beyond the simple state of quietude. Progress in prayer should give rise to an ever-ascending progress towards perfection. If tangible results are not obtained, the soul is nursing herself in illusions, or she is abusing grace; and, instead of feeding herself with vain fancies, she has need to strengthen herself in humility, in self-renunciation, and in obedience.

It is an illusion to think that these mystical states cannot come to an end. Actual contemplation is always of short duration. The severities of the passive purgations alternate with the sweets of consoling prayer. The mystical state itself may be lost, either by infidelity in corresponding with it, or by the special will of God, who ever remains master of His gifts, and alone knows whether they are injurious or useful to us.

It is an illusion to dream of visions, revelations, locutions, and the other phenomena of distinct contemplation. Usually the lives of the saints are full of these facts which entertain both the writer and the reader. Certain modern authors go to the opposite extreme and suppress the supernatural, as far as possible, in the life of a saint. The truth is, that the greater number of the great servants of God have been favoured largely with these gifts. Heaven honoured its elect, in order to accredit the mission with which they were charged, to awaken the faith of the masses, or in view of their own personal sanctification. Their sanctity did not consist in these extraordinary favours, but in their being completely dead to self, and in the heroism of their virtues; and the graces of prayer contributed much more than visions, to lead them on to perfection. Besides, visions, revelations and other facts of this nature, easily open a door to a thousand illusions; even canonised saints have not always been able to avoid the deceits of the demon or the reveries of the imagination. Who does not know how urgently St. John of the Cross exhorts his readers to distrust visions, revelations, or locutions, to resist them, and to get rid of them? St. Teresa gives her readers the same counsel: " In such matters there is always reason to fear, until the soul is certain that they proceed from the Spirit of God. This is why I say that, in the beginning, the best course to adopt is always to combat them. If God is their author, this humility of the soul in guarding herself against such favours will only the better dispose her for receiving them, and the more she puts them to the test, the more they will increase." [1] The saint, when speaking of Our Lord's apparitions, adds : " Never ask Him, never even wish Him, to lead you by this way. This way is, no doubt, good, and you ought to hold it in high esteem and respect; but it is unseemly either to ask or desire it." [2]

It is an illusion to dream of mystical states, in which there will be nothing but enjoyment; for in them there will always be a much greater share of suffering;—or, again, of states, in which the soul will have nothing to do but to passively receive favours. The soul, indeed, at times, will be more passive than active, yet, even then, she must keep her mind in a state of simple attention to God, and her heart in a loving disposition, or in acts of love. Far from remaining merely passive, she is really more active than at other times, but in a simple way and by direct acts, even when the mystical union is at its height. When the contemplative act has passed away, the soul should return to active prayer and exercise herself therein, in spite of the dryness she may experience.

It is an illusion to believe that in this state we cannot fall into sin any more. These favours do not confirm a soul in grace; she remains always weak, and even capable of being lost through mortal sins, except, perhaps, when she has reached the state of spiritual marriage. She must, therefore, distrust herself, take care to avoid the danger, and keep herself in humility and detachment. Let us

[1] *Castle*, 6th mans. c. iii.   [2] *Ibid.*, 6th mans. c. ix.

not forget what St. Teresa says of the union of all
the powers: " The soul in this state is not strong
enough to expose herself without peril to occasions
of sin." [1]

It is an illusion to believe that the mystical state
dispenses us from cultivating Christian virtues, from
discharging the duties of our state, from observing
our rules, &c.　On the contrary, the more God gives
us, the greater must be the return we make Him; if
He confides ten talents to us, He rigorously requires
that this capital shall not remain unproductive.
Humility, abnegation, obedience, recollection, the
spirit of prayer, and, above all, charity towards
Himself and towards our brethren should increase
in proportion to our gifts; these virtues are the
end to which God wishes to lead us, mystical states
are only the way; if our means of locomotion are
more perfect, all our virtues also should increase
their pace towards perfection.　An elevated state of
prayer, without this well-marked progress, is either
an illusion or a buried talent.—We must, therefore,
accept of these mystical states with humility, correspond to them with generosity, fear them while
desiring them, abase ourselves in proportion as
God elevates us, hide the divine gift from those
who have no right to be informed of it, love more
than ever our rule, which is our safeguard, fly
exemptions and singularities, put our trust not in
mystical graces, but in humility, self-renunciation,
obedience, and the other virtues which should be
their fruit.

[1] *Castle*, 5th mans. c. iv.

It is an illusion to neglect the duties of our state, in order to give more time to contemplation. "It is certain, on the contrary," says Father Balthasar Alvarez, "that we ought to quit contemplation to fulfil the duties of our charge or to help our neighbour in his necessities. . . . I have come to know by experience," he adds elsewhere, "that God gives more to a mortified soul, in one hour of prayer, than in many hours to another that is not so, and that the occupations, with which obedience burthens us, are more profitable to my soul than spiritual reading or repose."[1]

It is an illusion to believe that, in the guidance of mystical souls, everything should be out of the ordinary course, as if God had taken upon Him to guide them Himself by interior inspirations, and that they have no need of a superior or a spiritual father. Deplorable illusion, the daughter of pride! Very presumptious is he who believes himself to be inspired, and presumes to lay down the law for himself and others! Very foolish he, who welcomes inspirations but little conformable to common sense and to faith! Very rash he, who bases his conduct upon so shaky a foundation! "This person," says St. Teresa, speaking of herself, "never regulated her conduct by the inspirations she received in prayer; and, when her confessors told her to act in a way opposed to them, she used to obey without the least repugnance."[2]   She teaches elsewhere,[3]

[1] *Life of Fr. Balth. Alvarez*, by the Ven. Dupont, c. xiii. and xli. 5th diff.

[2] *Second Rel. to Fr. Rodr. Alvarez*

[3] *Castle*, 6th mans. c. iii.

that " such is the will of Our Lord," but adds :
" Whenever interior words tend only to console
you, or to admonish you of your faults, whoever be
their author, and even were they an illusion, they
cannot do you any harm."—God loves contemplative souls with predilection, is prodigal of His
graces in their regard, and leads them, more than
He does others, by the royal road of suffering and
humiliation; but He has not undertaken to guide
them miraculously. It is the law of Providence
that men should be guided by other men. Have
not these souls at their service the spiritual writers
with all their knowledge and experience? Above
all, God has given them superiors and a spiritual
director, and to these they ought to manifest their
interior with docility, in order to subject what passes
therein to due control.[1]   God sent an angel to Cor-
nelius to refer him to St. Peter.[2]   Our Lord Himself appeared to Saul, but sent him to consult
Ananias.[3]

Many other illusions might be pointed out. It
is easy to see that they all arise from pride, or from
an inordinate desire of enjoyment. A soul in such
dispositions is exposed to a thousand errors, to the
most diverse faults. With humility, detachment
and docility she has less to fear in the state of
obscure contemplation than in meditation. God,
who leads by these ways men of good will, owes it
to Himself not to let them go astray.

[1] St. Liguori, *Praxis*, 143 and 144.
[2] *Acts*, x. 3, 5.   [3] *Ibid.*, ix.

CHAPTER XIII

THE DESIRE OF CONTEMPLATION

WE have just said what we are to think of visions, revelations, and the other phenomena of distinct and particular contemplation. The saints recommend us to reject such things, as far as it is in our power, if they occur to us of themselves; for a stronger reason, they should not be desired. The same line of conduct should be followed as to ecstasies *in public*, miracles, and other open manifestations.

But with regard to *the graces of mystical union*, whose nature and degrees we have described, may we desire and pray for them? [1]

If a soul has already received a beginning of mystical union, it has always been admitted that she may desire further progress in these ways. God has given a true vocation and deposited a germ; to desire that this should be developed is to will what God wills. This is applicable even to those who are as yet in the passive purgation of the senses; they have only one foot in the ordinary kinds of prayer, the other is already planted in the mystical way; God is calling them, and wishes to lead them on to further heights.

[1] Fr. Poulain, *Graces of Prayer*, c. xxv.

Many authors clearly assert that it is not permissible to desire ecstasy. We do not see why a soul, already arrived at the state of quiet, or at that of full union, might not desire an increase of light and of infused love, even though the alienation of the senses should be the result. Her intentions are pure, this hope animates her to practise virtue, and, after the favours already received, is in no way presumptuous, nor does she desire this to take place in public; in what, then, is she to be blamed?

If a person has not yet entered upon mystical contemplation, may he desire and ask it?

Some celebrated authors [1] maintain that not only he may, but that he ought to do so. Scaramelli admits that this desire is permissible, but immediately surrounds it with a multitude of restrictions. St. Liguori teaches [2] that it is safer for souls, who have not yet been raised to mystical union, to desire only the active union.—But the common and almost universal opinion is, that they may desire and ask the gift of supernatural contemplation, provided that this desire does not arise from pride or sensuality, and that it is accompanied with an humble submission to the Divine Will.

These graces of prayer spring in fact from love; they have for principle the Holy Ghost and His better gifts; for object, God; for end, divine union, God tasted and possessed; they enrich the soul with many merits, urge it on to heroic virtues, dispose

---

[1] Vallogornera, *Mystical Theol. divi. Thomæ.* Philip of the Holy Trinity, *Summa Theol. Myst.* Anthony of the Holy Ghost *Direct. Myst.*   [2] *Praxis*, 143.

it to do great things for God and for one's neighbour, are a powerful lever to raise her from earth
and to unite her to the sovereign good; they are
even a foretaste of the occupations and the happiness of our heavenly home. How, then, is it
possible not to desire them ?

It is objected that these favours make us quit the
common ways and indulge in strange familiarities
with God; ought not humility then prompt us to
avoid them ?—No more than it should prompt us to
avoid Holy Communion and all commerce with
God by prayer. For, who would venture to
believe himself worthy to converse with Infinite
Majesty, or to be united intimately with the God
of the Eucharist ?   The voice of our needs cries out
more loudly than that of our respect.   Let us adore,
and let us also desire.

Contemplation introduces us into a world so very
supernatural.—In this state, indeed, the supernatural is certainly more manifest.   But is it not
true that a merely Christian life, grace, the sacraments, infused virtues, the gifts of the Holy Ghost,
are all a supernatural world quite as real, though
not so manifest ?

In contemplation, God shows us so much love !
Should we dare to receive His caresses ?—We dare
to receive Holy Communion.   During prayer, too,
as well as at the Holy Table, we adore, we humble
ourselves, we make ourselves quite little; but,
nevertheless, we love and eat because we need to
do so.

One may misuse contemplation !—One may also

2 C

misuse the consolations of ordinary meditation. Poverty and riches, offices and employments, rest and work, consolations and aridities, health and sickness, life and death, the sacraments, the Holy Scripture, all the gifts of God, without exception, may be abused and turned aside from their end. It is supremely unjust to condemn what is good on account of possible abuses. Let us guard against dangers and illusions, by humility, abnegation and obedience to a wise director. Let us keep our intention right, our heart detached, our will submissive to Divine Providence, and then we may desire ardently, and ask with confidence these graces of prayer.

But there is a danger for humility. " On the contrary, no kind of prayer is better calculated to crucify self-love and to penetrate a man with the sense of his own nothingness, none other is more apt to exclude every movement of pride." [1]

" At present," says Father Louis Lallemant, " if any one aspires to some gift of prayer a little above the common way, he is clearly told that these are extraordinary gifts which God gives only when He pleases, and to whom He pleases, and that we must neither desire nor ask them ; thus the door is closed for ever upon these gifts. This is a great abuse." [2]

This, too, is the opinion of St. Thomas.—St. Teresa maintains the same in more than twenty passages of her writings.[3] St. John of the Cross composed his work for the sole purpose of leading

---

[1] Lejeune, *Theol. Myst.*, c. ii. n° 11.

[2] *Doc. spirit.*, 7th principle, c. i. art. 3, § 2.

[3] Fr. Poulain, *Graces of Prayer*, xxxv. n° 17 18 19.

souls to the summit of mystical union. We must also mention St. Peter Damian, Richard of St. Victor, Louis of Blois, Blessed Albert the Great, Ruysbrœck, Lanspergius, St. Ignatius, Alvarez de Paz, the Ven. Louis da Ponte, &c., &c.[1]

Let us be satisfied with citing our own great St. Bernard. Everywhere he admits the lawfulness of this desire. He extols it, arouses it, gives it as one of the dispositions which attract the visits of the Spouse; he even admits that one who has been unfaithful may still hope to attain to mystical union. For the sake of brevity, we refer the reader to his sermons, especially those on the Canticle of Canticles.[2]

However, it is to be noted, that the more a soul advances the better she knows the greatness and sancity of God and her own nothingness and misery. The graces of prayer appear to her in the highest degree precious and she has an ardent desire of them, while at the same time she feels that she does not deserve them. Sometimes *this desire predominates*, and she exclaims: " Oh that He would give me one kiss of His mouth "; at other times, *humility prevails*, and she says: " O Lord, I am not worthy." It is this alternating rhythm of desire and humility, which ravishes the heart of God.[3]

The view of the responsibilities which so elevated a state entails, the humble fear of failing to corre-

---

[1] Fr. Poulain, *Graces of Prayer*, xxv. 20 and *ff.*

[2] St. Bernard, *Serm.* 9, n° 1 2 and 3 ; *Serm.* 32, n° 2 ; *Serm* 49, n° 3.

[3] Fr. Poulain, *Graces of Prayer*, xxv. n° 11.

spond sufficiently with its graces, the danger of
illusions, may all serve to lead the soul to moderate
this desire by a complete abandonment of herself
into the hands of God who knows what is best for
us. This filial and loving abandonment does not
exclude desire; but, fearing to be deceived in a
matter so far above her own feeble lights, she leaves
herself to the wisdom and goodness of Him, who
possesses all her love and confidence. No other
disposition seems to us so calculated to charm God
and induce Him to bestow His gifts.

CHAPTER XIV

CONCLUSION

If the reader has had the patience to read to the end this unpretending work of ours, he has seen how God leads the soul from meditation to affective prayer, and from this, to the different degrees of mystical contemplation, in order, by means of this ladder of prayer, to raise her up to the sublime heights of perfection. It only remains for us, dear reader, to express our sincere desire that God, in His infinite bounty, may deign to lavish upon you graces of prayer, which may enable you to lay down steps of ascent in your heart, and make you rise from virtue to virtue. May it please Heaven, that every one of our brethren in religion may walk in the footsteps of our wiser forefathers, who were great in holiness because they were eminent in prayer! May it please God, that they may apply themselves to purify their conscience, their mind, their heart and their will, that they may avoid pouring themselves forth entirely upon external things, that they may attend to these rather only through a sense of duty, and, their task once done, they may hasten to re-enter the solitude of their soul! There, closing the doors of the sanctuary, and banishing from God's house the tumult of cares and preoccupations, may they place their happiness in being alone with God alone, in pouring forth their heart in His presence, and altogether united to Him may they taste how sweet is the Lord. Earth has so little to say to him, who knows how to listen to God's voice; it is so easy to despise the vile things of this nether world, when one has once relished the Sovereign Good; and a heart, which is enamoured of the divine love, finds so great a charm and so much facility in conversing with Him whom it loves and serves !

" Those who aim at perfection," says the Ven. Louis Dupont,[1] " ought to commence and continue their career, by walking in the way of meditation (and the other kinds of ordinary prayer), until God, by a special vocation, raises them to a more elevated degree ; but as soon as this call is certain, it should be faithfully obeyed. To wish to raise oneself to contemplation, without being called thereto, or, to resist this attraction when God has deigned to give it, are the two extremes between which are to be found truth and virtue." One must therefore beware of wishing to abandon too hastily meditation for affective prayer, or, prematurely, to leave this for mystical contemplation. The form of our prayer is an instrument of perfection, and every instrument should be proportioned to our size and our strength. No doubt we may desire and ask progress in prayer; but we should much more earnestly ask and desire progress in virtue; and, while waiting in humble patience for

---

[1] *Life of Fr. Balth. Alvarez*, xlii. near the end,

the divine invitation, the spouse should employ her time in healing her wounds and adorning herself with all virtues, to the end that, when the hour of the spiritual banquet comes, she may not be found unprovided with the nuptial garment.

We would also exhort our brethren not to lose courage, not to turn back, notwithstanding the difficulties, the aridities, the disgusts and other pains, which are wont to beset the man of prayer. Does it cost a warrior nothing to win glory, a labourer nothing to fertilise the soil, a merchant nothing to make a fortune? Should we then fear fatigue and sacrifice, when there is question of working the golden mine of prayer? "If there are many who begin well, there are but few who reach the term, and yet, perseverance alone shall be crowned, it alone shall receive the prize. There is no virtue to be had without trouble, great rewards are not to be obtained but by great labours."[1]

Above all, we wish in conclusion to remind our brethren, that prayer, whatever be its kind or degree, is not perfection; it is only a most potent means, a wonderfully fertile soil; hence, we must labour to make it produce, both while it lasts and after it is ended, the rich harvest of virtue it promises. It is a tree, that should always bear an abundance of flowers and fruits. The various, and sometimes very intense, acts, which are made during it in great numbers, are fruits already garnered, merits really acquired; but, moreover, we are instructed as to our duty, we have taken resolu-

[1] Inter opera Sti. Bernardi, 8 *puncta perf. asseq.*, 1, 7, p. 170.

tions, our petitions have made grace abound, and all these are blossoms to be afterwards developed into fruits. The best prayer is not that which is most savoury, but that which is most fruitful; not that which consoles, but that which transforms us; not that which elevates us in the common or the mystical ways, but that which makes us humble, detached, obedient, generous, faithful to all our duties. Assuredly, we highly esteem contemplation, provided, however, it unites our will to God's, transforms our life, or, at least, advances us in virtue. As the Sovereign Judge has declared: "the tree is known by its fruits." We should, therefore, desire to advance in prayer, only in order to make progress in perfection. Instead of curiously examining what degree our communications with God have attained, we should rather consider whether we have derived from them all possible profit, in order to die to ourselves and develop in our soul the Divine life.

THE END.